THE DEMONS OF LEONARD COHEN

THE DEMONS OF LEONARD COHEN

FRANCIS MUS

WITH A FOREWORD BY
BRIAN TREHEARNE

UNIVERSITY OF OTTAWA PRESS
2020

Les **Presses** de l'Université d'Ottawa
University of Ottawa **Press**

The University of Ottawa Press (UOP) is proud to be the oldest of the francophone university presses in Canada as well as the oldest bilingual university publisher in North America. Since 1936, UOP has been enriching intellectual and cultural discourse by producing peer-reviewed and award-winning books in the humanities and social sciences, in French and in English.

www.press.uottawa.ca

Library and Archives Canada Cataloguing in Publication

Title: The demons of Leonard Cohen / Francis Mus ; with a foreword by Brian Trehearne.
Other titles: Demonen van Leonard Cohen. English
Names: Mus, Francis, author. | Trehearne, Brian, 1957- writer of foreword. | Vroomen, Laura, translator.
Description: Series statement: Études canadiennes | Translation of: De demonen van Leonard Cohen. Translation by Laura Vroomen. | Includes bibliographical references.
Identifiers: Canadiana (print) 2020018749X | Canadiana (ebook) 2020019335X | ISBN 9780776631202 (softcover) | ISBN 9780776629926 (hardcover) | ISBN 9780776631219 (PDF) | ISBN 9780776631226 (EPUB) | ISBN 9780776631233 (Kindle)
Subjects: LCSH: Cohen, Leonard, 1934-2016—Criticism and interpretation. | CSH: Canadian poetry (English)—20th century—History and criticism. | CSH: Poets, Canadian (English)—20th century—Biography.
Classification: LCC PS8505.O22 Z76813 2020 | DDC C811/.54—dc23

Legal Deposit: Third Quarter 2020
Library and Archives Canada

Production Team
Copy editing   Michael Waldin
Proofreading   Robbie McCaw
Interior layout   John van der Woude, JVDW Designs

Cover design   Steve Kress
Cover image   [Hans-Jurgen Dibbert—K&K]/ [Redferns] via Getty
Album covers courtesy of Sony Music Entertainment

FLANDERS LITERATURE
This book was published with the support of Flanders Literature (flandersliterature.be)

© Lannoo Publishers 2015. For the original edition.
Original title: De demonen van Leonard Cohen.
Translated from the Dutch language.
www.lannoo.com.

© University of Ottawa Press 2020. For the English edition.

No part of this publication may be reproduced or transmitted in any form or by any means, or stored in a database and retrieval system, without the prior permission.

In the case of photocopying or any other reprographic copying, please secure licenses from:

Access Copyright www.accesscopyright.ca
1-800-893-5777

For foreign rights and permissions: www.iprlicense.com

The University of Ottawa Press and the author wish to thank Dominique Boile for the use of the images on page 65.

The University of Ottawa Press gratefully acknowledges the support extended to its publishing list by the Government of Canada, the Canada Council for the Arts, the Ontario Arts Council, the Social Sciences and Humanities Research Council and the Canadian Federation for the Humanities and Social Sciences through the Awards to Scholarly Publications Program, and by the University of Ottawa.

For Lucas and Hanne
To M.

CONTENTS

Acknowledgements **XI**
Foreword by Prof. Brian Trehearne **XV**

INTRODUCTION 1
Leonard Cohen, who are you?

---

1. IMAGE 25
On the self-representation in the music

2. ARTISTRY 57
On the relationship between maker, work, and audience

3. ALIENATION 85
From local embeddedness and global exile to
universal aspirations and back again

INTERMEZZO I. "ANOTHER VOCABULARY" 121
A writer in search of his language (I):
Case study of an unpublished short story

INTERMEZZO 2. "DON'T FOLLOW THE STORY, FOLLOW THE EMOTION" 131
A writer in search of his language (2):
The international reception of *Beautiful Losers*

---

4. RELIGION 149
How the priest, prophet, and believer serve artistic expression

5. POWER 175
Artistic personas caught between vulnerability and authority

INTERMEZZO 3. "EVERYONE MUST FALL" 195
Freedom as consciousness: About longing and loss

---

6. ENCOUNTER 211
"The only song I ever had"

APPENDIX 229
À tout prendre [Take it all] – Leonard Cohen, Claude Jutra,
and the Academy of Motion Picture Arts and Sciences

Primary Sources **237**
Secondary Sources **239**

Perhaps a time is coming which will be more favourable to your kind of talent than the present or the last twenty years. I do have a feeling that a brighter day, a singing day, must come if there is to be any future at all, and then a poet will want to make his work resemble music instead of an equation enclosed in a cryptogram.
—Hugh MacLennan to Leonard Cohen, February 13, 1955

[T]hough I have seen the same actor a hundred times, I shall not for that reason know him any better personally. Yet if I add up the heroes he has personified and if I say that I know him a little better at the hundredth character counted off, this will be felt to contain an element of truth. For this apparent paradox is also an apologue. There is a moral to it. It teaches that a man defines himself by his make-believe as well as by his sincere impulses. There is thus a lower key of feelings, inaccessible in the heart but partially disclosed by the acts they imply and the attitudes of mind they assume.
—Albert Camus, *The Myth of Sisyphus*, 1942

ACKNOWLEDGEMENTS

The Demons of Leonard Cohen is a second book disguised as a translation. In February 2015, a Dutch-language version was published, aimed at a general readership in the Netherlands and Flanders with only a passing familiarity with Cohen. Because Cohen's work lends itself to an exploration in essays, my monograph found a place among the numerous biographies and academic publications. The English translation faced a twofold challenge: the book would have to appeal to a more international audience, while I also wanted to iron out some inconsistencies in the original edition by linking my gaze as an invested reader and listener to a more academic approach. The writing of these two publications, between 2010 and 2020, was a long and very intense process during which I received a great deal of assistance from a large number of people. I would like to take this opportunity to thank them.

This book would not have come about without the support of the University of Ottawa Press and Uitgeverij Lannoo. My special thanks go out to Lara Mainville, Caroline Boudreau, Pierre Anctil, Maarten Van Steenbergen, Katrien Van Oost, and Wim Degrave. Many thanks to Laura Vroomen for her meticulous translation. My research trips to Canada were made possible by funding from the Research Foundation–Flanders and the Canadian embassy in Brussels. It was also an honour to be invited by François Letourneux, Victor Shiffman, and John Zeppetelli to participate in the Leonard Cohen conference A Crack in Everything (Montréal, April 2018). I am also indebted to Chantal Ringuet, who gave me the opportunity to contribute to the collection *Les révolutions de Leonard Cohen*.

I admire Brian Trehearne for his exceptional ability to couple profound insights with constructive criticism.

I would like to thank Robert Kory and Alexandra Pleshoyano for their support with this and future academic work, and for their generosity in letting me use quotes and archive material.

During my research I received help from a great many fans, experts, and academics, as well as colleagues and friends of Leonard Cohen himself. Thank you for your unfailing input and enriching testimonies and insights: Allan Showalter, Alexandru Bublitchi, André De Bruyn, Anthony Glinoer, Aurelia Klimkiewicz, Bart Meuleman, Catherine Leclerc, Charley and Hattie Webb, Christian De Paepe, Christophe Lebold, Christophe Van Gerrewey, Christophe Vekeman, Cin Windey, Dirk De Wachter, Dominique Boile, Hazel Field, Ira Nadel, Jarkko Arjatsalo, Javier Mas, Jennifer Toews, Maarten Massa, Michel Biron, Michel Garneau, Rainier Grutman, Raluca Tanasescu, Roscoe Beck, Sammy Slabbinck, Sherry Simon, Silvia Albertazzi, Sylvie Simmons, and Vicky Broackes.

Amid the many demands of successive world tours, I had the chance to present my work to Leonard Cohen in person. As he nodded his approval, I remembered his words from 1963: "For my friends and family, I will always stand between them and work." The true encounter took place within the work itself.

My friends and family played a vital role in bringing this work to a successful conclusion. I would like to extend a special word of thanks to Pieter Boulogne, Asieh Harati, Maarten Vanhee, and Hanna Van Parys. I also have fond memories of the many book presentations

ACKNOWLEDGEMENTS

with Sophia Ammann and all the musicians I have worked with in recent years.

This book is dedicated to my two children, Lucas and Hanne, and is addressed to you, *still working for your smile*.

FOREWORD
by Prof. Brian Trehearne
McGill University, Montréal

The years since Leonard Cohen's death in 2016 have been marked by an international array of public and private acts of commemoration, as well as by a Cohen industry, including the publication of "new" works of literature and song, and a marked increase in academic activity on Cohen, that seeks to perpetuate both his sales and his recognition by hundreds of thousands as a secular saint (see Bilefsky 2018) for a "broken," "defeated," but still "longing" contemporary world. (Those are three of Cohen's signature words, of course.) Colin Hill, now a professor at the University of Toronto, first showed in his master's thesis that even from the earliest writings Cohen found the life of the saint to be a compelling model for an artist consciously shaping his career: for its licensing of a period of youthful sin, for its well-timed conversion—even successive conversions—and for making sense of the call he had always felt to some higher form of inner and outer life. Montréal staked its claim as a pilgrimage site for this particular saint not only because he lies in the family plot on the slopes of

Mount Royal but also by hosting the multimedia Cohen exhibition *A Crack in Everything* at the Musée d'art contemporain and decorating two prominently visible buildings with iconic images of Cohen, each mural many stories high, hand to heart in one case and with the well-known fedora on both for a halo. In the wider national context, Canada recently honoured itself as his birthplace with a series of postage stamps, the marketing of which required, apparently, his face on every normally red mailbox in the last months of 2019. The irony will not be lost on those who have read *Beautiful Losers* and recall F.'s welcoming of the mailbox bombs set off by the Front de Libération du Québec in Montréal in the 1960s.

In *The Demons of Leonard Cohen* Francis Mus asks and answers, in five different angles of light, a simple and essential question, one that should be asked by every member of his global audience: "Leonard Cohen, who are you?" Who was this man, and what are these songs and poems and fictions, that so many have agreed to adore with a reverence that may be unique to the gravesites of pop singers? Who am I, if I revere such songs or gaze so moved at such murals? Mus is not seeking merely biographical answers to his question; and anyway Sylvie Simmons has given us a host of possible answers of that kind in her extensive narrative of the artist's life, *I'm Your Man: The Life of Leonard Cohen* (2012). This capacious biography arguably leaves Mus's real question unanswered—if by it we mean, who was the enduring inner Cohen who wrote these songs, these poems, made these films and gave these interviews; who enticed us by projecting such intimacy with our real needs, and who distanced us, too—if we are honest with ourselves—with how thoroughly rehearsed that intimacy can feel? For Mus, that Leonard Cohen is best approached through a series of imaginative encounters with his *daimons*, the positions and personas and performances which he was always expressing—his "themes," a literary critic might call them, except they are themes with faces like Cohen's, and sometimes with masks too.

FOREWORD

As a scholar of Canadian poetry who has only recently begun to write about Leonard Cohen (I have taught Cohen's writings to students at McGill University for more than twenty years and taught the first course on Leonard Cohen *solo* in Canada), it is an honour to be asked to preface this book with a Canadian perspective on its subject. Canadians knew Leonard Cohen first, of course, as an iconoclastic young poet whose second collection, *The Spice-Box of Earth* (1961), took their breath away with its verbal beauty and lushly sensual vision, and soon after as a scandalous writer of experimental fiction who moved a former prime minister to rise in Parliament to condemn his second novel. Montrealers of the late 1950s might already have known him as the young Jewish poet who was performing his verses to jazz accompaniment and growing crowds in the cooler nightspots along rue Sainte-Catherine. His politically-posturing travel to Castro's Cuba in the early sixties ("I wanted to kill or be killed," he told filmmaker Donald Brittain, who included the remark in the publicity-driven "documentary" *Ladies and Gentlemen... Mr. Leonard Cohen* of 1965) and eventual willing exile to the island of Hydra in Greece troubled the nationalist expectations of Canadian cultural arbiters of the time but excited emulation and envy among Canadians of his own age and younger. *Flowers for Hitler*, with its savage and self-condemning excoriations of the post-Holocaust global mind, turned off many who had loved *The Spice-Box* (as he intended), but the courageous ugliness of that newly politicized voice spoke powerfully to a generation ready to overturn their own shibboleths and icons of institutional power and cultural hygiene. In all such reactions, diverse as they were, Canadians enjoyed for a while sole power of judgment over their young writer, for all that he had refashioned himself as a cosmopolite.

But when Cohen turned to the performance and recording of popular music in 1967, and the first three albums arrived in rapid succession to international acclaim while the novels ceased and new poems thinned out, Canadians found they were no longer in command of or even familiar with the terms of Cohen's global recognition. Most, it seems, were not unhappy to let him go. The heady success of *The Spice-Box of Earth* is now a bit of antiquarian and specialist knowledge known only to the most impassioned followers. *Beautiful Losers* sustains its readership in Canada, though chiefly for an academic public renewed annually in university classrooms across the country (and less by the year of even that much notice). The harsh, razor-blade-surmounted poems of *The Energy of Slaves* in 1972 did little to redeem Cohen with his *reading* public after his portentously worded refusal of a Governor General's Award, Canada's highest literary honour, for his bestselling *Selected Poems* of 1967: "Much in me strives for this honour, but the poems themselves forbid it absolutely." By the mid-1970s, with the album sales dropping, Cohen was an acquired taste at best among Canadians.

I first heard of Leonard Cohen in this period of public antipathy in Canadian literary circles to their former "golden-boy poet," and my lack of awareness of what his work would come to mean to me constituted, I now see, one microscopic instance of the decline of his Canadian reputation in the middle and late 1970s. The album *Death of a Ladies' Man* (1977) and the book *Death of a Lady's Man* (1978) were released while I was in the last years of study for a Bachelor of Arts degree at McGill University. None of my friends or professors, including his old mentor and then mine, Louis Dudek, encouraged the least interest in Cohen's new writing or music. For the professors of the still nascent and clannish discipline of Canadian Literature at that time, Cohen had betrayed a high literary and modernist purpose, and an exquisite gift, for the fleeting pleasures of success in the pop-cultural marketplace and the decline in his art's quality that such success "always" entailed (a sacred cow of modernist judgment that Cohen's entire career can now be seen to have slaughtered, ritually). I recall local reviews of both releases as almost entirely negative, even faintly condescending, and they seemed confident that Cohen had turned himself into a fad that had passed. People who had once known him remarked how old and worn the album cover made him look; the book spoke in the language of an embittered man turning on his own audience just as he was turning on his (textual) wife. *Recent Songs* of 1979 received even less notice and slighter sales; by the late 1970s, in Canada and in the United States, Cohen and his work were in profound eclipse. The breathtaking fifty prayers of *Book of Mercy* certainly raised a ripple of intrigue in Montréal newspapers and reviews when it appeared in 1984, but it was taken for the most part as another eccentricity—a book of prose psalms from an anything-but-sacred singer who had seemed for years to have turned away from the merely written word altogether. I had no idea that these two books would become, for me, the greatest of his works, as essential to my experience of twentieth-century literature as Joyce's *Portrait of the Artist as a Young Man* and T. S. Eliot's *Four Quartets*.

Perhaps justly, then, Canada had little control over Cohen's reputation at the time of his death; partly from years of growing physical pain, he rarely returned. Sightings of the singer on the Main (formally known as Boulevard Saint-Laurent, still a boundary at that time between French and English or bilingual neighbourhoods) had long been trumps in party conversation because they were so few and far between. His triumphant 2008 concerts at the city's central Place des Arts reaffirmed the bond of love both local performer and fellow citizens had once felt for one another. Canadians were by that time and remain much like Europeans in knowing him chiefly for the songs; they are as susceptible to the over-indulged pleasures of "Hallelujah" as any other people of the world, and as likely as any other contemporary audience to listen to popular music a great deal more than they are willing to read poetry or arcane novels of the 1960s. One of the chief pleasures of *The Demons of Leonard Cohen*, then, is its statement to us of a variant European perspective on the local boy who made good: it is an uncannily distinct Leonard Cohen we learn of here, both deeply like and slightly unlike the poet and singer to whom we have returned, especially since his death, with an anachronistic national pride. We will recognize Cohen in Mus's book, but we will also hear him recognized, from perspectives that are not quite our own.

Europeans I've had the chance to speak to about Cohen can project a special sense of proprietorship over his fame, since they helped so much to sustain his reputation and perhaps his sense of musical purpose when it appeared in the late 1970s and early-to-mid-1980s that North America had little interest left in his early poetry and fiction, in his straining "golden voice," or in his increasingly sombre and recondite songs. Although according to Sylvie Simmons each successive album up to *Various Positions* (1984) rose to a lower point on the European sales charts, those sales always surpassed his dismal North American figures, and the European concerts retained an exuberance that American and Canadian crowds would not muster. In this light, Francis Mus's book has a dual purpose. Like all good criticism, it illuminates some of the central issues that guided Leonard Cohen in his journey toward the light (even if for much of the time he wanted it darker); but it is also a statement to Canadians, in this new English translation, from one thoroughly informed European fan of Leonard Cohen who is also a wide-ranging scholar, of the grounds and expressions of Europe's long engagement with and sympathetic comprehension of Cohen's voice.

Mus has made many good decisions in writing his book. The European perspective allows him to clarify Cohen's relation to folk music and to the ethos of the *chansonnier*. His multilingual alertness helps us to see, in his valuable intermezzo on *Beautiful Losers*, the ways in which European and Québécois translations of Cohen try to deal with Cohen's own sense of language, and particularly of prayer, *as* translation from some primal form of utterance we have lost. Mus allows the songs equal prominence with the poetry and fiction, partly because the songs have had a currency in Europe across several decades that the printed works have lacked. He is adept and precise in detailing for us the songs' distinct performances over the years, both by Cohen himself and by the various musicians and backup singers he worked with, many of whom Mus has interviewed. His full engagement with the most recent albums allows him to articulate the total arc of Cohen's performing career, an expertise still emerging among Canadian critics. He presents an impressive range of vital, fresh material from Cohen's private papers and archives, including a thorough analysis of a hitherto unpublished short story from the apprenticeship years in one of three intermezzos. Mus quotes such documents not to shore up a narrow book-long thesis but rather to multiply and give nuance to the voices he represents as Cohen's own. He is attentive to what critical editors call the paratexts—liner notes, cover art, promotional material, cover blurbs on the books—as well as to the hundreds of interviews and to little-known correspondence. He has learned a great deal from Cohen's literary critics, and engages them candidly, but is not confined to their discourses: to articulate Cohen's fame he draws as often from the popular media, which can speak more clearly than academia to the singer's meanings for his audience.

To me, however, the most important feature of the book is its frequently articulated skepticism—which is not the same as disbelief—regarding the idealized and saintly Cohen who was celebrated in the popular media after the last great concert cycles began in 2008 and who has been fixed as a cultural icon since his death. With our current reverence for Cohen's authentically performed wisdom, our sense that he came through some darkness and returned to tell us where the light gets in, we may have lost touch with the lacerating experience of existential and spiritual damage—damage survived and sometimes made beautiful, to be sure, but not without long years of self-destructiveness and lashing out—that most of his work expresses. Cohen's life on Hydra and the years of relative seclusion in the late 1990s at the Buddhist monastery on Mount Baldy in California speak to us of a man who felt the need for refuge from pain (another Cohen keyword) as strongly as the longing for fame, performance, and adoring audiences. We know more, now, too, of his struggles with mental illness and of his patterns of substance abuse in his middle years. Right from the earliest poems we hear a voice imagining, praying, that there might be some place of calm, beauty, and safety where fulfilled erotic desire and creative zeal can coexist without cost. Because he never finds it (or finds it stifling if he does), the typical Cohen avatar is a *traveller*, and as he moves on from one archetypally beautiful woman to the next, he unfortunately wields his private damage and does harm with it to others. He sings all these stories beautifully, goldenly, of course, but... "CAVEAT EMPTOR" (let the buyer beware), as Cohen once wrote in felt pen onto a bathroom wall as he was being filmed taking a bath. If we read and listen to the whole of his creative output, we'll find that there is no such sacred refuge whose praise he sings that is not in some other song or poem devastated by the scathing irony and bleakness of a wholly fallen man. Mus's multiple approach to Cohen's daimons—and perhaps, for the moment, we can allow the audible likeness to "demons" to stand—forces us to recognize the mask of the secular saint as just one of many excellent performances.

Mus is right: the question for the attentive Cohen reader and listener will always be, is there one face under all these masks, and can we lift them one by one to hear an unfiltered voice? Can we know who Leonard Cohen *was*? To be reminded of the masks, the demons, and the daimons is instructive and prudent. To be exposed to so much of the long performance that was Leonard Cohen's life as well as his art is informative and encourages cultural acumen. And to learn in the course of our reading that the book's guiding question cannot be answered finally but cannot finally be avoided—this accords well with Cohen's own idea of what questions are for. They are an expression of the restlessness that suffuses his works: a restlessness that the shifting and dissonant voices of Mus's daimons allow us to hear afresh.

INTRODUCTION

LEONARD COHEN, WHO ARE YOU?

Are we justified in saying that Leonard Cohen's oeuvre is overshadowed by his personality, or is this merely a temporary side effect, a consequence of the worldwide success he enjoyed during the final years of his career, which came to an abrupt end in 2016? Barely five years after his death it may be too early yet to determine Cohen's place in the literary and musical canon, in Canada and beyond. In "Almost Like the Blues" he speaks scornfully about a "great professor," and in the posthumous collection *The Flame* he appears to address his reader from the grave: "whatever happened to my place in the Anthology of English Literature"[1] (Cohen 2018, 257). It is ostensibly no longer a priority for the poet, unless he is falsely modest rather than sincere here—and why not? Cohen's oeuvre is haunted by unreliable narrators. One thing is certain: his early literary work, in particular his two novels and first books of poetry, has been canonized. In fact, this institutional recognition came relatively early. In 1964, at the age of thirty, Cohen won the Quebec Literary Competition Prize; four years later he was awarded a Governor General's Award; in 1971 he received an honorary doctorate from Dalhousie University; a year later the University of Toronto decided to acquire his archive; as early as 1967 the *Oxford Companion to Canadian Literature* gave him a separate entry; his two novels were included in McClelland and Stewart's prestigious New Canadian Library series before 1970; various symposia and monographs have been dedicated to him; and the list goes on.

Temporal distance is what is really needed for such a judgment, but this does not necessarily explain the absence of his later literary oeuvre—roughly from around *Death of a Lady's Man* (1978)—from quite a few reference books on Canadian literature. Because Cohen's works from the 1950s and 1960s subscribe to a number of local literary traditions, it was not too much of a stretch to see him as representative of Canadian literature, or a segment thereof, such as Canadian modernism (Scobie 1991, 70), "the Montreal group" (Djwa 1967, 34), or, more broadly, "Jewish-Canadian writers," who, as Daniell notes in 1957—shortly after Cohen made his literary debut—form a full-fledged third category alongside the traditional dichotomy of "anglophone" and "francophone" literature (Daniell 1957, 72), although this distinction was to continue apace, both on an ideological level and in the institutional development of French and English Canadian literature. The young Leonard Cohen also merits his place in *littérature québécoise*. After all, prior to the Quiet Revolution it had been characterized by frequent intercultural contact between both language communities. On the anglophone side, this even gave rise to what Biron et al. ([2007] 2010, 476–483) described as an *"imaginaire anglo-montréalais,"* with Mavis Gallant and Mordecai Richler as its main proponents alongside Cohen. To this day, Cohen's contacts with a range of francophone artists (Claude Jutra, Marcella Maltais, Sylvain and Michel Garneau, the Automatistes group, and others) have been largely neglected, both in academic research and in the many biographies.

Cohen's first book of poetry, *Let Us Compare Mythologies* (1956), is a typical product of Canadian anglophone modernism from the 1950s. A great deal of poetry from that era originated in academic circles. Cohen is no exception: the influence of the so-called McGill Movement, including most notably F. R. Scott and Louis Dudek, is evident from the erudite style, the classic form, and the intertextual references to Auden, Eliot, and Yeats. In subsequent works, he used explicit references and conspicuous stylistic devices to express his indebtedness to local traditions. He included a "Song for Abraham Klein" in *The Spice-Box of Earth* and dedicated *Parasites of Heaven* to Irving Layton, to give but two examples. At the same time, he also differentiated himself from the literary production *du jour*, according to Sandra Djwa in a frequently cited article:

> Cohen's technique is considerably more complex than that of Layton or Dudek, and the vision and sensibility which he expresses are sufficiently different from those of Klein to suggest that he moved into a different tradition. (Djwa 1967, 34)

According to Djwa this other tradition is "Black Romanticism," and it is precisely its intense and dark character that made Cohen unique in Canada and that brought him closer to a more European style. Others, including Stephen Scobie (1978, 5), have argued that the perilous exploration of the "wilderness"—a geographical, but above all, an interior wilderness—is not only a typical feature of Black Romanticism, but also a truly Canadian phenomenon, as exemplified by Margaret Atwood's *Survival* (1972). By the same token, for many critics and academics Cohen's second novel represented a radical break with what Canadian literature was known for. In 1988 Linda Hutcheon described *Beautiful Losers* as Canada's first postmodern novel. Many would adopt this label. Five years later Burnham (1993, 65) went a step further by positing that "the post-modern qualities of Cohen's poetry, and specifically *Flowers for Hitler*, have yet to be recognized," while Scobie (1991, 70) continued to see Cohen as a modernist, albeit "in the trappings of postmodernism."

From the 1970s and 1980s onward, when Cohen's career really took off internationally, the Canadian affinities became less obvious, and he was also far less present on the artistic scene in Canada and in his home country *tout court*. This international dimension, evident in both his life and work, resulted in a problematic relationship with Canadian identity, traditionally linked to domestic references. In addition, Cohen's stubborn adherence to a (pseudo-)romantic ethos of the artist proved hard to reconcile with the then popular movements of postmodernism and postcolonialism. Finally, this is of course the time when his oeuvre developed a distinctly musical character, with explicit references to popular culture. This affinity had always been a feature of the literary work, but it became far more noticeable when Cohen began to carve out a profile as a musician. And while the number of literary and musical titles may be quite evenly balanced, sales figures between the two reveal an unbridgeable gap. In his foreword to this book, Brian Trehearne makes it clear that this popularity is directly to blame for Cohen's relative absence from university-based research during the fairly long period between his international recognition in the 1970s until the comeback in 2008, which led to a boom in publications, academic and otherwise.

Simply put, the force with which Cohen's literary career was launched by a bevy of professors was more than matched by their implacable refusal to welcome him back to the academy later on. In fact, Cohen and the literary-academic establishment always had a tense relationship. He turned down a Governor General's Award, and his honorary doctorate at Dalhousie did not go unchallenged. In a letter, the chairman of the Department of Music expressed "vigorous opposition": "The Department does take strong exception to the implication that Mr. Cohen has in some way made a truly significant contribution to the art of music. Whatever his particular creative talents may be, it remains to be demonstrated that Mr. Cohen is making or will make such a contribution" (Byham 1971). The literary value of Cohen's oeuvre did not go unchallenged, either, as suggested by the correspondence on *Beautiful Losers* between Malcolm Ross and Jack McClelland, the founders of the New Canadian Library. Ross is unsparing in his criticism: "My objection is at once aesthetic, moral, philosophical *and* theological. It is also visceral. The book turns my stomach. Quite literally, Jack!" (Lecker 1994, 206). Others, highlighting the formal and thematic originality of works such as *Death of a Lady's Man* and *Book of Mercy*, are much more positive. This being said, the nonconformity of these projects meant that Cohen could not be easily incorporated into existing movements and threatened to fall through the cracks of dominant and more visible literary and artistic categories.

THE MASTER'S HAND DISAPPEARS
ON THE 2008 COMEBACK

The result is reminiscent of two communicating vessels: since the late 1960s it was Cohen the *person* who would be picked up by the popular culture and music press, largely eclipsing academic interest in his *work*. But this conclusion is incomplete. It is not entirely clear just how these two vessels are connected since work and persona often intersect in complex ways. Besides, it would be unfair to paint an overly polarized picture of the jealous, elitist academic high up in his ivory tower versus the popular, philanthropic Leonard Cohen somewhere down in the Tower of Song. So, academic studies of his work continued to appear (though obviously outnumbered by interviews in the popular press), while the lure of fame frequently cropped up as a self-reproach in various books of poetry, long before Cohen actually achieved international renown.

Indeed, while the canonical status of Cohen's oeuvre may be up for discussion, this is far from true for the significance of celebrity—not just in the attainment of commercial success but also, and especially, as a leitmotif in his work. Joel Deshaye (2013) speaks of the "metaphor of celebrity," which has impacted the artistic practice of several Canadian authors. This tendency is most evident in the period 1955–1980, when, alongside Cohen, Irving Layton, Michael Ondaatje, and Gwendolyn MacEwen were rising stars on the Canadian literary scene. "The demands of celebrity on the self began to interest poets at a time when authors in Canada and elsewhere were gaining publicity through the converging media of television and radio" (5). Cohen's case is remarkable because this celebrity was an element that tied him to a national poetic tradition, before it grew so big he became nothing short of a global product.

Cohen's celebrity status started life as an ambition before becoming a fact, a burden, and finally a comfort. In the poems of the 1960s and 1970s an intertextual dialogue evolved between Cohen and Layton about the role of celebrity in their lives and work (see Deshaye 2009). Layton saw it as a form of freedom, while Cohen experienced it as a form of slavery. The signifier "disgrace" appeared frequently, perfectly capturing the artist's perceived inadequacy toward his audience. In "How to Speak Poetry" (from 1978), for instance, Cohen addresses himself: "If ambition and the hunger for applause have driven you to speak about love you should learn how to do it without disgracing yourself or the material." The longing for a form of purity was immense yet seemingly hard to realize. It was precisely this that Cohen admired in Alexander Trocchi's work, as the eponymous poem from *Flowers for Hitler* attests: "Your purity drives me to work. / I must get back to lust and microscopes." The relationship with the other's gaze—"the eyes of men," as we read later in *Book of Mercy*—becomes an obsession in a great many texts. But in the final phase of his career Cohen appeared to take a remarkably positive view of things. In 2001 he described the effect of celebrity as follows:

> If you hang in there long enough, you begin to be surrounded by a certain gentleness and invisibility. This invisibility is promising,

because it will probably become deeper and deeper. And with invisibility—and I am not talking about the opposite of celebrity, I mean something like The Shadow, who can move from one room to another unobserved—comes a beautiful calm. (Simmons 2012, 449)

At the time when Cohen spoke these words his claim must have sounded plausible. He had not released a new album or book in ten years, let alone graced a stage with his presence. It goes without saying that at that point he could not have known that seven years hence he would swap a decade of seclusion for ten years of uninterrupted public activity. The story is well known: having been defrauded by his financial manager Kelley Lynch, he was forced to start performing again. The unexpected success soon pushed the monetary motivation to the background. The final decade of Cohen's life was characterized by unprecedented artistic activity: dozens of global tours; three studio albums and twice as many live albums; a posthumous poetry collection and ditto record, *The Flame* and *Thanks for the Dance*, respectively; countless tributes by other artists and cultural institutions, and more.

But even during this final stage of his life, Cohen's statement from 2001 held true. Although he was ubiquitous, his presence also brought about a certain invisibility. It was not long before audiences grew accustomed to the figure of the old man with the dark fedora who would skip off stage after each concert and disappear into the wings like a shadow. The occasionally erratic course of the first half of Cohen's career—literature and music, success and failure, admiration and disapproval—had been replaced by a strangely homogenous picture of a modest, perfect gentleman, somewhat inscrutable and thus all the more attractive. This image was reinforced by tour manager (and later trustee of the Leonard Cohen Family Trust) Robert Kory, who had taken the necessary steps to organize, in contrast to earlier tours, a closed tour—without backstage visits from journalists, fans, colleagues, friends, or family. This created a space, quite literally so, of delightful calm and intense creativity, allowing the mythology to grow and Cohen's image to become progressively more homogenous. The iconic cover of *You Want It Darker* is a case in point, as is the use of Cohen's work by third parties. Kory has explained that such requests are not just a financial and legal matter, but that each enquiry is carefully considered for correspondence between the spirit of Cohen's work and the intention of the reuse—Kory (2018) himself talks of "aesthetic judgments."

In Europe Cohen's image has been more consistent. After his 2008 comeback, a younger generation in their twenties and thirties either discovered his work for the first time or remembered the commercial heyday of *I'm Your Man* twenty years previously, whereas the veterans looked back with nostalgia on the mythical sixties and seventies and saw Cohen as an inimitable interpreter of folk and protest songs. In both cases, the status of iconic singer-songwriter was confirmed. In Europe, too, the literary work had been available at a relatively early stage, even in translation, but the novels and books of poetry had never really been an object of discussion on the literary scene. In the best case they were seen as an intriguing sideline from the singer-songwriter, and for many fans soon became collectors' items that were certainly not always read. The French translation of *The Favourite Game* is illustrative here. The headline from France's leading literary journal *La Quinzaine littéraire* contained a hint of contempt: "The singer is a novelist too" (Anon. 1971). This was eight years after the novel was first published, that is to say by the time Cohen had acquired enough legitimacy as a musician. Could it be that Cohen's musical fame helped him gain access to France's literary system, but that once recognized as an author that very same fame was an obstacle to being taken seriously?

In the past decade the iconic image of Leonard Cohen as singer-songwriter has been reaffirmed and reinforced. During concerts no efforts were spared to consolidate the unwavering aura of the performer and his songs. The tracks were dusted off, polished, tweaked, and perfected until the wavering hand of the master had been completely erased. The music had to be untouchable and remain untouched. Half a century after the start of Cohen's musical career, in 1967, the songs had become "classics" to the general public, and their performer's intriguing personality greatly contributed to this standing. "A classic," in the words of Pascale Casanova (2004, 92), is "literarily speaking, [...] a work that rises above competition and so escapes the bidding of time. Only in this way can a modern work be rescued from aging, by being declared timeless and immortal." That said, this honorary title does incur some risks: in the worst case the sought-for perfection in the composition and rendition means that the song no longer comes across as a lived experience. From 2008 onward, there was no longer any trace of the improvisations that Cohen had been known and even notorious for in the 1960s and 1970s. I am thinking here of the illustrious tour of 1972 (covered at length by Tony Palmer in his documentary *Bird on a Wire*), when Cohen had no qualms about interrupting or even cancelling a gig because he was not in the right mood. In the best case there was something anachronistic about the 470 shows after May 2008, performed in thirty-one countries and attended by four million fans. They offered a final chance (over and over, since it was never certain whether Cohen would tour again) to find out in person what those classics must have once sounded like. Every now and then, the seventy-year-old singer would turn directly to the audience and send up his image of timeless icon. At times he would present himself as "a sage, a man of vision," only to undermine this constructed solemnity again, for instance by cheerfully launching into "Tower of Song" or concluding with some piano tinkling or incomprehensible mutterings.

On April 6 and 7, 2018, seventeen months after Cohen's passing, an international symposium took place in Montréal. The forum, Leonard Cohen—A Crack in Everything, was the culmination of a successful exhibition with the same title, hosted by the Montréal Museum of Contemporary Art. As a museum initiative, the event was able to reach a wide audience without compromising on academic gravitas. It was part of the annual Max and Iris Stern International Symposium, which, so the conference brochure explained, sets out "to make the latest research of today's leading thinkers accessible to the public." As in previous editions, the delegates worked in a variety of disciplines, "such as art history, aesthetics, sociology and literature", but with the marked difference that many presentations did not really take the form of an academic paper; they were more like testimonies. The recurrent use of the first name "Leonard"—pronounced in either English or French—appeared to be symptomatic of this. Was this a spontaneous form of expression by those who had known him for many years? An appeal to authority to lend credence to the presenters' messages? Compensation for the excessive regard in which he had been held in recent years? An implicit assumption of the convergence of man and artist?

The contrast with the perfect gentleman on stage could hardly be starker. As early as the 1970s, when the concerts were far more intimate, there had been an unbridgeable gap between the artist on stage and the audience in the auditorium. It did not take the extremely self-aware singer long to understand that the sense of community and the spontaneous expression inherent in the genre of folk music in the 1960s (the context in which Cohen's musical career took off) were an illusion, after all. Either way, it would be best not to ignore the unbridgeable gap that remained. Hence the degree of theatricality[2] his performances contained from the outset.

During a chaotic gig in Aix-en-Provence in 1970, Cohen rode onto the stage on horseback and addressed the audience with condescension, a stunt that earned him the reputation of being an aloof "bourgeois singer" in the French press. Even music journalist and writer Jacques Vassal, one of Cohen's most prominent defenders in the magazine *Rock et Folk*, had compared Cohen to Dylan and concluded that they had radically different relationships to the audience: "We would never dare say 'Leonard' the way we say 'Bob'" (Vassal 1969, 38). This detail actually transcends anecdote and is symptomatic of the way critics and scholars approach Cohen's life and work. It would appear that much has changed between 1970 and 2018.

So how can we talk about Leonard Cohen's oeuvre today? How can, may, and must we interpret the relationship between persona and work? The question is not really new given that Cohen was also immensely popular fifty years ago, first as the "golden boy" of Canada's literary scene, and later as a charismatic singer-songwriter in Europe. In 1978, Stephen Scobie noted that the interviewers always outnumbered the critics: "they have been obsessively interested by Cohen the man" (1978, x). Scobie himself, however, is of the view that biography is "largely irrelevant" (xi) to an understanding of Cohen's writing, which suggests a simple solution for the scholar: forget the biography and the interviews and stick to the work. Sure, "Leonard Cohen" the public person is pervasive in the work, but he ought to be distinguished from Leonard Cohen the private person, "who remains unknown" (xi).

But how absolute is this distinction? From a psychoanalytical perspective, each work contains by definition an autobiographical dimension. It may also have been easier for Scobie to make such a claim in 1978, before the ubiquitous media blurred the line between public persona and private person. Today chance encounters are shared by fans on social media; unpublished footage (ranging from discreetly filmed soundchecks to old family videos) regularly appear online; there is no keeping up with the biographies. In other words, this ubiquity inevitably colours every reading of the oeuvre to a greater or lesser extent and, who knows, perhaps also partially shapes the creative process and the *mise en scène* of the countless speakers. The inner self, the media figure, and the artistic personas cannot be strictly differentiated.

In 1993 Scobie himself revisited the question, describing the absolute distinction between the maker and his work as "naïve" and making a case for viewing the author as text, "as part of the work, perhaps indeed as the *centre* of the work" (1993, 11). Such self-referentiality has always been part of Cohen's work. Up to and including *The Flame*, Cohen made an art of presenting himself in a public context—in both text and music, during shows and interviews—in different guises and under different names. The examples are legion. There is the "Sincerely, L. Cohen" at the end of "Famous Blue Raincoat." And in an improvised track during a gig in 1972 he described himself as "the man who wrote Suzanne." More recently, there has been the self-mockery of "Going Home," the opening track of *Old Ideas* ("I love to speak with Leonard, he's a sportsman and a shepherd, he's a lazy bastard living in a suit"). The literary work features quite a few other forms of address. Cohen has rarely been as outspoken as he is in the poem "The Cuckold's Song" (from *The Spice-Box of Earth*): "I repeat: the important thing was to cuckold Leonard Cohen. / I like that line because it's got my name in it." In *Book of Longing* he occasionally refers to himself as Leonardos. *The Energy of Slaves* may well boast the most salient example. Paraphrasing "Call me Ishmael," the well-known opening line of Herman Melville's *Moby-Dick*, Cohen wrote mockingly, "You can call me Len or Lennie now, like you always wanted." In his private correspondence, he was sometimes addressed as *"Canadien errant"* (the title of a folk song he once recorded), while he usually signed his neatly handwritten letters with his first and last name, spelled out in full.

THE MASTER'S HAND APPEARS
ON *THE FLAME* (2018)

The significance of the posthumously published *The Flame* may lie in the fact that it introduces a new dimension in the distinction between the private and public person *through the work*. The new collection throws open the doors to the author's private chambers: the inclusion of a separate and extensive section with texts from "The Notebooks" gives the reader a first structural glimpse into the creative process—at least that is the illusion being created here. While the wavering hand of the master had been erased from recent gigs, here it comes into sight again. Obviously, this image of the searching and faltering artist had been around for some time. On the back of the sleeve of *Songs from a Room* we saw the maker sitting at his writing desk, and both *Book of Longing* and the insert of *Popular Problems* included facsimiles of the odd manuscript fragment. Yet *The Flame* affords us an exclusive and extensive look at the work-in-progress: we get to see the naked thoughts, or so it would appear, original versions of texts that would later be inscribed in the definitive poems and songs. This sense is further enhanced by the inclusion of twenty scans of Cohen's notebooks in and among the printed text, "showing his unique handwriting and the presentation of his lines on the page," according to Alexandra Pleshoyano (2018, xiii),[3] the academic ambassador for the Leonard Cohen Estate and Archive, who helped put *The Flame* together. On reflection, however, it is the complete *absence* of any corrections that catches the eye, as if the poems found their way straight onto the page, whereas Cohen often described himself as a "worker in song," a *poeta faber* who found writing anything but easy. Then what is the point of the photos, and indeed of the entire section of notebook fragments?

In an early version of the editorial note Pleshoyano observes that "these notebooks reveal a new depth to Leonard as an artist." Unfortunately, she does not elaborate on the idea. What does this new depth look like? Both thematically and formally, this is primarily a continuation of the early work (although the word "continuation" is ill-chosen here: the fragments are drawn from the whole of his career and not presented in strict chronological order). What better example than the title itself: Cohen used the image in *The Favourite Game*, speaking of "the Mosaic bush each of us grows in our heart but few of us care to ignite" (Cohen 1994, 185), and the drawing was previously published beside more than one poem in *Book of Longing*. What is more, the large volume of material suggests that the works published during the author's lifetime paint a misleading picture of the size of the complete oeuvre: this is merely the tip of the iceberg. This assumption raises all kinds of heuristic questions regarding the status of the author and his oeuvre. To what extent can a text published in book form and carefully designed (with, admittedly, the occasional typographical reference to the unfinished nature of the texts) still be considered a notebook? And conversely, to what extent can the rest of the unpublished material be granted the same status as the published "Notebook" fragments?

Death of a Lady's Man offers an interesting point of comparison. In a letter to Stephen Scobie, Cohen shed light on that book's genesis. It emerged that the definitive text was based on another, rather different manuscript (after the proofs had already been sent to the critics, Cohen went so far as to block publication and completely revise the text), which in turn was a compilation of two other texts: *The Woman Being Born* and *My Life in Art*. Ken Norris correctly notes that "there is an interesting interplay between the three titles. The 'death' of the lady's man is complemented by the woman 'being born,' while the 'life in Art' exists beyond these births and deaths" (Norris 1987). The genesis of *Death of a Lady's Man* alone illustrates that genetic textual analysis can yield fascinating insights into artistic practices and the creation of semantic networks. By starting out from a particular order and hierarchy of the different "versions," a sequence of formal and semantic shifts can be reconstructed that shows something of the intended coherence and the texture that was introduced to the text. But because the notebooks in *The Flame* become an integral part of the publication, this hierarchy is no longer entirely evident. Is there a fundamental difference between the texts in the first section (sixty-three new poems) and those in the final section ("The Notebooks")? Are we, the readers, meant to judge "The Notebooks" more leniently? Are we discouraged from identifying a (different) narrative in this section compared to the others?

Again, a comparison with *Death of a Lady's Man* is illuminating. Although this collection, for which Cohen initially suggested the subtitle "a curious book," is not divided into separate sections, it does possess a fundamentally heterogeneous character. On the one hand this is reflected in the internal composition (prose poems poised between formal poetry and more narrative prose); on the other hand, the definitive structure consists of an intriguing combination of these prose poems (on the left page) and an accompanying commentary (on the right page), which together form a polyphonic whole. The author thus alternates between a narrative and a reflective perspective, and always remains one step ahead of the reader. Every now and then, fragments from the "Notebooks" are integrated in the "commentaries." Indeed, they were not called this in the first edition; this is just one instance of the impact of *Stranger Music* on our conceptions of Cohen. The four-line poem "The Dream," for instance, is printed on the left page, followed by a commentary in which the poet refers to himself in the third person. The right page features three paragraphs and just as many subheadings: "from the Notebooks of 1975"; "he refers to the incident again in 1977," and "from a Diary Tape of 1978." The notebooks, memos, and diary excerpts are slipped in among the poems as texts of equal merit. What is more, while chronologically speaking they come before the definitive poems, here they appear in their status of commentary *after*, to the right of the text on the left page.

Although *The Flame* came out after Cohen's death, the editorial note stresses that the publication came about in accordance with his instructions (only the drawings were added by the editors). Yet how can we be sure that an author as notorious as Cohen for his cunning and conning (para)texts—as pointed out by various critics (including Linda Hutcheon and Eli Mandel)—is not trying to guide our interpretation via all kinds of intermediate agencies? The paratext played an important role from the start: think of the programmatic poem as the prelude to *The Favourite Game*, the "note on the title" in *Flowers for Hitler*, the Faulkner quote in *Let Us Compare Mythologies*, and the Ray Charles quote in *Beautiful Losers*, for instance. There are numerous examples, in the music as well, of added quotes. Likewise, album sleeves contain a fair amount of useful information (see chapter 1). In short, the use of paratexts to guide reading is anything but exceptional in Cohen, which suggests that we ought to be wary of unambiguous interpretations.

Perhaps the "new depth" lies in the broadening of the oeuvre: *The Flame* appears to be saying that Leonard Cohen the man was always writing and therefore merged with his identity as an artist. "My father, before he was anything else, was a poet," says Adam Cohen in the foreword, and on the Book & Film Globe website, Don McLeese (2019) sums up the collection as "a handsome volume that humanizes the artist." Such a conflation of man and artist is not new. Cohen cultivated it in his work, just as it is a structuring principle in many of the biographies. The list is long, but Ira Nadel and Sylvie Simmons are undoubtedly the best-known biographers. Nadel's *Various Positions* (1996, update 2007) was long seen as the benchmark, but has since been eclipsed by Simmons's voluminous *I'm Your Man* (2012, update 2017). Both authors owe their prominence not just to their extensive research, but even more so to the fact that they were the only biographers to secure direct access to their subject. While this put them in a privileged position, they still opted to use a quote from the work as the title of their biography. Although biographers generally foreground the man behind the artist, these titles reproduced a familiar voice: that of the artist himself. This is most apparent in Simmons: for her the "man" is none other than the "your man" from the album and song of the same name. In the conclusion of the prologue she leaves us in no doubt. "Darling, I was born in a suit," Cohen is said to have confided in her in some mysterious way.[4] Nadel's choice of title is more original. The various positions do indeed allude to the different guises in which Cohen presents himself to his family, friends, and audience. Equally, the title of the first edition of his book *A Life in Art* hinted at the distinction between man and artist ("My Life in Art" is also a poem from Cohen's poetry collection *Death of a Lady's Man*).

Whatever the case may be, the visible presence of the handwriting in the notebook scans and in the reproductions of the drawings confronts the reader with the materiality of the writing. Not only does the writing hand appear to erase the distinction between man and artist, but above all it creates an effect that cuts across Cohen's entire oeuvre, something I will come back to at length in the following section: the maximization of the power of expression of his art, comparable to something Roland Barthes once said about the few words painter Cy Twombly added to his works:

> The strokes are a little childish, irregular, clumsy. This is quite different from the typography in conceptual art: the hand which has drawn them confers on all these names the lack of skill of someone who is trying to write; and from this, once again, the truth of the Name appears all the better. Doesn't the schoolboy learn the essence of a table by copying its name laboriously? By writing *Virgil* on his canvas, it is as if Twombly was condensing in his hand the very immensity of Virgil's world, all the references of which his name is the receptacle. (Barthes 1979, 11)

MASKS, MIRRORS, AND DEMONS

Whether it is Leonard Cohen's enigmatic personality or the fact that pop music is often read biographically, there is no doubt that a great many readers and listeners are immensely curious to know *who* speaks to us in words and music. The question hits us once more in the most recent book of poetry. Reading *The Flame* from cover to cover, one cannot help but be amazed by the presence of so many speakers, which is further reinforced by the numerous self-portraits that fix the reader with their penetrating stare. Cohen made them throughout his life, like some form of continuous self-scrutiny. And the rest of the oeuvre similarly abounds with first-person narrators and speakers in different guises.

Who speaks here? By identifying the many guises in which Cohen presents himself to his audience, I will try to provide an answer to this question. My hypothesis in this book is that these numerous roles, more than an innocent game, are experiments designed to confront the tensions and conflicts inherent in Cohen's "life in art." They serve as masks, which have traditionally had the function of covering the performer's face and representing his state of mind in an expressive, magnified yet detached way (moreover, "mask" is also the meaning of the Latin word *persona*). In the following pages I discuss the ways in which these masks take shape in and around the artistic work. I will limit myself to five themes, which are embodied in different guises: image (the poser), artistry (the writer and singer), alienation (the stranger and the confidant), religion (the worshiper, prophet, and priest), and power (the powerful and the powerless). In the final chapter (encounter) I argue that Cohen's artistic practice can be read as an ongoing attempt to forge interpersonal contact, which often, though not always, falls short.

The word "mask," like the concept of "image," has rather negative connotations. Anyone talking about image runs the risk of missing the essence, so it seems, as images are confined to outward appearances, to the semblance and the lie. Put differently, the image overshadows the content or simply masks the absence of content. That said, the creation of an image can also be tied to a tentative quest for authenticity which one has no choice but to make explicit. In Cohen's case, it often boils down to the search for an authentic embodiment of an artistic ideal that becomes eroded and can only be captured in clichés. In 1970 Michael Ondaatje wrote that Cohen dons a mask as often as he takes it off again and that over time this has become a fully fledged part of his personality (Ondaatje 1970, 61). Morton Rosengarten, a close childhood friend of Cohen's, attests to this in the Simmons biography. In the early 1970s Cohen asked him to make a mask, a plaster cast of his face. "Leonard felt it was helpful in deciding his persona on stage. A mask is neutral, it's the person that wears it that gives it life, the way you move your head and your eyes and all that stuff. It becomes very powerful," according to Rosengarten (Simmons 2012, 218).[5]

Figure 1. The mask was made at Cohen's home outside of Franklin, Tennessee, during a period when he was recording in Nashville; it was cast in aluminum at Morton Rosengarten's foundry in Way's Mills, Quebec. Photo credit: Morton Rosengarten.

Previously, in *Beautiful Losers*, Cohen had already stressed this relationship between the mask and the face it hides:

It was a dance of masks and every mask was perfect because every mask was a real face and every face was a real mask so there was no mask and there was no face for there was but one dance in which there was but one mask but one true face which was the same and which was a thing without a name which changed and changed into itself over and over. (Cohen [1966] 1991, 140)

These different masks are separate threads linking an oeuvre spanning sixty years, which is why I have opted for a thematic rather than a strictly chronological reading (only the first chapter is structured chronologically). The advantage of this approach is that such a comprehensive reading can shed new light on the selected themes. It threatens to push the work's internal evolution and contextualization to the background to some extent. While I do touch on this every so often I also hope to show that Cohen's oeuvre is characterized by a striking continuity that justifies a thematic reading and offers scope for an interpretation that complements the existing bibliography. Besides, the wide international circulation of the music has meant that the connection with the history of its creation has been at least partially severed and that much of the work's reception has been filtered through the images created by both the artist and critics in concerts, interviews, and reflective texts. In that sense, this monograph is far less a biography than a reception study.

In this book, I refer to these masks as "demons," in the original Greek mythological meaning of the term, in which the *daimon* is not necessarily a negative figure (unlike its representation in popular culture today). The daimon nestles on somebody's shoulder, incarnating that person's identity while remaining invisible to the individual it has taken possession of. It is only in the outside world, through contact with other people, that the daimon's presence manifests itself. Without using the actual term, Cohen formulates this idea in an interview from 1972, chronicled in the documentary *Bird on a Wire*:

> I think that everybody understands the songs. We don't understand perfectly what we say to each other in words, but we always understand each other. And it's the same way with my songs. The texts are

sometimes difficult, but even when you sit with somebody and you listen to them speak about their lives, you can't follow the meaning from word to word or from sentence to sentence. *But something else comes through, something of the person himself or herself comes through. And so it is with my work*, although the meaning of each line may be obscure. (my italics)

"It's very hard for me to locate a view of myself," Cohen told a journalist more than fifteen years later, explaining, "I'm reminded of that story I read in *Dalva*, a novel by Jim Harrison, who is speaking of certain tribes where the white man tried to introduce the mirror, and certain native American tribes refused to accept the mirror. The reason was, they said, that your face is for others to look at" (Schnabel 1988, 51). In Cohen this other can be read in different ways, given that this contact is more than just a dialogue between himself and his audience. It is also Cohen in the capacity of the artist who is seeking to come into contact with Cohen the man. All of these "various positions" provide a glimpse of Leonard Cohen's "dialogical self": his identity keeps assuming new forms, depending on the other to whom the "self" turns time and time again—hence the plural *demons* in the title of my book. As such, the use of the term "daimon" is meant to highlight the intriguing dynamic of artist, work, and audience, and not to defend a psychological-biographical reading of his work.

The name Leonard Cohen is perhaps the ultimate mask: it can be pronounced in different ways, and it refers to both the man and the artist. The name, which is supposed to speak for itself, may well evoke too many associations. It not only evokes those meanings, but generates them too. At times the first and last name sound like an open-ended question (who are you?), at other times like a commandment (thou shalt answer to the image circulating of thyself!). Maybe Cohen once began a novel in this way because he too struggled with this question and commandment. In 1966, in a haze of sun, drugs, and alcohol on a Greek island, he put the finishing touches to

Beautiful Losers, a book described by some as the most experimental novel ever written in Canada (Scobie 2002). In the opening pages the ambition of the unnamed first-person narrator is clearly described as an epistemological enterprise. The objective is to reconstruct the life story of Kateri Tekakwitha, in an effort to understand who this Iroquois saint may be. These are the novel's opening lines:

> Catherine Tekakwitha, who are you? Are you (1656–1680)? Is that enough? Are you the Iroquois virgin? Are you the Lily of the Shores of the Mohawk River? [...] I've come after you, Catherine Tekakwitha. [...] Do I have any right to come after you with my dusty mind full of the junk of maybe five thousand books? [...] Is it any wonder that an old scholar who never made much money wants to climb in your Technicolor postcard?

This search for Leonard Cohen could begin in a comparable way:

> Leonard Cohen, who are you? Are you (1934–2016)? Is that enough? Are you the man with the golden voice? Are you the little Jew who wrote the Bible? I've come after you, Leonard Cohen. Do I have any right to come after you with my dusty mind full of the junk of maybe five thousand books? Is it any wonder that an old scholar who never made much money wants to climb in your Technicolor postcard?

This Technicolor postcard is real. It was made in a photo booth in a New York subway station. A year after the publication of *Beautiful Losers* it appears on the very first album cover of the singer Leonard Cohen, *Songs of Leonard Cohen*, from 1967. For many fans it really has become an iconic prayer card, one that marks the start of each attempt at forging contact with Leonard Cohen.

NOTES

1. The quote is taken from "The Notebook" section, which features fragments from various periods. It may have been written at an earlier stage.
2. Others, like David Bowie and Prince, would only widen that gap. For a detailed analysis of this ambiguous relationship between pop musicians and their audience, see Keunen (1998).
3. The quote was taken from one of the proofs but was removed from the definitive version.
4. For my interview with the author, see Mus (2012a, 2012b).
5. Simmons adds that Cohen declined to actually put on the mask, although he continued to entertain the idea for decades.

ONE

IMAGE
ON THE SELF-REPRESENTATION IN THE MUSIC

I begin this chapter in 1967, the year of one of the twentieth century's most successful world fairs: Expo 67 in Montréal. It was also the year Leonard Cohen launched himself on the international scene as a singer with his first album, *Songs of Leonard Cohen*. It goes without saying that the construction of a public image had also been an integral part of his authorship, but 1967 was a turning point in more than one respect. From then on Cohen would have to express himself within the context of popular culture, where the relationship between maker and work is far more obvious than it is on the literary circuit. In those years, pop music was almost exclusively covered in the (non-academic) music press, where the dominant formats of the review and the interview gave musicians a platform to promote themselves and explain their work. Gigs, too, enabled them to flesh out their image through direct contact with audiences. The release of live albums (both official and bootleg) shows that these have a greater impact than the traditional poetry evenings and literary happenings in writing circles. In that sense Cohen's unconventional performances as a writer, which carried a whiff of stand-up comedy, had already been rubbing up against the popular circuit, not unlike the American beat poets who popped up in talk shows and magazines such as *Playboy*.

At least as important was the new audience, international and anonymous, to whom Cohen was still a complete unknown. *Songs of Leonard Cohen* was released in the United States, but thanks to some influential mediators[1] Cohen soon gained a foothold in Europe. But for this European audience the song lyrics were not as accessible as the literary work had been for his Canadian readership: not all listeners mastered the (often well-wrought) English, nor were the song lyrics readily available in printed format, not even on the first LPs. Journalists and critics in Europe were asked to round out their reviews with transcripts and translations of these lyrics. Jacques Vassal recalls the situation in France: "and the way we [...] strained our ears to copy the texts bit by bit. Then came Cohen's first 'songbook,' which had been imported. Here, finally, was our chance to verify that we had understood everything, and to learn to accompany those songs on guitar" (Mus 2018a). The lyrics are obviously only one part of a broader musical experience, and a lack of understanding can actually be productive. Translation scholar Susam-Sarajeva suggests that "non-translation in the case of music may allow the imagination more leeway" (2008, 192). This imagination crystallizes in an overall experience, as the interplay of word, image, and sound.

All these dimensions must be considered in an analysis of pop music. This is something Vicky Broackes (2018), senior curator at the

Victoria and Albert Museum in London, is acutely aware of, having curated several successful exhibitions on the likes of David Bowie and Pink Floyd that cater to a growing trend in the museum world. The traditional role of the viewer as one who passively consumes exhibits was systematically swapped for a more active museum experience revolving around immersion and interactivity. This idea of "experiencing knowledge" also informed the scenography of the Cohen exhibition *A Crack in Everything*. Although its primary focus was the impact of Cohen's oeuvre on international artists who had assimilated his universe in their own artistic practice, for many the first room was the highlight of the exhibition. This imposing space was set up as a kind of experiential chamber aimed at visualizing Cohen's artistry: a selection of video excerpts in which Cohen delivered the same song live at different moments in his career was projected simultaneously on to the high walls. This was without a doubt the room where visitors spent the longest and happily immersed themselves, without additional explanation either on the wall or via audio guide, in Leonard Cohen's world, which is mainly a world of sound and vision. The exhibition makers appealed to a sense of recognition and capitalized on the direct expression made possible by the available audio-visual material and technology.[2]

In the same way, Cohen's publishers were aware of the communicative power of imagery at an early stage. When his poetry was first published in the United States, in 1965, the poems from *The Spice-Box of Earth* were complemented with a series of drawings. In later collections, such as *Book of Longing* and *The Flame*, Cohen's drawings would be printed alongside the poems, and at recent gigs images would occasionally be projected onto the backdrop. The hundreds of portrait photos of the man with the "lines in his face," and even the lettering of his first and last name, have become equally iconic. Obviously, these graphical elements all help direct our reading. An analysis of Cohen's international reception should therefore consider the interaction between a range of semiotic *dispositifs*, all the more so since Cohen's artistic practice has developed in various directions: his literary and musical work are well known, but his output as a draftsman, dramaturge, actor, and even translator have been overlooked in the existing literature.

In this chapter I would like to take a closer look at one aspect of this practice and its reception, in particular the impact of images on (the perception of) the musical oeuvre. I shall do so by comparing the album covers and the music. It is correct to say that in today's music world, the idea of a discrete album is much less of a unifying principle than it used to be. Individual songs are sent into the world via all manner of music websites and streaming services without necessarily being part of a greater whole. Likewise, a carefully orchestrated publicity campaign circulated a few select songs ahead of the release of Cohen's final albums. But that does not alter the fact that up to and including *You Want It Darker* the albums were always released as independent entities. Another major difference between the 1960s and today is the formats on which the music is disseminated. For a long time the vinyl LP (which is gaining traction again these days) was the prime format until it was replaced by the CD. One of the differences between the two was their size. The LP may have come in different editions, but it was always larger than the CD. This meant that the covers looked more impressive and served a dual purpose. They observed a commercial logic (attracting the potential buyer's attention) while at the same time creating a visual encapsulation of the new album. They are, each one of them, powerful images, consumed at a glance and thus literal representations of the art. The music is captured in advance in a way that appeals to a wide audience.

CAVEAT EMPTOR
READER AND LISTENER, BEWARE!

Did Leonard Cohen wonder in December 1967 how much control he would have over his new international career as a singer-songwriter?

A few months earlier he had walked off stage after playing a few chords of "Suzanne." Having lapped up his shy appearance, the audience encouraged him to carry on playing, which he eventually did. The thirty-three-year-old Canadian, considered by many to be too old to be making his musical debut, must have thought about the charms of naïveté: a precious quality almost always remarked on by others. In interviews he frequently let on that he had no truck with enigmatic figures, yet he was all too aware of possessing such a talent himself: "I used to be a good hypnotist," he once told a journalist (Brusq [1996] 2009). His mysterious utterance appeared to evoke Lawrence Breavman, the protagonist from *The Favourite Game*, who had taught himself the art of hypnosis to win over women.

Be that as it may, the cover of the first LP displayed a disarming simplicity. This does not look like a carefully constructed image at all. Maybe the cover had not been given much thought (which is highly unlikely). Maybe it did not matter much (less than in our current visual culture perhaps). Or maybe the use of a dark, sepia-coloured passport photo on a jet-black background was a deliberate strategy. We see a shy young man, staring intently into the lens with a determined look on his face. The title, *Songs of Leonard Cohen*, likewise bespeaks simplicity. No great proclamation, just an almost redundant statement, which serves to herald a new name in a world in which the likes of Bob Dylan (*Blonde on Blonde*), the Beach Boys (*Pet Sounds*), the Rolling Stones (*Aftermath*), and The Beatles (*Revolver*) were already well established. Although Cohen would always have his name on the cover, he would never again use it in an album title. What is more, his name would never again so unequivocally evoke the image of a young but celebrated writer from Canada who wanted to make music too.

But even on this "naive" cover, the form is carefully considered. The simplicity of the front is complemented by a remarkable picture on the back—a so-called *anima sola*, a female figure depicted in the flames of purgatory. The solemn style and the religious content of the drawing lend the album a serious aura and establish a connection with the literary work, in which religiosity, femininity, and the searing power of love had figured prominently for some time. Several months after the release of *Songs of Leonard Cohen* an article appeared in the *New York Times*: "Disks Wear Art on Their Sleeves to Woo Buyers." The journalist concludes that something is afoot. He talks about a "revolution" in album-cover design, with copious experimentation with various art forms (painting, sculpture, photography) and no clear rules, except a duty to be experimental. "The static art of romantic mood is out." Like Bob Dylan, Leonard Cohen proves to be an exception: "Leonard Cohen, the folk singer, insisted on taking his own picture for a Columbia album. He went to an amusement arcade, spent a quarter in the automatic photo machine, and brought the result back as the cover picture" (Shepard 1968). Two years previously, Cohen himself had warned his readers that such naive imagery should always be approached with the necessary circumspection. Released in 1965, *Ladies and Gentlemen... Mr. Leonard Cohen* is one of the first documentaries dedicated to him. Cohen is filmed during performances, while meeting friends, and even in the hotel room where he was staying at the time. On the bathroom tiles he writes "CAVEAT EMPTOR" in block letters, which is to say that the viewer is warned, as he is merely watching the constructed image of a writer. On the inner sleeve of the first LP he again alludes to the fact that it is hard to differentiate between semblance and being when he tells the listeners: "The songs preferred to retreat behind a veil of satire." In short, it is not just the singer who struggles with his image. Even the (personified) tracks find it hard to come to the fore. He was to repeat his *caveat emptor* trick several times. In a songbook from 1969, with the same title as his first album, a note he jotted in the margins of the introduction made it into the printed version: "This is pure fantasy. Never heard of the man mentioned here. All good things. Leonard" (Kloman 1969). And in 1975, on his *Best Of*, he included a photo taken in the hotel bathroom mirror, as if he would only be pictured in an indirect way.

IMAGE

LEFT: *Songs of Leonard Cohen* (1967), RIGHT: *The Best Of* (1975)

Michael Ondaatje remembered Cohen's warning: in 1970 he noted that Cohen pursues some measure of sincerity not in the media but in his performances, especially when he improvises and engages in spontaneous dialogue with his audience. The interaction at such live shows allows him to continuously adjust his image, depending on who is sitting or standing before him and what reactions he receives. That dialogue is lost when the listener at home or in the shop sees an album with just a single captivating image. Let us therefore assume that his album covers are not at all random. The question then is: What do they communicate? What story do they tell us when we line them up? How can Leonard Cohen's fifty-year musical career be reconstructed using some twenty carefully chosen illustrations through which he has tried to shape his image? It is certainly striking to see that a photo of Cohen graces the front cover of just about every album. Only the jackets of *New Skin for the Old Ceremony* (1974), *The Future* (1992), and *Dear Heather* (2004) do not feature him—at least not at first sight. While he may have been new to the music world in 1967, as a poet and novelist he certainly knew the ropes. His books of poetry always had an author photo on either the front or back. He told his publisher that he wanted it this way because it would give at least some indication as to who had written the text. This attention to the persona behind the work has contributed in no small measure to Cohen's success, but it has also fostered a few stubborn caricatures. A reviewer once opined that the cover illustration of *Parasites of Heaven* was a perfect reflection of Cohen's career in free fall. The image of the man on the dust jacket who appears to be suffering a splitting headache contrasts sharply with the cover photos of his two previous books, *Let Us Compare Mythologies* (1956) and *Flowers for Hitler* (1964), which show a youthful poet with a broad smile and a self-assured writer, respectively. In a recent biography Tim Footman takes stock and enumerates about twenty of these caricatures:

> the Pope of Mope; the Bedsit Bard; the sometime Buckskin Boy; the composer of music that allegedly makes you want to slash your wrists; the Jewish Buddhist; the philanderer; the drinker; the smoker; the occasional opium fiend; the man who talks to Greek daisies; the poet; the novelist; the raconteur; the unlikely gun fetishist; the bad monk; the worse singer; the potential permanent advisor to the Minister of Tourism of the People's Republic of Trinidad that never happened; the guy who wrote that song in *Shrek*. (2009, 7)

THE QUEST FOR AUTHENTICITY IN THE THREE-PART SONGS CYCLE

The picture on the first LP may be personal (after all, the purpose of a passport photo is to enable identification), but only to a degree. It is like a business card, creating a stylish air of individuality while at the same time setting clear boundaries: the fact that you have an address is no guarantee you will be allowed in. This boundary is clearly crossed with the second album, *Songs from a Room* (1969). Now that Columbia Records had cottoned on to the fact that Cohen's image was just as important as his music, a promotional text appeared in

Songs from a Room (1969)

Rolling Stone magazine with the question: "Is Your Name Leonard Cohen?" Every reader and listener could identify with the description that followed: "From time to time you get the feeling that you want to disengage yourself from your life. Because you're no different from anyone else" (Rolling Stone 1969). The front of this second cover is a virginal white and shows Cohen staring at the world from a black, cropped-out square in the middle. The perspective is reversed on the back, giving the listener a direct and intimate glimpse into Cohen's life: we are looking into the artist's own study. It is furnished with a writing table and chair, a bed, and a semi-naked woman (Marianne Ihlen). This is where it is all happening.

The myth of artistry that Cohen evokes here was one he had already cultivated in his first novel, *The Favourite Game* (1963). The book was compared to James Joyce's *A Portrait of the Artist as a Young Man,* and to *On the Road,* Jack Kerouac's cult book, which had come out five years earlier. In his novel Cohen chronicles Lawrence Breavman's search for his identity as a writer. On *Songs from a Room* the image is also somewhat stereotypical. The woman in the photo is sitting at a desk, a typewriter in front of her, and is momentarily distracted. Cohen himself is not in the photo—might he be the photographer? This cover raises more questions than the first album (Who is this woman? What room is this? Why does Cohen look so dejected?), but overall it feels much more personal too. Some people claim this is the closest we have ever come to Cohen's personal life. This openness returns in the music: "I choose the rooms that I live in with care, the windows are small and the walls almost bare," we hear in "Tonight Will Be Fine."

The tone changes with 1971's *Songs of Love and Hate*. On the front cover Cohen no longer gazes into the lens, but the look on his face is all the more expressive for it. Besides, the title does not shun the big words: love and hate. He deploys blunt tools to describe his new album, and that includes the high-contrast black-and-white design. The motto on the back (a short poem from *The Energy of Slaves*) is anything but neutral either. In bold capitals we read: "They locked up a man / who wanted to rule the world / The fools / they locked up the wrong man." Every word appears to be intended as a provocation: the he/they dichotomy, the "fools" reproach, and of course the conflicting intentions of he who wants to rule the world and they who want to lock up that "man" (who else but Cohen?). This is heavy subject matter—leaving literally not much room for anything else on the cover—but the unshaven artist himself looks relaxed. A closer look, however, reveals that the broad smile and the wide eyes hide a visibly fatigued singer. After the formal introduction of *Songs of Leonard Cohen* and the raw yet clichéd offerings of *Songs from a Room* the style has become bolder, and that shift can also be found in the music. Cohen experiments with his voice and deliberately explores his vocal limits. The fragile, deeply human tone of the singer-songwriter is replaced by the screams of someone at odds with himself and his image. The romantic cliché of the solitary artist, as evinced on *Songs from a Room*, is no longer a given. Lines are ripped apart and the magic is gone. "Where is your famous golden touch?" Cohen asks himself. Emotions and doubt overshadow the aesthetic. The album cannot end with anything other than an unanswered question, in which love and hate are not pitted against each other but linked. He concludes "Joan of Arc" by singing, "Myself, I long for love and light / but must it come so cruel, and oh so bright?" The listener is challenged by both word and image. No wonder this album was not a commercial success.

The connection between the three albums is evident from the repetition of the first part of the titles (*Songs…*) and from the logical transitions in the second (from the artist as an individual via his workplace to the subject matter of the tracks). The titles also betray the explicit ambition to give some internal cohesion to the albums, which could be labelled "concept albums" for that very reason. In Martina Elicker's definition, it is "an album by either one artist or a group which contains a unifying thread through the songs—be it musical, thematic, or both" (Elicker 2001, 229). The term was first used in 1967: "with the release of *Sgt. Pepper*, pop/rock critics and fans alike became familiar with the idea of a concept and unified structure underlying a pop album. The term 'concept album' was born" (231).

Quite a few boundaries were pushed between 1967 and 1971. The new made way for a sense of intimacy, which then derailed on *Songs of Love and Hate*. On each of these three albums Cohen found a suitable mode of "authentic" expression. The term was not always interpreted in the same way, but there was always a sense that language was still up to its job, even if it sometimes engendered a crisis. Every time, the singer would find a way to mold it to his will, so he could reach out to his audience. It looks as if the musician went through a similar kind of evolution as the novelist, who swapped a classic writing style (*The Favourite Game*) for an experimental approach (*Beautiful Losers*) in the space of three years. The poet evolved from a romantic soul who praised love and nature in beautiful, enchanting words (*The Spice-Box of Earth*) into a self-hating writer eager to adopt the "anti-style" (*Flowers for Hitler*). Both on the dust jacket of *Flowers for Hitler* and in "Dress Rehearsal Rag" (*Songs of Love and Hate*) Cohen single-handedly buries his golden-boy image.

 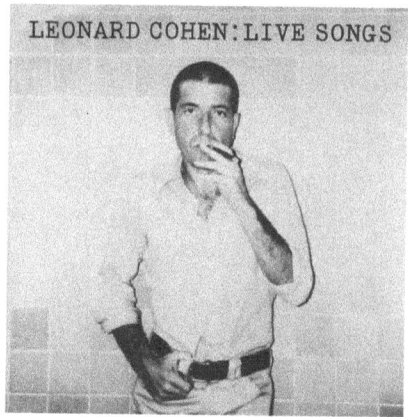

LEFT: *Songs of Love and Hate* (1971), RIGHT: *Live Songs* (1975)

DESPAIR IN THE 1970S

Is it at all possible to say something similarly credible after these three milestones? There is a way around it and it is called parody. *Live Songs* came out in 1973. Once again, the front sleeve shows us a tired-looking Cohen, portrayed in a hyper-confident pose, with close-cropped hair and sucking on a cigar. The photo was also used for the cover of *The Energy of Slaves*, the book of poetry published the year before. The tone of both the book and the album is self-conscious: "I can't write a poem anymore / You can call me Len or Lennie now / like you always wanted." After three masterpieces the artist appears to be burnt out. "I am in pain," he said about the creation of this book of poetry, and likewise on *Live Songs* nothing seems to be working anymore: the figure of the artist has been all but erased, and there is little sign of substantial innovation. Beside a few new tracks, the record features mostly live versions of Cohen's established repertoire. Nonetheless, this fourth album is about more than mere reuse of older material. Just as a parody is an imitation that differs from the original in some details and that can therefore lend precisely those details a polemic or destructive dimension, *Live Songs* is more than the sum of the previous productions. Like *Songs from a Room*, this transitional album affords us another glimpse behind the scenes. This time that glimpse is indirect and unintentional, but unavoidable: the parody gives us a different, more fundamental sound. Something has certainly been added to the otherwise familiar tracklist. The few new titles are less finished songs than they are slips of the pen, a direct outlet for the maker's pain. This is true for the fragile "Minute Prologue" and the repetitive "Passing Through," as well as the shouty "Please Don't Pass Me By (a Disgrace)," in which the artist shatters his own image. The "disgrace" can be read as the confession of a singer with nothing left to say. In these new songs repetition plays a crucial role. By constantly reiterating the same words and lines the singer may yet manage to recapture the intensity of yesteryear. The liner notes appear to confirm this: a handwritten text with the telling title *Transfiguration*, and below it the key word *intensity*. All in all, *Live Songs* may be seen as a necessary rite of passage, a purifying metamorphosis.

This transition does not come off all that easily though: the subsequent two productions are less original. To begin with, the title of the next album again alludes to the challenge of creating something new. *New Skin for the Old Ceremony* (1974) sounds like old wine in new bottles, something the working title *Return of the Broken Down Nightingale* also hints at. That said, there are some signs of innovation. Producer John Lissauer opted for new instrumentation (violin, banjo, and mandolin), and for the first time Cohen used a drawing rather than a photo for the jacket. The maker has disappeared from the front cover, replaced by an engraving of two angels making love— at least it is on the original LP. The symbolic character of the *coniunctio spirituum* did not stop the British and American censors from covering its explicit parts with a pair of extra wings (in Great Britain) or replacing the drawing with a photo of Cohen himself (in the United States). Yet the picture perfectly encapsulates Cohen's imagination: the coupling of body and mind, the combination of sexual ecstasy and religious exaltation, which influence and reinforce each other.

The drawing dates from the sixteenth century but came to prominence following Carl Gustav Jung's analysis of it as part of a reflection on alchemy. Interviews reveal that Cohen had read Jung's work: "The alchemical process is a process of internal change. This process can only be expressed through symbolism. Alchemy is an allegorical process for lifting the fundamental human emotions to a higher level. That's something I believe in" (Cohen, in De Bruyn 1980, 32). In that sense, the cover of *New Skin* does herald an (attempted) return to substance, and it can be interpreted as the work of someone who is recovering. At the time of *Songs of Love and Hate* Cohen detested his voice and felt as if the muse had abandoned him. Rumour had it that he was leaving the music business. Both his professional and private life were undergoing change: *New Skin* had been recorded in New York (and not, as before, in Nashville) with a new group of musicians, and shortly after the release Cohen became the father of a daughter, Lorca Cohen, two years after his son, Adam, had come into the world.

Death of a Ladies' Man (1977) flies in the face of all this. The album is generally seen as the biggest flop of Cohen's career. Cohen himself often referred to it as "Phil's album," despite the fact that it is clearly attributed to "Spector & Cohen" on both the front and back, and he described it in interviews as his best record (which he often did after a new release). It was a leap in the dark. In search of a new style that might allow him to transcend his vocal limits, Cohen turned to Phil Spector, the producer known for his "wall of sound," with its bombastic instrumentation. Was Cohen dreaming of being a star, like his childhood heroes such as Ray Charles, who is frequently name-checked in his novels? Whatever it was, a memo from publisher Jack McClelland to an employee says that Cohen "became so dissatisfied with the album that according to Irving [Layton] he paid $20,000.00 to buy his way out of the contract. Incredible" (McClelland 1977). And it must be said that although the album was inspired by the desire to try a different, original image, it is full of clichés and gimmicks. The most conspicuous ones are Cohen as Casanova and pop star,

LEFT: *New Skin for the Old Ceremony* (1974), RIGHT: *Death of a Ladies' Man* (1977)

Phil Spector as mad producer, and folk singer Bob Dylan and writer Alan Ginsberg doing backing vocals on "Don't Go Home with Your Hard-On"—a stark contrast to the original parody of *Live Songs*. The cover photo shows Cohen, seated at a table in a bar and flanked by two ladies (the woman on the right is Suzanne, the mother of his children—not the woman of the song by the same name), casting a sardonic glance at the camera. The inside has a photo of the same location, but without Cohen. A symbolic void remains; the ladies' man appears to have died. Funny it may be, but that is the best that can be said: it is nothing more than a copy of an existing caricature.

What the two albums of 1974 and 1977 have in common is that they articulate the despair of an artist in search of an authentic form of expression. In contrast to other works in which he grappled with the same problem Cohen here fails to translate this feeling into his art. In the poetry collection *Death of a Lady's Man* (1978) he does a better job of it. The singular *Lady* is significant: it differentiates the book from the nearly identically named musical album and it refers to one woman in particular, the Suzanne who appeared on the cover of *Death of a Ladies' Man*. By using the *coniunctio spirituum* engraving again, which appears in gold on the cover, the bundle also references

New Skin. Through literature Cohen does manage to reinvent himself. He gives himself a starring role in his work, which then becomes a hall of mirrors of "a narcissist who hates himself," as fellow writer and mentor Irving Layton once put it (quoted in Flynn 2000, 11). But while *Death of a Lady's Man* is a highly personal book, it is no spontaneous emotional outburst. Its complex genesis alone suggests that everything has been carefully thought through. The innovative composition through which Cohen highlights the fictitious or rhetorical nature of the facts and characters automatically overrides the false semblance of reality. This was not quite so apparent yet in his first literary and musical works.

THE POWER OF THE SYMBOL

Recent Songs (1979) has all the hallmarks of a new beginning. At the time the record received little or no attention—given his incompatibility with the music that was hip at the time, like rock, punk, and disco, Cohen was immensely unpopular—but he later came to see the album's mood and musical arrangements as a benchmark for his late-career gigs. The faded colours of *Death of a Ladies' Man* have been replaced by a bright-blue backdrop with a stylized drawing by Cohen himself. The similarity with the debut album is striking. *Recent Songs* is just as neutral a statement as *Songs of Leonard Cohen*. The record covers are alike, too, and show little more than the title and Cohen's portrait. But there are a few differences. The realistic photo has been replaced by an iconic drawing in which Cohen's distinctive facial features are exaggerated. His image has caught up with him. In addition, there is a small drawing of a hummingbird in the bottom left-hand corner, which is proof that some things have definitely changed since 1967. Cohen here discreetly introduces a new dimension to his oeuvre: the symbol. It would appear that in order to tame his image he resorts to imagery in which the relationship between representation and meaning is, if not completely, at least partially fixed. In his texts he had been drawing on such symbolic language for some time, but this is the first time he uses it on an album cover. On *New Skin for the Old Ceremony* he had enlisted the symbolic character of alchemy, while here he seeks to create a symbol of his own. In his novel *Beautiful Losers*, which is twenty-five years old at this point, Cohen had already evoked the image of the hummingbird: "I am (or let me be) tender as a hummingbird. Don't I have some hummingbird in my soul?" (Cohen [1966] 1991, 61). In poetry collections (*Death of a Lady's Man*, *Book of Longing*, and *The Flame*) and on later records (*The Future*, *You Want It Darker*) the little bird becomes more and more prominent. "Listen to the hummingbird / Don't listen to me," Cohen urges his listeners on the final track of the same name on *Thanks for the Dance*. The hummingbird is a symbol common to many cultures. Was it this universal character that appealed to Cohen? In the poems it always serves as a role model: either for its mobility (illustrating a flexible attitude to life), its energy (its wings flutter so fast they are invisible), or its purity (the hummingbird is also known for its beak's ability to quickly penetrate to the core, the flower's nectar).

The recent moments of crisis may explain this evolution toward a more symbolic language. *Death of a Ladies' Man*, the failed attempt at embodying a pop star, was a low point. Cohen once let slip to a journalist that he no longer had control over his image:

> The image I've been able to gather of myself from the press is of a victim of the music industry, a poor sensitive chap who has been destroyed by the very forces he started out to utilize. But that is not so, never was. I don't know how that ever got around. I would also contest the notion that I am or was a depressed and extremely frail individual, also that I am sad all the time. (Jones 2017)

Thematically, too, *Recent Songs* heralds a return to a few traditional symbols that were evoked by the romantic poet of *The Spice-Box of Earth*. What is only a minimal addition at this stage will be taken further on the cover of *The Future*, which is packed with symbolism. But before that, there are two more albums, and not the worst ones either.

Featuring tracks like "Hallelujah," "Dance Me to the End of Love," and "If It Be Your Will," which went on to become classics in his repertoire, *Various Positions* (1984) shows Cohen in good form. The *New York Times* described the album as a masterpiece, despite record company Columbia refusing to release it in the United States. The title of the new record confirms all that has gone before it: having been through a lot in recent years Cohen is now taking stock. But this is about more than what lies behind him. The various positions also reflect an approach to life articulated by a man Cohen had been spending time with for some years. His Buddhist teacher, Roshi, claimed that a zen master knows no attachment: flexibility and detachment are the new watchwords. The album cover of *Various Positions* features a photo, but the image is unsharp, so it is reminiscent of a sketch, an impression which—like the cover of *Recent Songs*—reduces reality to "the lines in his face." The picture is a bit unbalanced: a slightly tilted head, half shrouded in darkness. Although the eyes are lowered and the gaze is anything but intense, Cohen appears to have some control over himself again. At the very least, the artistic project is balanced. The nine original songs on this album (it contains not a single cover) are very personal, at times openly autobiographical. Although some read the title as an outright reference to the Kama Sutra, Cohen, by his own account, wanted to articulate nine different perspectives, nine approaches to freedom and attachment. There was a clear ambition to turn *Various Positions* into a concept album.

This delicate, fragile balance (Cohen was still not truly popular with the wider, pop-loving audience) was bolstered in 1988. In "First We Take Manhattan," the opening track of *I'm Your Man*, Cohen labels the past twenty years, that is to say his entire musical career, as "boredom," a clear statement if ever there was one. The moment has arrived to seduce Manhattan and Berlin—two epicentres of the music industry. Everything on the cover refers to the indomitable

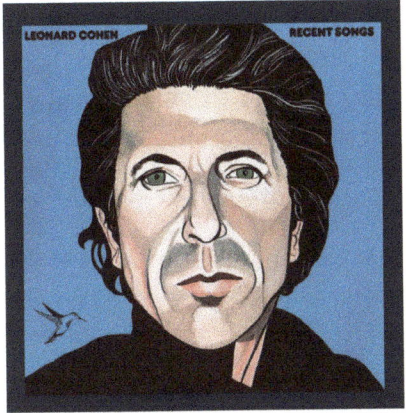 

TOP LEFT: *Recent Songs* (1979), TOP RIGHT: *Various Positions* (1984), BOTTOM LEFT: *I'm Your Man* (1988), BOTTOM RIGHT: *The Future* (1992)

performer, whose name in block letters occupies half of the front. In the title, Cohen addresses his audience in the first person. The cover design is as slick as the suit he is wearing. While *Various Positions* was not a commercial success when the album came out, *I'm Your Man* was an immediate hit. This was a true rebirth and a break with the past. On *I'm Your Man* the icon in the shades and Armani suit no longer opts for a cigar as an accessory (as he did on *Live Songs*), but openly provokes with a banana in his hand.[3] It may be an allusion to the "arty" cover of the first album by The Velvet Underground, whose iconic singer Nico was once courted by Cohen. Whereas in 1973 he resorted to parody, now he simply reincarnates himself: Mark Cooper observed that Cohen had perfected "the art of being Leonard Cohen" (Simmons [2012] 2017, 342). Around that time he even appeared in the popular police series *Miami Vice*, playing a minor role as the head of Interpol. Cohen is turning into a brand, and he is only too aware of it—not to mention being very successful at it.

The self-assured image he mocked on *I'm Your Man* is taken further in 1992 on an album packed with symbolism. With *The Future*, Cohen assumes a prophetic role and proclaims himself to be "the little Jew who wrote the Bible" in the title track. Now that he has transcended his own persona in that capacity, the photos and drawings of the earlier albums make way for three powerful blue-and-white symbols: a hummingbird, a heart, and a pair of handcuffs. Although symbolic language was introduced on *Recent Songs* and given a modest place in its classic cover design, the hummingbird now looms larger and is joined by two more symbols. It is difficult to attribute an unambiguous meaning to them, but what is certain is that once again the tension between freedom and attachment is pivotal on this record. On *The Future* the bird is free(d) and spreads its wings. The longing for freedom we heard as early as 1969 in "Bird on the Wire" is now within reach. We are still dealing with a future perspective though: the title suggests as much, as does the design of the drawing, which could be read chronologically (from the bottom up). At the bottom the handcuffs have been opened. This is remarkable: in 1967 Cohen still saw love and chains as inextricably linked (on "Hey, That's No Way to Say Goodbye"), and on "Born in Chains" (on *Popular Problems*) he reminds his listeners that he was born in chains. This is now a thing of the past ("my hands *were* tied," Cohen sings on "Waiting for the Miracle") as he describes love as simply "the only engine of survival." Both its title and design make *The Future* the most cryptic album to date. Cohen's texts are oracular at times. In the eponymous title track, for instance, he preaches, "I've seen the future brother: it is murder." The mysterious aura he surrounds himself with is only reinforced by the silence that follows this record. A live album is released in 1994 but contains no new songs. It raises renewed questions as to whether the curtain has fallen over a long career.

TWO PEOPLE IN ONE MIND
IS LEONARD STILL HERE?

Little is then heard of Leonard Cohen for nearly a decade. From rare interviews we learn that he has withdrawn to Mount Baldy, Roshi's Buddhist monastery in northeast Los Angeles. For the first time since 1967, when music became an integral part of his career, he appears to have embarked on a new route. But once again it is more of a reordering of priorities (he discovered Buddhism in his thirties) rather than a radical shift. In private he carries on writing and making music. In 2001, in the run-up to a new project, he issues a live album with songs from the 1979 tour, called *Field Commander Cohen*. The similarity between the photo on the cover and the drawing on *Recent Songs* from the same year as the tour is striking. Only the title is different. But while Cohen assumed his own name with *Field Commander Cohen*, he does so in the guise of a commander. Whereas *I'm Your Man* and *The Future* were decidedly self-assured, the approach here is a little more indirect. Cohen does not identify with his role, but begins by talking about himself in the third person ("he was our most important spy") before addressing himself directly ("Leave it all," "I know you need your sleep now," "I know your life's been hard"). This look back on the 1970s shows that art is a demanding mistress.

The same year, 2001, sees the release of *Ten New Songs*. On this album Cohen takes yet another new direction. Similar to *Songs of Leonard Cohen* and *Recent Songs*, the title does not reference a specific theme but is purely descriptive. The return is remarkable in and of itself: the prophet of *The Future* has literally come down from the mountain and is standing among his audience again. For the time

LEFT: *Field Commander Cohen—Tour of 1979* (2001), RIGHT: *Ten New Songs* (2001)

being he addresses this audience via an album only, as there is no talk of gigs. And then there is something else: Cohen shares the cover with Sharon Robinson. Her role comprises a great deal more than background vocals, having composed much of the music to Cohen's lyrics. It is not surprising, therefore, that during the recent tours he habitually announced her as "my collaborator." Cohen's then-producer Leanne Ungar described their collaboration for this project as "two people in one mind" (Gilmore 2008, 364). But there is another way of looking at it. In 1978 Stephen Scobie stated in no uncertain terms that "Cohen's vision is so completely self-centred that there is no room in it for *any* individualized personality, male or female, than his own" (11). *Ten New Songs* marks the first time that there is room for somebody else besides Cohen, and that is remarkable. He arrives at a new insight on this album: the more he explicitly pursues perfection, the less likely he will succeed. To allow spontaneous creation to happen, easing up on the determination or tenacity is essential. The art is to let go. In "A Thousand Kisses Deep" Cohen formulates the idea as follows: "You lose your grip, and then you slip into the Masterpiece." Biographer Sylvie Simmons comes to the same conclusion, linking the period in which *Ten New Songs* came about to Cohen's spiritual journey, which brought him to India among other places. "Something 'just lifted' the veil of depression through which he had always seen the world," Cohen is said to have revealed (Simmons 2012, 402). The reviewers of *Ten New Songs* made similar observations.

Dear Heather builds on this. Besides Sharon Robinson, Anjani Thomas (one of Cohen's backing singers and later life partner) also plays a significant role on this record. The face on the cover is hers, a portrait drawn by Cohen. The collaboration with Anjani also translates into artistic choices, making *Dear Heather* a multifaceted album. It boasts experimentation with different genres (spoken-word poems, bluesy tracks) and the lyric booklet contains drawings by Cohen; the collage-like style is reminiscent of the mix of word and image in *Book of Longing*, which is published two years later. Does this mean that Cohen has been pushed from the front to the back cover? No, not quite. Two symbols can be found in the bottom left-hand corner. The first is that of the "order of the unified heart," which also takes up the entire penultimate page of the lyric booklet. The interlocking of two hearts, inspired by the Jewish Star of David, also graced the dust jacket of *Book of Mercy*. It is a symbol created by Cohen himself to represent his artistic-philosophical quest. The second symbol is the Chinese sign for *Jikan*, the silent one, the Dharma name Cohen was given on Mount Baldy. In short, on *Dear Heather* Cohen again tolerates somebody beside him, while at the same time continuing to harness the power of the symbol for the benefit of self-representation. The two symbols give some indication of what he stands for.

A few of these symbols had already made an appearance on the covers of *Cohen Live* (1994) and especially on *More Best Of* (1997), albeit in a narrow strip, while on *Dear Heather* they are slightly more conspicuous. *More Best Of* contained a stylized version of the *anima sola*, the intertwined hearts, a waltzing couple (a small version of which appeared on the inner sleeve of *I'm Your Man*), the full cover of *The Future*, and finally two unpublished images, a synagogue and a guitar, referring to Cohen's Jewish roots and his artistic vocation respectively. The guitar, specifically, could be an allusion to the famous poem "La guitarra" by Spanish poet Federico García Lorca, a strong influence on Cohen. The symbol of the *anima sola* has been illustrative of Cohen's evolution. Where once it served as a direct religious reference on the first LP (we were looking at a traditional representation), this time the symbol is stripped of its original coloration and now has the same schematic design as the other figures on the strip. By restyling the *anima sola* Cohen has incorporated her into his own symbolic universe. But the question is whether these symbols can continue to fulfill their function and carry on representing the maker's artistic identity. This is no easy task. The maker's name continues to exert a hold over the imagination of both audience and press, who demand that he live up to the image they have created of him.

That tension can also be found on some record covers, namely those of the three live albums that came out shortly after *Dear Heather*. *Live in London* (2009) and *Songs From the Road* (2010) chronicle Cohen's recent world tour, while *Live at the Isle of Wight* (2009) is a recording of a gig from 1970. There is a significant difference between the 1970 cover and the other two. While Cohen is literally in the full glare of the spotlights at the Isle of Wight festival, the 2009 photo was shot in the semi-dark, and in 2010 all we see is a silhouette. This is as dramatic as it gets. It is as if in recent years Cohen has gradually lost control over an image he had helped create, although it also led to a kind of invisibility that culminated in the "beautiful calm" I mentioned in the introduction.

THE LIGHTNESS OF THE THREE-PART FAREWELL CYCLE

There are a few parallels between Cohen's musical debut and the end of his career, some fifty years later. One of them is the sheer productivity. Three studio albums are released at two-year intervals: *Old*

IMAGE

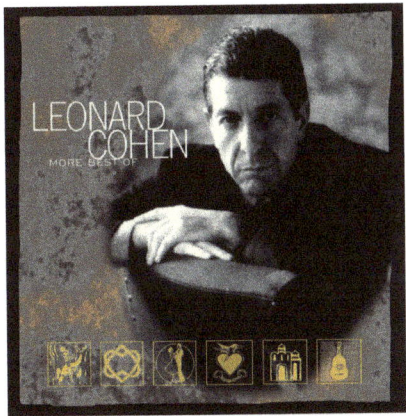

TOP LEFT: *Dear Heather* (2004)
TOP RIGHT: *More Best Of* (1997)
ABOVE LEFT: *Live at the Isle of Wight* (2009)
ABOVE RIGHT: *Live in London* (2009)
LEFT: *Songs from the Road* (2010)

Ideas (2012), *Popular Problems* (2014), and *You Want It Darker* (2016). But while the three albums from the *Songs* cycle of the late 1960s show an artist at pains to adopt a new image for each release, there are not that many shifts on the last three albums. Sammy Slabbinck, the collage artist who designed the sleeve of *You Want It Darker*, was explicitly instructed by Adam Cohen to preserve his father's iconic status in his design: in other words, to maintain continuity[4] (Slabbinck 2017). He did, however, include a knowing nod to the artwork of *Songs From a Room* by replacing the black frame against the white backdrop with a white frame against a black backdrop. We have come full circle.

The release of *Old Ideas* (the title had been considered for what became *Dear Heather* in 2004) in early 2012 is tied in with Cohen's comeback of 2008. Nonetheless, its cover differs markedly from the two previous live albums. As on *Live at the Isle of Wight*, he is well lit. Bright-red and green colours dominate the photo, taken in Cohen's garden in Los Angeles. Two years after his final gig in Las Vegas and no fewer than eight years after *Dear Heather* he speaks to us again. Key themes are the balance between man and artist, and the familiar tension between the image he has created for himself and what others have made him into. In the opening track, "Going Home," the status the media have foisted on him contrasts with the reality that fails to live up to it: "He will speak these words of wisdom / Like a sage, a man of vision / Though he knows he's really nothing / But the brief elaboration of a tube." The tube in question could be a TV tube (the printed lyrics speak of "a televised invention"). Cohen appears to have regained some control over his iconic status, as his shadow no longer precedes him but falls clearly visible behind him. That said, the critic's menacing, lethal gaze still looms large. The black silhouette on the front cover seems to want to capture the maker and his work in a single stroke of the pen or in a single image (is he/she not holding a camera?). "Going Home" digs deeper too. The artist here addresses the man inside himself: "I love to speak with Leonard /

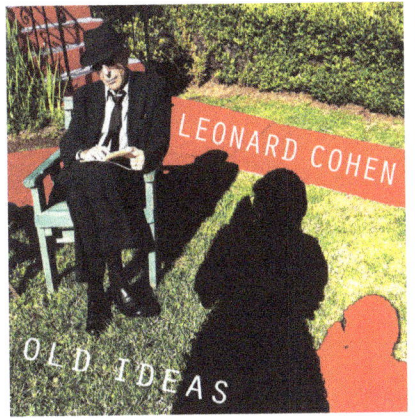 

LEFT: *Old Ideas* (2012), RIGHT: *Popular Problems* (2014)

He's a sportsman and a shepherd / he's a lazy bastard / living in a suit." The artist expresses the wish to no longer be burdened by the demands of the artistic profession. *Old Ideas* heralds the finale of a "life in art," a therapeutic album on which Cohen tries to throw off all demands and obligations, and, for the first time, actually manages to do so. This trend continues on the next two albums—"I struggled with some demons," he states on the title track of *You Want It Darker*. Many of the titles on the last three albums bear witness to this longing for a return to the essence: "Going Home," "Amen," "Show Me the Place," "Anyhow," "Nevermind," "Treaty," "Steer Your Way," for example. The final song on *Old Ideas*, "Different Sides," can be viewed as the counterpart to "Going Home": the man addressing the artist. As death becomes more and more imminent, the public image becomes less and less important—a tendency that had been present since *Ten New Songs*. *The Flame* contains a drawing in which this change in perspective is specified: "Waiting for his orders / amid the symbols of the past," Cohen wrote beside a large, poignant self-portrait flanked by five frequently used symbols. The image of the artist becomes of secondary importance, and the presence of a higher authority ever more pronounced.

From *Old Ideas* in 2012 to *Popular Problems* in 2014, with his poetic reflections on ancient ideas and current problems, Cohen appears to be delivering a universal message. Genuine hope and cheerful resignation are resounding loud and clear. The black silhouette of *Old Ideas* is still present but has been pushed further into the background. That said, Cohen's final albums cannot be dismissed as saccharine words of wisdom. The emphasis on lasting pain and disillusion in life and love is just as important. "You Got Me Singing" locates his work within the context of both liberating music and painful confession, in line with the demand for coming clean that he placed on his readers fifty years earlier in *Flowers for Hitler*.

On November 7, 2016, just over two weeks after releasing his final album at the age of eighty-two, Leonard Cohen died. There is no doubt he knew that *You Want It Darker* would be his final studio album, although there were concrete plans for another production, which was eventually released in 2019 as *Thanks for the Dance*, on which the spoken word is serenely carried by the music.[5] The listener is given a taster in the final track, a reprise of the third song, "Treaty," in a slow, instrumental version that concludes with a brief parlando. The silences are just as audible as the music and words. Why? Is this not rather awkward for a writer and a singer? The knowledge that Cohen was aware that this would be his farewell record makes the questions raised at the start of this chapter all the more pertinent. To what degree did he wish to make himself the subject of his work? How did he shape his image—in words, music, photos? And above all, what is the shelf life of such an image?

Identity is a recurring theme in the lyrics. The opening track sets the tone: "If you are the dealer / I'm out of the game / If you are the healer / I'm broken and lame." The relationships are not entirely clear-cut: just about every single line is in the conditional tense. From the first line onward, a resigned ignorance settles in and among the singer's words. He has doubts and wonders out loud whether he ought to see his "Lord" as a (strict) "dealer" or a (mild) "healer."

 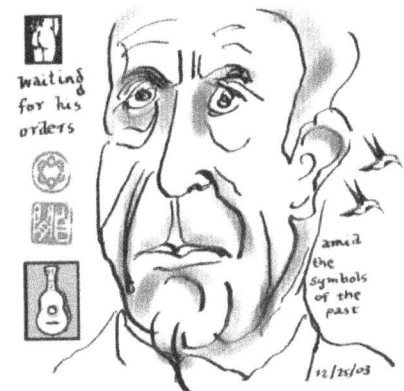

LEFT: *You Want It Darker* (2016), RIGHT: Waiting for his orders amid the symbols of the past (*The Flame*, 2018)

In 2016 it is clear that he can only understand himself *in relation to* the one he addresses. This interdependence is also reflected in the explicit admission that he is ready to surrender, "I'm ready, my lord." In the few interviews he gave he voiced similar sentiments: "I'm ready to die," Cohen said to a journalist from *The New Yorker* around the time the album was released (Remnick 2016). For someone who spent years trying to understand himself in and through his work such a surrender is anything but evident. The acute self-awareness of many of Cohen's characters means that while a well-defined identity is initially reassuring, ultimately it gives rise to unrest: predetermined relationships and frameworks threaten to undermine who they are or want to be. "Treaty" revolves around this tension. Looking back on a tumultuous relationship, the singer proposes a treaty to bring peace and calm to a turbulent situation and to define relations between two (ex-)lovers: "I wish there was a treaty we could sign." But such a clear-cut contract seems all but impossible. Peace and quiet appear to be feasible only by relinquishing all kinds of abstract ambitions and ideas. Who or what eventually prevails is beside the point: "I do not care who takes this bloody hill." "Love" is seen as an urgent moral or spiritual imperative for which the price of years of pain, disillusion, and guilt has been paid and from which the "I" and "you" have now been liberated. "We sold ourselves for love but now we're free," is the resigned conclusion.

You Want It Darker is often described in the press as a testament: on this last album death is ubiquitous. This makes it all the more salient that Cohen is *not* taking stock here, not comparing lovers or placing life in a broader perspective. On the contrary: he describes both past and present as accurately as possible but does not draw any sweeping conclusions. "Accurate" here meaning that the experience of the moment takes precedence and that any interpretive framework would obfuscate rather than illuminate. The challenge lies in the singer's attempts at being honest with himself, with his nearest and dearest, and with the life he has lived. "Let's keep it on the level," he sings in the song of the same name before concluding that the break between himself and his lover cannot be seen as either a wholly "good" or a wholly "bad" decision. "When I walked away from you / I turned my back on the devil / turned my back on the angel too." In "Steer Your Way" he addresses his audience directly—and perhaps himself too, when, at the end, "your heart" is replaced with "my heart"—with an unequivocal message: "Steer your heart past the truth/ you believed in yesterday / Such as fundamental goodness / and the wisdom of the way." In "Leaving the Table" the refusal to draw conclusions is just as clear: "I'm not making a claim," "I'm not taking aim," "I don't need a reason," "There is no reward," "You don't need a lawyer."

Despite the iconic cover photo, the artist's image is ultimately also a retrospective construct that no longer matters much. Has the need to prove himself gone? This may be a premature conclusion, because in the end the artist tells it like it is one last time, through an album with undeniable musical and poetic clout, and at the very least gives the impression that he has something more to say: "So blow out the flame." It is very tempting therefore to regard *You Want It Darker* as the "ultimate" album in which the "wisdom" of the old songwriter enjoys a last hurrah. That interpretation is likewise too narrow. It denies the impact and the echoes of the earlier work that continue to resonate in the recent lyrics, and also suggests that the singer formulates a kind of consistent message, thereby denying both Cohen's efforts to eschew such reductionist teachings and the dynamic resulting from the simultaneous acceptance of and rebellion against the non-existence of ultimate truths. The frail voice on the final album illustrates how, in his work, Cohen tried to float freely between the trap of indifference and the ease of one-dimensional truths. On *You Want It Darker,* and perhaps in the oeuvre as a whole, it is not the end result in words, music, and image but the incessant new beginnings that move the listener most.

NOTES

1. Many biographers have noted that Judy Collins played a key role in launching Cohen's career as a musician. In Europe several well-known and lesser-known names and institutions were responsible for the dissemination of his work. In France this happened in part at so-called hootenannies. These cultural gatherings, or open mics where people could sing whatever they fancied, were born in the US in the late 1950s and were introduced in Paris at the American Center in Montparnasse in 1963. In December 1967 the French singer Martine Habib sang her version of "Suzanne" at one of these events (Gasnault 2015).
2. In the other rooms, too, the exhibition frequently called on the active participation of the visitor. Janet Cardiff and George Bures Miller designed a "poetry machine," a vintage Wurlitzer organ that was altered so that on pressing a key the visitor would hear a poem from *Book of Longing*. Candice Breitz created a video installation with huge screens arranged in a circle showing fans giving their own renditions of Cohen songs. The Sanchez Brothers even made a Leonard Cohen hologram. Broackes is justified in wondering how far a museum can or should go along with this "experience economy": Where is the balance for the visitor between critical distance and subjective proximity?
3. A very different yet similar visual joke can be seen on *Cohen Revisited*, a tribute album from 2009 released by French cultural magazine *Les Inrockuptibles* and featuring ten cover versions by various artists: the front boasts an ascetic Cohen (close-cropped hair, wearing a Buddhist robe, gaze directed heavenward) with ostentatious Nike sports shoes, a suggestive smile, and a very mediagenic pose.

In short, high and low culture are mixed indiscriminately, while the protagonist himself appears to derive a certain pleasure from shattering illusions and images.

4   Likewise, Slabbinck had to delete some scenes from the video for "Traveling Light," for which he was supplied with some recent, previously unreleased footage, because they showed an overly fragile Cohen.

5   I see *You Want It Darker* as the final chapter in Cohen's music career, with *Thanks for the Dance* as something closer to an elegant epilogue. In light of the fact that Cohen has always sought to shape his oeuvre in distinctive ways, a posthumous release by definition occupies a different position in his discography. At the same time, it is clear that stylistically the album is subtly different compared to previous work. Producer Adam Cohen has gone on record as saying that even though his father never wanted to hark back to styles he had used on previous albums; *Thanks for the Dance* drew on a combination of them: the raw spoken word of the older Cohen on the one hand and the more melodic and narrative approach of the earlier albums on the other.

TWO

ARTISTRY
ON THE RELATIONSHIP BETWEEN MAKER, WORK, AND AUDIENCE

"Obody swayed to music, O brightening glance, / How can we know the dancer from the dance?" asked William Butler Yeats in "Among School Children," his famous poem about the transience of life and the acceptance of death. Cohen, whose early poems bore the stamp of a Yeatsian poetics, would occasionally cite the final verse in interviews. It is a pithy statement on the role of the artist's identity in his work. Practically every component of this brief quote will be addressed in this chapter: the importance of the body, of music, of image, and of dance as a movement in which the maker wants to lose himself with his audience. The previous pages revealed a tension between the artist and the man, who tries, where possible, to become one with his artistic identity, or who might even try to hide behind it, for instance via the creation of symbols. That said, Cohen's vision and shaping of his artistic identity is much more complex than that and has been redefined over the years. For instance, if we compare the opening lines from *Let Us Compare Mythologies* with the song "Banjo," off *Old Ideas*, we find that in 1956 poetry is clearly a performative utterance—"I heard of a man / who speaks words so beautifully / that if he only speaks their name / women give themselves to him"—whereas fifty-five years later the artist's ambition is more cognitive in nature, and he does not spare himself in the process: "Its duty is to harm me / My duty is to know." Nonetheless, there are some constants in Cohen's approach to his artistic identity.

Beside a drawing in *The Flame,* Cohen scribbled an unmistakable message about the relationship between the maker and his work: "We do not bless / we convey the blessings."

The drawing evokes the image of the *poeta vates*, the poet inspired by the gods or the muses, who sees himself as a conduit rather than a creative agent. Creativity is not a choice but a vocation, not a pastime but a verdict, as Cohen would often reiterate, right up until *The Flame*. Adam Cohen quotes his father in the preface, describing his "vocation" as a "mission from G-d" (Cohen 2018, v). This myth of his artistry can be traced back to a symbolic act after the passing of Nathan Cohen, Leonard's father, in 1944.[1] Ira Nadel opened the first real Cohen biography with this anecdote and every biographer since has come back to it. The story also pops up in Cohen's first, semi-autobiographical novel. To come to terms with his grief, Cohen cut open one of his father's bow ties before stuffing a handwritten note inside and burying it in the garden. Henceforth, writing would always remind him of everything that transcends the here and now. "I've been digging in the garden for years, looking for it. Maybe that's all I'm doing, looking for the note," he told Nadel ([1996] 2007, 6). There is more to the myth: the birth of the artist in 1944 appears to be no more than the manifestation of an artistic identity that had *always* been present. "I was born like this, I had no choice," Cohen explains in "Tower of Song." To begin with, the tone is self-assured, but a few verses later this changes: "Twenty-seven angels tied me to this table right here." The divine muses from the ancient classics go above and beyond what is asked of them here. As well as provide inspiration, they see to it that Cohen performs his duties conscientiously. But the picture of the *poeta vates* is just as likely to be replaced by that of the *poeta faber*, the "poet-craftsman" in whose work technical skill prevails over inspiration. In interviews Cohen frequently

We do not bless, we convey the blessings (*The Flame*)

dwelt on the often laborious creation of his texts. As much as anything, he characterized himself as a craftsman who sat down at his desk every day to commit words to paper. In "My Guitar Stood Up Today" (from *The Flame*), Cohen drew on a personified guitar to express the great and inescapable demands Art makes on its practitioners, not unlike F. G. Lorca's "guitarra" (in *El poema del cante jondo*).

Yet none of this guarantees success, as evidenced by a track like "Came So Far for Beauty" (1979), whose opening lines are taken up by Adam Cohen in his preface to *The Flame*: "I came so far for beauty / I left so much behind / my patience and my family / my masterpiece unsigned / I thought I'd be rewarded / for such a lonely choice." Cohen continued to struggle with his vocation until late in his literary career too. "Thousands" (from *Book of Longing*) is a case in point:

> Out of the thousands
> who are known,
> or who want to be known

>   as poets,
>   maybe one or two
>   are genuine
>   and the rest are fakes,
>   hanging around the sacred precincts
>   trying to look like the real thing.
>   Needless to say
>   I am one of the fakes
>   and this is my story.

The poem, a fine variant of the classic Epimenides paradox, sees Cohen freely and frankly describing himself as a fake poet and leading his readers into a hall of mirrors from which they cannot escape. In retrospect, his "story" is not only pertinent to the collection that includes this poem, but to his career as a whole. In the early years, he also frequently adopted an extremely self-conscious tone by ironizing the clichéd figure of the poet, as in "The Flowers That I Left in the Ground" from *The Spice-Box of Earth*: "Gold, ivory, flesh, love, God, blood, moon— / I have become the expert of the catalogue," he mocks. At the same time, this ironic style enabled Cohen to address different target audiences with conflicting views on art. Especially at the start of his career, high and low culture were irreconcilable worlds to many, as Benson and Toye note:

> Much of the work of the fifties originated in the academic community, and displayed some of the effects of the continuing power of high modernism in the influence of Yeats, Auden, and Eliot. [...] This strain of fifties' poetry was erudite, and assumed a well-educated audience in its rich use of literary and other allusions. Another of its features, one that has been sustained, was the organization or subjection of individual short lyrics into a larger unity, and the use of a wide range of traditional forms—ballads, hymns, nursery rhymes, eclogues. Traditional forms did not necessarily support traditional

values. On the contrary, those poets who used them usually did so for purposes of parody, to question accepted bourgeois values, and to suggest in the world of art and imagination alternative values. (Benson and Toye 1997, 933)

In short, his artistic self-representation assumes many forms, and the tangled mix of *poeta faber* and *poeta vates* alone, whether as parody or not, raises the question: how do these *postures*, a concept defined by Jérôme Meizoz (2007, 18) as "the literary identity as constructed by the author himself, and often conveyed by the media who give it to the public to read," relate to one another? Unlike others, such as Bob Dylan, Cohen never adopted a pseudonym or another name: the biographical person and the actor in the artistic field always bore the same name. In the work itself, on the other hand, the *inscripteur* (a term put forward by Dominique Maingueneau [2004]) is given different names and guises, depending on the scenography that varies from text to text. But for Meizoz, a true understanding of these "modalities of self-creation" requires more than just enumerating them and accepting them as gospel truth: "But the posture is significant only in relation to the position actually occupied by an author in the contemporary literary field. This is why we cannot just describe the most visible or superficial elements of a posture, as if it were all intentionally staged" (2007, 21).

When we compare the ambivalent character sketches in Cohen's work to the visible, more objective position he occupies in the artistic field, we see that from 1967—especially in Europe—Cohen is recognized first and foremost as a "serious" singer-songwriter. While there has never been a precise definition of the label, there is certainly a clear affinity with Cohen's literary status as a poet. According to pop-music expert Gert Keunen, the marker "singer-songwriter" is less about a specific style than about an attitude, and one in which authenticity is key: "How this [attitude] is interpreted, packaged, or shaped as a poet is open and the result of an individual's vision," as

Keunen puts it (2002, 73–74). It stands to reason then that Cohen's singer-songwriter peers, like Joni Mitchell, J. J. Cale, Van Morrison, Jackson Browne, and Randy Newman, do not have a lot in common with each other. Both then and now, and despite some confusion about the concept, many artists and critics have used "authenticity" as a barometer for gauging the appreciation of and for artists. The maker's authenticity adds to his symbolic capital (Bourdieu) and is essentially independent of commercial success, which is in fact more of a threat to it. As such, it is remarkable that the aura of authenticity, especially that surrounding Cohen later in his career, has been conducive to his fame without critics calling the integrity of his artistic ambitions into question. In *Flowers for Hitler* this synergy was far more problematic: during the production process Cohen realized that while he would be taking a commercial step backwards with this new book, it was the inevitable consequence of his artistic vocation. In a letter, whose personal and provocative style did lend it a certain commercial potential, he tried to persuade his publisher Jack McClelland to proceed with the project. McClelland agreed, and had Cohen's words printed on the book's cover—albeit without his permission:

> This book moves me from the world of the golden-boy poet into the dung-pile of the front-line writer. I didn't plan it this way. I loved the tender notices *Spice-Box* got but they embarrassed me a little. *Hitler* won't get the same hospitality from the papers. My sounds are too new, therefore people will say: this is derivative, this is slight, his power has failed. Well, I say there has never been a book like this, prose or poetry, written in Canada. All I ask is that you put it in the hands of my generation and it will be recognized. (Cohen 1964)

Despite the promotional text, the book was not a commercial success. The collection was not reprinted until Cohen's death. A few poems were included in the anthology *Stranger Music* from 1993, although significantly fewer than from *The Spice-Box of Earth*. Perhaps with hindsight Cohen considered *Spice-Box* to be more successful than *Flowers for Hitler*, or at least as a work that had better stood the test of time. By the time *Parasites of Heaven* was published, two years later, he had embraced a far more conventional style again.

In any case, from the outset of Cohen's career it would appear that the need to be authentic called for each book to be different from its predecessor: *The Spice-Box of Earth*, *Flowers for Hitler*, *Death of a Lady's Man*, and *Book of Mercy* share little if any common ground. In the best case, this requirement leads to a rich and diverse oeuvre, in the worst case to writer's or singer's block, on- or offstage. The most notorious instance of such a public moment of crisis dates from 1972. During the final gig of that turbulent tour, Cohen appeared to have lost touch with his material. In tortuous and dramatic wording he explained this to his audience:

> Somehow, the male and female part of me refuse to encounter one another tonight, and God does not sit on his throne. So listen: we're going to leave the stage now and try to profoundly meditate in the dressing room to get ourselves back into shape, and if we can manage, we will be back. (Palmer [1974] 2010)

In the end, he returned to the stage to play the last few songs. A performance, as he described it a few years earlier, depends on a "state of grace" (Anon. 1968, 82; also mentioned in the 2019 documentary *Marianne and Leonard*). The line between pretense and sincerity is extremely fine, but if anything this remarkable quote proves that Cohen was aware of the importance of authenticity, where the identification of the maker with his work seems to be crucial. In what follows, I will draw on a simplified sender-message-receiver communication model to distil from the work, both written and sung, three basic ideas that Cohen has variously explored.

"THE GIFT OF A GOLDEN VOICE" ("TOWER OF SONG")
ON THE HAT, THE GUITAR, AND THE VOICE

Artistry demands great sacrifices and high standards from both the *poeta vates* and the *poeta faber*. It is not surprising, therefore, that many texts explore how the artist can deal with the pressures of his artistic vocation. One of Cohen's many self-portraits goes some way toward answering this question. He added what at first sight may appear to be an odd caption: "It was the hat, after all." And under another portrait: "One of those days when the hat doesn't help." It seems as if the hat—like the suit, the guitar, the Olivetti typewriter, the cigarette, the blue raincoat, and even the black patent shoes on *Popular Problems*, in short everything to do with the pose—is meant to expedite the identification of man and artist. The symbol of the hat is therefore not an "expression" of an artistic identity—like an accessory, a signature added later—but the opposite. One could argue, with some exaggeration, that it is the hat that makes the man an artist. The hat imprints the identity on the person[2] and then becomes a symbol. Donning and doffing it introduces a pause: the man can momentarily shake off the artist's identity. The hat is an aid, which usually—if not always—works.

The same goes for the guitar, which helps the man to be a complete artist. It is a beloved attribute of many singer-songwriters, artists who shoulder every single element of the artistic process: writing, composing, singing, and performing the music. With this in mind, it is interesting to note that in the mid-1980s Cohen swapped his acoustic guitar for the electronic sound of a Casio synthesizer. He had already experimented with a more macho image on *Death of a Ladies' Man*. At the time, French music magazine *Rock et Folk* (1979, no. 154) had openly wondered how it could reconcile Cohen with the image of a rocker and put a bizarre drawing of a rock star with Cohen's head superimposed on it on its front page. French music

LEFT: "It was the hat, after all," RIGHT: "One of those days when the hat doesn't help." Private collection of Dominique Boile

critics seemed skeptical about this new identity. The Casio makes its first notable appearance on *Various Positions*, although Cohen's distinctive guitar arpeggio can still be heard on the album's best-known song, "Hallelujah." Later he would go even further down the electronic path: *Ten New Songs* features not a single acoustic instrument. Besides, much of the music on this album was written by Sharon Robinson. It is an intriguing evolution. Does it mean that on a musical level, too, Cohen is turning himself into a brand and no longer views his music and performances as unique but as duplicates? Or does he believe that an electronic sound or an incomplete identification with the entire musical process can be just as authentic and need not get in the way of a good performance? Conversely, it is worth noting that his last concert band was almost fully acoustic (again). "We didn't pursue this as a conscious goal but the songs came out like that," said Javier Mas (2013, 2), the Spanish bandurria player who joined the band in 2008.

Man and artist also meet in the voice which, unlike the hat, is not an attribute he can switch on and off at will. The folk tradition has always accorded a central position to the voice. Like the guitar, it had to be as natural and serene as possible. Initially, there was no place for stars, hits, or technology in the folk world, but all that changed with some influential names in the 1960s, among them Bob Dylan, Phil Ochs, and Joan Baez. But Cohen cannot be classed as an outright folk singer, despite having been named folksinger of the year by *Le Nouvel Observateur* in France in 1969. Vassal (1977, 319–321) lists four reasons that, in his view, contributed to this misunderstanding: Cohen writes lyrics that greatly matter to him and accompanies himself on the guitar; he made his musical debut at a folk festival (in Newport) with the help of folk celebrity Judy Collins; he worked with Bob Johnston, who had previously produced folksingers like Bob Dylan, Johnny Cash, Marty Robbins, and Simon & Garfunkel; finally, in folk circles he was regarded as a member of "the family." But compared to the traditional folk music from the 1960s, Cohen's work is quite different, both technically and poetically, although the importance of the voice to his work cannot be overestimated. He was familiar with the way it was incorporated in the music in the European and especially the French repertoire of the *chansonnier* (including Jacques Brel, Serge Gainsbourg, and Yves Montand) as opposed to the American popular balladeer or crooner. Given Cohen's limited vocal skills, the European approach suited him better (the chansonnier both recites and sings) and allowed him to reconcile his musical ambitions with his literary craftsmanship in an elegant way.

    The sound of his voice seems to translate everything he sings *about* into *how* he sings it. Both instrumentation and background vocals are carefully balanced on most albums. They serve the intensity and the credibility of the performance. This is why the "wall of sound" approach on *Death of a Ladies' Man* found little favor with either fans or critics. The heavy arrangements undermined the emotions. It also explains why the minimalist instrumentation on *Ten New Songs* seized listeners by the throat. The vocal-technical aspects clearly play second fiddle to the style and timbre that add depth to the songs' subject matter. In fact, for Javier Mas the entire body takes center stage with Leonard Cohen: "It's his body. It's the center of himself. If he came outside for a gig and he didn't play any songs but just told a story on the microphone, it would be the same" (Mas 2013, 3).

Authenticity and credibility are, in short, key concepts in artistic communication, which is why the appreciation of readers and critics often rests on emotional grounds—it is difficult to determine with any objectivity just how authentic or credible an artist is. This reflects the way Cohen himself does or does not appreciate others as a reader or listener. He seldom proffers detailed analyses or interpretations of fellow artists—not in public and apparently not in private conversations either, as suggested by a letter from 1961, in which he describes his experience reading a poem by William Kelly, "The Creation of Man":[3] "I'm not in the comparison business and I don't know anything about the immortality of poetry. All I can say is whether I *believe* a poet or not. I believe Kelly" (Cohen papers, 11-5, Cohen's emphasis). But does credibility automatically imply the maker's identification with his work? This may attest to an overly naive understanding of art. During the creative process, in the act of writing, the work comes into being via its maker—be it *vates* or *faber*—but this organic bond disappears at the point of performance. "A singer must die," Cohen sings in the song of the same name, "for the lie in his voice." For Stephen Scobie, this lie is inherent to any form of performance, and all the singer can do is die. Ultimately, says Scobie, the creative process is also marked by a distance between the maker and his work:

> On the one hand, performance is seen positively, as a source of spontaneous contact and intimacy between artist and audience, as a guarantee of personal presence, and as a healing force. On the other hand, performance is also artificial, an exercise in lying, and its ideal of "presence" depends upon a structure of absence, even of death. [...] The metaphysics of presence postulates a "personal encounter" as something which takes place between two independent, fully self-present individuals. It has no place for the invented

self, for the doubled or divided self. But the activity of writing is always a doubled and divided one: the structure of writing, even at the instant of creation, inscribes a split between the I who writes and the I who is written. There is no pure, unmediated moment of "original" creation. And even if there were, performance is necessarily distanced from it. Performance evokes the nostalgia for such a moment of pure self-presence, but it can only do so by repeating, and emphasizing, the original division. (1997, 58–62)

Earlier I wrote that the hand of the maker sometimes disappears in polished live performances, in contrast to earlier gigs that offered more leeway for variation. It is when the artist starts improvising that he most closely approximates the moment when maker and artwork interact in a natural way. Scobie touches on a remarkable instance of precisely such an improvisation in 1972, when Cohen unexpectedly started riffing on the original lyrics of "Suzanne." On the one hand, improvisation marks the moment when theatricality disappears and the maker merges with his creation, which unfolds before the audience's eyes, while on the other it provides the best possible proof of Scobie's argument: this maker is no longer the same person as the man who, years ago, put the opening words of "Suzanne" on paper. Cohen's performing practice yields a few more examples in which the performance is ruptured and the "dancer" is briefly visible again. While the voice may produce a lie, the *sound* of the voice can certainly cut through the performance. Year upon year it got a bit lower, until the tracks became *spoken-word poems* rather than songs. The evolution of the voice is the physical evidence of a life lived. Since he does not produce a smooth sound but a rasping, faltering one, it sticks in the ear. It is this faltering that reveals man and performer concurrently: in this context the celebrated "crack" from "Anthem" can be seen as the grain in the voice that cuts across the entire oeuvre and whose significance has been cited in practically every single review between 1967 and 2016.

ARTISTRY

"THE NEWS IS SAD BUT IT'S IN A SONG SO IT'S NOT SO BAD" (*THE FAVOURITE GAME*)
ON THE AUTONOMY OF THE ARTWORK

"Go little book ...," Cohen wrote in a 1963 letter to his sister, Esther (Cohen papers, 11–13). With those words he bid farewell to his first manuscript. *The Favourite Game* had just been published and had seceded from its maker. At other moments Cohen talked about the "unfolding" (Cohen 2009) or "break[ing]" (Rasky [2001] 2010, 84) of a song, acknowledging that it was not always easy to "find his way" (Lake 1980, 12, 36) in a finished song during a live performance; "It's just a matter of finding a door into the song." Despite the close bond between maker and product during the creative process, the work of art acquires an air of unassailability once it is released into the world (I look at this in detail in the second intermezzo through the international reception of *Beautiful Losers*). All the artist can do during a performance is to unfold the song, like one would unwrap a present and see it emerge in one piece.

The autonomy of the artwork comes into play on another level: the very act of creation itself separates it from everyday life, giving rise to a separate universe in which delicate ideas and intimate feelings can be expressed. Did Cohen allude to this when he turned down the prestigious Canadian Governor General's Award for poetry prize in 1968 with the words, "The poems themselves forbid it absolutely" (Simmons 2012, 213), as if the award would tie the poems to a concrete, temporal, and spatial reality? Whatever the case may be, the autonomy in the writing process furnishes the artist with a fundamental freedom, something that separates him from non-fiction authors. This is not a new idea and is often mentioned. In *Jews and Words*, for example, an essay Amos Oz wrote with his daughter, the historian Fania Oz-Salzberger, this idea is cogently expressed. Fiction, the authors state, can "invent plots and mess around with evidence, while telling us things about the universe and humankind that we recognize as genuine and profound. As the novelist among us once wrote, facts at times become the dire enemies of truth" (Oz and Oz-Salzberger 2014, 125–126).

Other elements also allude to the autonomy of the artwork. There is something enchanting or even hypnotic about the theme of the dance and the recurrent "la-la-la" motif. It literally sets these songs apart by spinning a musical thread around them, and their cadence sucks the listener in. Just as Orpheus could seduce with his lyre, Cohen's listener is subtly drawn into the track, be it dancing or singing. This movement from outside (world) to inside (world) is nothing more than the allure of the music itself. "Dance Me to the End of Love" is a case in point. In it the singer pleads to be led elsewhere via music. With the help of music and dance, beauty can be embraced ("Dance me to your beauty with a burning violin") and panic avoided ("Dance me through the panic till I'm gathered safely in"). What is more, the ecstasy of music and dance can coincide with the excitement of love, their aesthetic and erotic experiences reinforcing each other. Dancing and lovemaking intersect in the ambiguous movement of "let me feel you moving like they do in Babylon." Throughout the song, Cohen keeps playing on this ambiguity. The motion of the "moving" is accentuated by the recurring "o" sound and the repetition of slowly/only: "Show me slowly what I only know the limits of."

This being said, Cohen never specifies whether this ecstatic inner world turns out to be positive or negative. Is this a plea to be led *into* the world of love, where he has been so many times, or *outside* it? In other words, does "the end of love" refer to the ultimate love (till death us do part), or to a bitter split (love itself that withers)? The "burning violin," which reflects both beauty and destruction, casts a menacing shadow over the song. Cohen's inspiration for this song is said to have come from the experiences of the Jews who were forced to play music in the concentration camps. The reference to the "children who are asking to be born" is not innocent either. With future Jewish generations nipped in the bud, the camp survivors saw it as their duty to conceive children—a theme also addressed by A. M. Klein in "Sonnet Unrhymed."[4] All in all, "Dance Me to the End of Love" is not a round dance but a procession, a dance indicating a direction. This is also true for "Memories" ("Dance me *to* the dark side of the gym") and "Take This Waltz," Cohen's well-known adaptation of F. G. Lorca's poem "Little Viennese Waltz." Despite the complex metaphors it is clear, as so often in both Lorca and Cohen, that this is about a longing for a love that is either lost or yet to be won. "Take This Waltz" is an invitation: the love(r) is asked to dance. Will the dance partner be seduced by the dance and surrender to the movement? This is what the track sets out to do. Like "the end of love," the waltz, "with its very own breath of brandy and Death / dragging its tail in the sea," is anything but innocuous: death is everywhere. Likewise, the image of the sea carries death within it and is a recurring image in Lorca as the end point that ultimately subsumes everything.[5]

Given that the dance in Cohen is usually a movement that draws the listener into the song and carries him or her to the strains of the music to new places, "Dance Me to the End of Love" is an ideal opener to gigs. "That's where I want to go," he told a British journalist (Walsh 1994, 58). Occasionally, like in "Closing Time," we find ourselves in the middle of the dance from the outset. It is no coincidence then that Cohen often sings it at the end of his gigs. Many of his tracks are written in a somber three-quarter time (a remarkable choice in the world of pop music, where a binary rhythm is far more common), so the listener dances "into" the song, as it were. On *Ten New Songs* this waltz disappears. Cohen is far more direct here. Everything, from subject matter to instrumentation, is reduced to the essence. In places his style is raw and realistic. Perhaps Cohen's dance steps during his recent gigs reflect this: no longer a means to an end (luring the listener to another, artistic, universe), the dance has become a means in itself. At the press conference for *Old Ideas* he compared himself to Zorba the Greek: "When things get really bad, you just raise your glass and stamp your feet and do a little jig, and that's all you can do." Remember, these were the words of a near octogenarian.

In short, because the artwork is autonomous it can accommodate truths or experiences that cannot thrive elsewhere. This is not a new idea either. David Grossman captured it particularly well in an essay on freedom:

> As we read, we feel the book seep into us, meld with us, melt away knots, taking us back to our primeval, unprocessed, pre-verbal foundations. That is the moment when the book *reads us*. That is the great offering of literature: like a wolf howling outside our window at night, standing on our manicured square of lawn, it extracts from us—from the depths of our protected, secured existence—a wail of response and surrender.
>
> This wave of yearning may last a single moment (or for one single book). But what spiritual elevation and freedom that moment contains, when for an instant we are someone else; when for a brief moment we break free from the prison of ourselves. (Grossman 2015, 14-15)

But it need not stop there. These truths or experiences can also extend beyond the borders of the artwork, so the reader or listener is not only affected during the clearly demarcated moment of reading or listening, but afterwards too. In relation to this, Javier Mas (2013, 5) draws a distinction between somber and sad music. He stresses that whereas somber music does not transcend its somberness, all folk and roots music (blues, flamenco, country, klezmer), while usually also profound, can still make you feel better. In the delicate "Minute Prologue" Cohen articulates this as follows:

> I've been listening
> to all the dissention.
> I've been listening

to all the pain.
And I feel that no matter
what I do for you,
it's going to come back again.
But I think that I can heal it,
but I think that I can heal it,
I'm a fool, but I think I can heal it
with this song.

In "Bird on the Wire" too the healing power of music is fleshed out. It is the ultimate attempt at reconciliation: "I swear by this song / and by all that I have done wrong / I will make it all up to thee." The same applies to "Lover, Lover, Lover": "And may the spirit of this song, / may it rise up pure and free. / May it be a shield for you, / a shield against the enemy." In view of the track's genesis, the shield against the enemy may be taken literally—Cohen wrote it in the Sinai desert during the Yom Kippur War. Art has immense power, since it can lead to new insights, before realizing something in and through the act of speaking or singing.

"I WAIT FOR EACH ONE OF YOU TO CONFESS" (*FLOWERS FOR HITLER*)
ON THE PLACE OF THE READER AND LISTENER

For music and literature to wield this power, the reader and listener must first get carried away and surrender. While crucial, this move is often anything but obvious. The importance of this connection with the audience has its origins, in part, in the folk tradition of the 1960s, although by then the music was no longer developed by a community, but by an individual, the singer-songwriter. The community has to take shape during the actual performance. This is no mean feat, something Breavman in *The Favourite Game* was acutely aware of: "Humans are lucky to be connected in any way at all, even by the table between them. [...] What else is there? Conversation? I'm in the business and I have no faith in words whatever" (Cohen [1963] 1994, 116). His author declared that *The Favourite Game* sets out to elicit a certain engagement in the reader: "I want to challenge the reader's honesty. I want him to say: 'I was that man. I was there'" (Cohen papers, 10A-34). He issued a similar statement in response to the negative reviews of his second novel, *Beautiful Losers,* which he attributed to the demands the book placed on the readers, who were expected to fully surrender to it (with body, mind, and soul). Many readers gave up. How else can contact be made?

There are several answers here. First of all, there is a direct question, which can be asked in all kinds of ways. For instance, in the 1960s Cohen conceived a plan to co-host a TV show, with the aim of establishing close contact with the viewers and having them participate in the show. Likewise, the opening lines of a book or the opening track on an album are often outspoken statements, directly addressing the reader or listener. In *Flowers for Hitler*, for example, the opening poem "What I'm Doing Here" concludes with a clear appeal: "I wait for each one of you to confess." And in *The Energy of Slaves*: "Welcome to these lines / There is a war on / But I'll try to make you comfortable." Equally, in his music and (between-song) words, Cohen often turns directly to his audience.

But the reader and listener can also be involved in an indirect, more subtle way. Music is most effective when it moves us spontaneously, which may go some way to explaining why Cohen began to make music in 1967. Unlike poetry, according to Cohen, the quintessence of a popular song is "that it moves swiftly from lip to lip and from heart to heart" (Adria 1990). The powerfully seductive melodies, for instance, are what make many of his songs so subtle. Because the vocals are usually at the front of the mix this is not always evident, but it does come across in two side projects Cohen worked on. The first, *Famous Blue Raincoat*, is one of the first cover albums featuring only Cohen songs. It was released in 1986 by Jennifer Warnes, one of Cohen's main backing vocalists, who is known primarily for the tours of 1972 and 1979, but who also sang on the more recent *Old Ideas*. Warnes accentuates the melodic dimension, most prominently so on the live version of "Joan of Arc." Roscoe Beck, who co-produced the record, explains that this alternative interpretation of Cohen's work pulled in a new audience at a time when Cohen's career had stalled somewhat (Beck 2012, 4). The album played an important role in Cohen's renewed popularity in the late 1980s. On *Blue Alert*, an Anjani Thomas album from 2004, a few Cohen tracks are given a similar treatment: a warm and soft female voice singing powerful melodies. It would appear that Cohen wanted to apply this formula during the gigs of the past decade by having some tracks performed solo by other backing vocalists, like Sharon Robinson with her interpretation of "Alexandra Leaving," and Charlie and Hattie Webb with their take on "If It Be Your Will."

It goes without saying that the language itself must also appeal to the listener. At the most explicit end there are those moments when Cohen recites a few verses from his songs before singing them—a clear sign that he wants to be understood, above all else. The artistic lexicon borrows from various registers. The religious register is an excellent tool for increasing the lyrics' power of expression. It is also one of the most characteristic traits of Cohen's oeuvre as a whole: *Book of Mercy* is a good example of how the charged religious language can accommodate the strong feelings the author is trying to express (see chapter 4). Beside religious language, the singer sometimes resorts to romantic imagery, which is all the more effective for its familiarity. It is no coincidence that he does so pointedly in *Recent Songs*, after he lost some of his audience with the previous *Death of a Ladies' Man*. "The Guests" is the perfect opening track for *Recent Songs*, dealing as it does with the arrival of guests at a party and, by extension, listeners to the album. The instrumentation—especially the prominent violin—reinforces the intensity of some powerful romantic symbols throughout the album (the rose in "The Window," the Swan—capitalized in "The Traitor," and so on). During the 1979 tour older tracks would be played with similar violin arrangements, which upped their emotional charge. Cohen harked back to this atmosphere during the concert series of 2012 by adding a violinist, Alexandru Bublitchi, to his backing band for the first time since 1979. This is how the Moldovan himself sees it: "I think he uses it [the violin] to provide exactly the sound and the energy he needs to project in his songs. The violin can translate so many things: the spirituality in 'Come Healing,' the energy in 'I'm Your Man,' the Jewish and gypsy sound in 'Dance Me To The End Of Love'" (Bublitchi 2013, 3). To avoid cheap, meaningless clichés, Cohen often delivers these charged, romantic themes in an unconventional style, by embedding them in an ordinary, banal framework, for instance, or by ironizing them without stripping them of their emotional charge or recognizability. Conversely, he might deliberately opt for romantic clichés to express extremely unromantic ideas, such as a desire based purely on lust (see also Hutcheon 1980). Beside religion and romanticism Cohen also finds his language in world literature. It is as if he longs to be included, together with his audience, in a world of words that preceded him. He frequently sneaks well-known names and popular references into his lyrics, which should sound familiar to the reader or listener. I will come back to this in the next chapter.

The search for the right language is also evinced in the writer's power to shape reality through naming, an act in which artistic communication clearly becomes performative. A name change is often coupled with a breakup. This is true in "So Long, Marianne" (the name change equals the end of the relationship), in "The Partisan" (where it is associated with a new lifestyle), in "Lover, Lover, Lover" (a way out of an awkward situation), and in "Love Itself," another reference to the process of naming. But the most obvious example may well be "Hallelujah," in which the singer, at least in the original studio version, is accused of profanity: "You say I took the name in vain / I don't even know the name / But if I did, well really, what's it to you?" The religious dimension is prominent throughout the song, and in this passage Cohen seems to be explicitly referring to the ban, in the Jewish tradition, on uttering God's name. At the same time the act of naming can relate to the writer's core task of naming and (re)creating reality through language. But in the conclusion that follows, the artist puts both his own position and that of the listener into perspective: "There is a blaze of light / in every word / it doesn't matter which you heard." What is tentatively worded here as a prelude to the powerful "Hallelujah" will be more explicitly foregrounded two albums later in the well-known lines of "Anthem": "There is a crack in everything / that's how the light gets in." Both the syntax and choice of words are remarkably similar. It is perhaps no coincidence that these have become two of Cohen's most successful tracks.

Besides proper names, personal pronouns are another important element of Cohen's dialogic writing practice. There are plenty of examples. Right from the first track on the first album, the listener is actively involved: "Suzanne takes *you* down"—not *me*, despite the song's autobiographical foundation. And it is no different on the final record: You *Want It Darker*. With the exception of "It Seemed the Better Way," a reverie on a life lived, every single one of the tracks on this album is structured around Cohen's cherished one-to-one scenario. Although the personal pronouns often evoke a dialogical situation between singer and audience, many critics continue to read some of the tracks as purely biographical. Think of the anecdotal meeting of the young Cohen with the "real" Suzanne, or the assumption that Cohen is the one with the dark thoughts on his final album. In an email exchange between Peter Dale Scott, son of the Canadian poet F. R. Scott who was honoured on *Dear Heather*, Cohen addresses this. The correspondence was included as an appendix in *The Flame*, perhaps because Cohen formulated it rather well and in rhyme to boot:

> who says "i" want it darker?
> who says the "you" is "me"?

god saved you in your harbor
while millions died at sea
(Cohen 2018, 159)

"Light as the Breeze" gives us one of the best examples of the way relations between the I, you, and he/she figures are played out. It is a typical Cohen track. At its heart lies the longing for a woman, the relationships are described using religious terminology, the characters' identities are vague and interchangeable at times, the balance of power between man and woman is unequal, love is captured in both positive and negative superlatives, but above all the encounter is ultimately short-lived. That, at any rate, is the thrust of the song: the (amorous) encounter between two people, presented in the most vivid way possible. Initially, the singer excludes himself from the narrative and like a director places the listener opposite a woman. From the very first line the listener is addressed with the familiar *you* and some of the senses (sight, taste, touch) are stimulated: "She stands before you naked / you can see it, you can taste it / and she comes to you light as the breeze." It is not until the second verse—when the listener has found his place in the song—that the *you* is replaced with an *I*, a first-person speaker with whom the listener can easily identify from that point onward. This is followed by the speaker directly addressing the anonymous *you*, which from then on refers to the woman more than the listener: "O baby I waited so long for your kiss." In the remainder of the song, Cohen keeps trading places in much the same way, by acting as director and first-person speaker, respectively. In the end, a third voice is added to the mix, when the woman herself gets to speak for the first time: "Drink deeply, pilgrim, but don't forget there's still a woman beneath this resplendent chemise." In short, the woman agrees to the encounter and the love can be consummated, at first via a kiss and then, in an unmistakable allusion, via cunnilingus.

The rest of the oeuvre boasts plenty more examples of this dialogical play. The track "Please Don't Pass Me By (A Disgrace)" is like a refrain that is repeated dozens of times in an almost psalmodic way, interspersed with increasingly emphatic commentaries from the performer. The aim is to eliminate the distance between listener and musician: "I know that you still think that it's me. I know that you think that there's somebody else. I know that these words aren't yours. But I tell you friends that one day you're going to get down on your knees." In "Diamonds in the Mine" Cohen once again assumes the role of director and includes his instructions at the start of the track. The audience is also assigned a clear role: "The woman in blue, she's asking for revenge / the man in white—*that's you*—says he has no friends." In "Alexandra Leaving" the listener is confronted with an experience of loss: Alexandra can symbolize any lost love. And in "In My Secret Life" the listener is heartened, seemingly out of nowhere: "Hold on, my brother. My sister, hold on tight."

A final way of involving the listener is closely related to the previous one. Every now and then Cohen uses the epistolary form, as he does in the lengthy second chapter of *Beautiful Losers* ("A Long Letter from F.") and in a track like "The Letters," which deals with the dynamic of the correspondence. "Famous Blue Raincoat" is also written like a letter, as suggested by the conclusion "Sincerely, L. Cohen" (sometimes he replaces his name with "a friend"). Like in "Light As the Breeze" Cohen plays with the pronouns, so it is unclear who he is writing to. His own place in the song is not clear either: Why the explicit mention of "L. Cohen"? At first sight, there appear to be three characters. The sender is a first-person speaker who addresses a nameless "he" and talks about a woman, Jane. Some critics, among them Maurice Ratcliff, believe the speaker is writing to himself, to an earlier self (2012, 27). If, as this suggests, performer and listener partially coincide then the song automatically fulfills its ambition in the singing itself. The accusation and exhortation "you're living for nothing now, I hope you're keeping some kind of record" is made good by the song, which forms the actual record.

"... WHERE THE LIGHT IS STRONG"
ARTISTRY AND ALIENATION

It may seem strange that although Cohen's work is sometimes described as repetitive and inaccessible, many feel it speaks to them. It is an intriguing paradox: the multiple layers in his texts and the often complex genesis of many of his works do not get in the way of the direct and intense eloquence of the words and music. The power of the artistic language in Leonard Cohen's work lies mainly in suggestion. Early on, Michael Ondaatje described Cohen's first collection of poetry as "a book of moods" (Ondaatje 1970, 14). The moods evoked lend the work greater depth for some, while others see it as grotesque or kitschy for the same reason.

As shown in this chapter, Cohen systematically bypasses traditional forms of communication as mere transfer of meaning. He couples the meaning of the words to the semiotic and intertextual facets of language, an artistic process described by Julia Kristeva in *Revolution in Poetic Language* ([1974] 1985). Kristeva herself moves beyond semantic analysis, looking at the psychobiological factors at play in the act of reading. She posits that morphology, syntax, and phonetics are more important than semantics because these components can touch or move the reader, without them being able to pinpoint just what causes this compelling effect. It stands to reason, then, that in a discussion of Kristeva's work Maarten De Pourcq compares this semiotic effect to pop music which, he states, stirs us "when we have not even listened to the lyrics. We do not know what it is about and yet we 'know'" (van Dijck, De Pourcq, and de Strycker 2013, 30).

All this puts the reader and listener right at the heart of the artistic practice. In the 1970s poet and scholar Frank Davey (1974, 69) argued that Cohen's imagery is "of the imprecise but suggestive kind that can be easily projected into by the subjective reader." In a recently published monograph about Leonard Cohen, Silvia Albertazzi arrives at the same conclusion: "From the Canadian academics of the seventies to the biographers (sometimes more akin to hagiographers) of subsequent decades, to the exegetes, admirers, journalists, colleagues, and enthusiastic writers of the new millennium [...], *all, at a certain point, start speaking in the first person*" (Albertazzi 2018, 8; my italics).

As such, some artistic choices can be explained by the artist's desire to involve the reader or listener in his work, be it directly or indirectly. In "The Old Revolution" he admits that he asks a lot of his audience, who must venture into the "furnace" of the art: "Into this furnace I ask you now to venture." Cohen elaborated on this imagery to a Belgian journalist in 1976: "That furnace is the furnace of the self. It is a pool of longings, desires, and ambitions that we must examine. You must try to penetrate to the roots of your own being. That is what I ask of each and everybody" (De Bruyn 1976, 6). Cohen's ambition to operate on such an existential level explains why he has rarely expressed any explicit political-party opinions; nor has he ever been a "protest singer" like so many of his colleagues in the folk tradition, whose communiqués operate on a different level and are more geared to public action. At the press presentation of *Popular Problems* twenty-five years later, Cohen jokingly confessed that he weaves his political views into his songs in such a distorted way that nobody ever manages to decipher them.

In short, Cohen's artistry can only be understood by looking at the relationship between the work and the audience from both sides. For the maker this means that the "Tower of Song" where he resides is anything but an ivory tower. He stands by the window, "where the light is strong," and occupies a strategic intermediate position. He keeps in contact with the outside world, while retreating into the inner sanctum of his study. It is an ambivalent position that not only saddles the artist with a heavy burden but also threatens to undermine his coherent identity.

NOTES

1 According to Sylvie Simmons this was merely how his artistry manifested itself. "He turned his writing into a ritual, but perhaps the death of his father did not have as big an impact as some people would have us believe" (Simmons in a telephone interview with the author; for a synopsis see Mus 2012b). Tim Footman (2009, 7) situated the birth of the artist in 1949, the year in which Cohen discovered Lorca, bought his first guitar, and attended his first concert. In an old interview from 1969 Cohen himself gave more mundane reasons. When asked about the real start of his career as a writer, he replied: "I do remember sitting down at a card table on a sun porch one day when I decided to quit a job. I was working in a brass foundry at the time and one morning I thought, I just can't take this anymore, and I went out to the sun porch and I started a poem" (Batten et al. 1969, 30). Cohen did not come forward with the "garden story" until 1980 (Simmons 2012, 16).

2 I have borrowed this distinction from Rudi Visker's (2007, 105–110) reflections on mourning. Visker writes about the now obsolete practice of what is known in French as *porter le deuil*: the mourning that was once seen as a matter for the entire community, with people wearing black clothes or a black ribbon throughout a specified period. The author identifies a contemporary aversion to any form of symbolization: such (externalized) symbols are seen as something that does not come from within and therefore cannot be authentic. The idea that someone would "interfere" in personal feelings in this way is considered problematic. Some of this filters through in *The Favourite Game* when Breavman writes about burial rites in a letter to his beloved Shell:

> I went to a funeral today. It was no way to bury a child. His real death contrasted violently with the hush-hush sacredness of the chapel. The beautiful words didn't belong on the rabbi's lips. I don't know if any modern man is fit to bury a person. The family's grief was real, but the air-conditioned chapel conspired against its expression. I felt lousy and choked because I had nothing to say to the corpse. When they carried away the undersized coffin I thought the boy was cheated. (Cohen [1963] 1994, 224–225)

On a more anecdotal level, there is the care Cohen lavishes on clothing in general. At times he appears to have become one with the bespoke suit in which he is habitually seen. In an interview from 1969 he described clothing as "a magical procedure, they really change the way you are in a day. Any woman knows this, and men have discovered it now. I mean, clothes are important to us and until I can discover in some clearer way what I am to myself I'll just keep on wearing my old clothes" (Batten et al. 1969, 29). More than forty years after this interview

Sylvie Simmons opens her biography with a brief conversation she had with Cohen, which he concludes in his inimitable way: "Darling, I was born in a suit."

In this and the previous chapter, I want to highlight the (often subtle) distinction between the constructive, identificatory role of the symbol on the one hand, and its exploitation, for instance by the media or by Cohen himself, on the other.

3 Although Cohen provides no further information, the author in question is most likely the Irish theologian and writer William Kelly (1821–1906).

4 In this poem, A. M. Klein writes about a Jew making love. In the light of those who lost their lives in the camps, he feels compelled to give life and not waste his seed by using contraception or masturbating

5 There are two editions of the poem "Pequeño vals vienés" (from the collection *Poeta en Nueva York*). The best known of these was published in Spain by José Bergamín. Although widely recognized as the standard text, it came out later than the version of Rolfe Humphries, in May and June 1940 respectively. For his adaptation, Cohen was inspired by the Humphries edition, perhaps because it was published alongside an English translation. In Lorca, the image of the sea can be found in "Cuerpo presente," the third poem of *Llanto por Ignacio Sanchez Mejias*. In Cohen's work, the liberating force of the sea can be read as the liberation of/in death, for instance in "Suzanne": "All men shall be sailors then until the sea shall free them." In "A Thousand Kisses Deep" he talks about "the limits of the sea," while "Hey, That's No Way to Say Goodbye" evokes the cyclical nature of high and low tide ("like the shoreline and the sea"), and "Light As the Breeze" mentions "the cradle of the river and the seas."

THREE

ALIENATION
FROM LOCAL EMBEDDEDNESS AND GLOBAL EXILE TO UNIVERSAL ASPIRATIONS AND BACK AGAIN

"On the alienation scale, he rates somewhere between Schopenhauer and Bob Dylan, two other prominent poets of pessimism." So judged Donal Henahan, the cultural editor of the *New York Times,* in 1968. "In capsule it might be said that whereas Mr. Dylan is alienated from society and mad about it, Mr. Cohen is alienated and merely sad about it" (Rasky [2001] 2010, 19). But as the foregoing has shown, Cohen does much more than wallow in the human condition. He credited art with a liberating potential, while the combination of different identities also meant that for the singer with Jewish and Canadian roots, who tended to cultivate the (semi- or pseudo-) romantic ethos of the artist as *einzelgänger,* the act of departure soon became second nature. Yet in his well-known farewell to Marianne, he also sings: "I used to think I was some kind of gypsy boy, before I let you take me home." It remains unclear whether it is love that has prompted him to abandon his nomadic life, since he is the one who voluntarily grants Marianne permission to let him come home to her.

At the same time, he is saying something essential about this restless life. Underlying this inner urge to keep venturing out is an even deeper-rooted desire to come home somewhere. The former aspect will be familiar: the many accounts of Cohen's life often take the form of one long road trip, not unlike Bob Dylan, who for some time now has been on a "never-ending tour." Nonetheless, the undercurrent of domesticity in Cohen's work is at least as important, and it is a subject he often revisits. Does his artistic vocation allow him to find a lasting home somewhere? In 2012, on the opening track of *Old Ideas*, it seems as if the question finally has a positive answer. Right from the first lines of "Going Home" Cohen indicates that he wants to hang up his suit to go home. Judging by the album's atmosphere as a whole, this home can be seen as an ultimate endpoint, death.

Originally this home was in Montréal. Although Cohen travelled a great deal in the early years of his literary career, in nearly every interview during this period he claimed that he had to keep going back to his hometown "to renew his neurotic affiliations" (various interviews, as well as the back cover of *The Spice-Box of Earth*). In fact, despite his international success, he long presented himself as a local writer, although it must be said that his regular visits to Montréal had more to do with family and friends than literary motives. The institutional literary centre of Canada was in Toronto, which is where his publisher, McClelland and Stewart, was based.

In any case, this mixed feeling, somewhere between longing and commitment, between travelling *and* coming home again, manifested itself early on. "Stranger Music" is not just the title of a collection of works; the two words are carved into Cohen's guitar case like a calling card—name and line of work. The figure of the stranger provided him with a suitable narrative both for telling his life story and for positioning himself in the work, one in which the nomadic life is a recurring theme. Since the very early days of his public appearances, Cohen cultivated the artistic persona of the stranger. "The Stranger Song" is one of the first tracks he performed live. He sang it in 1968 during a BBC TV show with Julie Felix, around the time his debut album was released. The image seems very romantic: a traditionally dressed and neatly coiffed young man quietly playing his guitar, gazing into the distance and, at the end, when he calls himself a stranger, wiping away a tear.

Another arresting image is the opening scene of *McCabe & Mrs. Miller*, a 1971 western directed by Robert Altman. An impressive travelling shot captures the vast American landscape. In the middle of that vast expanse the figure of a lonesome cowboy appears: McCabe. Destination unknown. Above all, the scene reflects the monotony of being on the road. The horse's steady pace is underpinned by Cohen's rhythmic strumming in the background. McCabe the cowboy feels lost, displaced, disoriented. The contrast between the insignificant man and the impressive landscape he confronts is a typical North American trope of alienation, but it does visualize this complex feeling in a simple and direct way. Throughout the film Cohen's music heightens and visualizes the expansiveness of nature, the loneliness of the cowboy, and the rhythm of being on the road. *McCabe & Mrs. Miller* had a substantial impact on his name recognition abroad. Over time, the sense of alienation is separated from the singer's concrete work and social situation and starts to sound like a universal condition that many readers and listeners will recognize.

FROM CANADIAN ALIENATION IN *THE FAVOURITE GAME* TO EXISTENTIAL ALIENATION IN MUSIC

Philosopher and writer Alain de Botton (2002, 9) writes: "If our lives are dominated by a search for happiness, then perhaps few activities reveal as much about the dynamics of this quest—in all its ardour and paradoxes—than our travels." Is this wanderlust inextricably linked to happiness and to the demands made by art? What drove Cohen to represent himself as a stranger? To whom or what is he a stranger? And is it possible to take such an uncomfortable feeling and use it as the basis for a viable lifestyle? Let us not draw any premature conclusions. Is the stranger Leonard Cohen not the umpteenth cliché of the artist who places himself outside of society so that from this independent position he can impart something of (artistic) consequence to his public?

Either way, there is no denying that the existential condition of the stranger precedes the artistic vocation: immigration and emigration are also common threads running through Cohen's ancestral history. When he was born in Montréal in 1934, it was into a family with Russian roots, a distinguished family that was part of a significant Jewish population in the city. On *Popular Problems* he reminisces about them: "I listened to their stories of the Gypsies and the Jews." Pierre Anctil points out that the Jews have had a presence in Montréal for some 400 years:

> Firmly anchored in Quebec's soil is a set of community institutions and recognized democratic rights that form the basis of contemporary Jewish identity in our society. Grafted onto these long-standing foundations of Québécois Judaism that appeared at the beginning of the British Regime were the great Eastern European migrations, which took place in tragic circumstances and in a context of sometimes pernicious anti-Semitic tension. (Anctil 2017, 391)

As a young artist Cohen would distance himself from this Jewish community.[1] Of course this does not alter the fact that Jewishness is an inspiration in his oeuvre, although it is not always easy to pinpoint this influence. Unlike Hebrew and Israeli culture, which are easier to define (through language and geography—Hebrew and the state of Israel, respectively), Jewish culture is habitually described using a number of recurring themes that have marked the history of the Jewish people: the diaspora experience, centuries of migration and exile, the Holocaust, as well as an ironic take on life. Each one of these subjects profoundly shaped the poetry of some of Cohen's older colleagues in Montréal. Irving Layton, A. M. Klein, Eli Mandel, and Miriam Waddington formed a community of Jewish writers which, according to Layton, was as cohesive as it was self-conscious (see Rasky [2001] 2010, 37). This self-consciousness is partly explained by the fact that in Montréal in the 1950s language and religion were a source of division more than a source of diversity.

In *The Favourite Game* Cohen painted an accurate picture of the way in which the Jewish community was embedded within the city. Although many have read Cohen's debut novel exclusively as a *Bildungsroman* or, more specifically, a *Künstlerroman*—and it is often taken to be wholly autobiographical—the city, and space in general, can also be seen as a full-fledged character, one that has a significant influence on protagonist Lawrence Breavman and his best friend, Krantz. We are not just talking about the broad theme of arrival and departure, but also about the specific urban context of Montréal and New York, two cities that have a strong presence and help shape the narrative. In the 1970 foreword[2] Rowland J. Smith concludes:

> It is, however, the description of growing up in Westmount which must remain the unique feature of *The Favourite Game*. Lyric and ironic, tender and yet sharply focused, the picture of Breavman's childhood and adolescence vividly evokes an aspect of Canadian life, and yet embodies an intensity of experience which far transcends the limits of Montreal. (Smith 1970, s.p.)

Smith identifies an interaction between the space of the city and the "intensity of experience" it gives Breavman. Equally, the paratext illustrates how a particular space can shape an experience. The novel opens with an epigraph, "As the Mist Leaves No Scar" (from *The Spice-Box of*

Earth), one of Cohen's most popular poems from the 1960s, in which he effectively hands his reader a key to the book's interpretation[3]: "As the mist leaves no scar / On the dark green hill, / So my body leaves no scar / On you, nor ever will." Although some read the "dark green hill" as a clear allusion to the imposing Mount Royal, the poem is first and foremost an existential question about personal encounters, or the possibility thereof, and the traces that such contact can leave. These traces are described in less than innocent terms as "scars," which is in fact the novel's central motif, as we can see already from the opening paragraphs. *The Favourite Game* links abstract, existential themes to a concrete, spatial context: streets, neighbourhoods, squares, and districts are mentioned by name.

In the sections that follow I will take the effect of space as my starting point; in the final chapter, I will turn this around and focus on the encounter itself. For now I will limit myself to saying that physical space plays an active role in creating a parallel imaginary universe. Put more generally, Cohen mythologizes reality (just like, conversely, he demythologizes the myth; see chapter 4, on religion). Take, for instance, the passage that describes protagonist Lawrence Breavman's view of the local park from his room:

> At night the park was his domain. [...] The empty baseball diamond was blurred with spectacular sliding ghosts. He could hear the absence of cheers. [...] Just beyond the green rose the large stone houses of Westmount Avenue. [...] The park nourished all the sleepers in the surrounding houses. It was the green heart. It gave the children dangerous bushes and heroic landscapes so they could imagine bravery. It gave the nurses and maids winding walks so they could imagine beauty. It gave the young merchant-princes leaf-hid necking benches, views of factories so they could imagine power. It gave the retired brokers vignettes of Scottish lanes where loving couples walked, so they could lean on their canes and imagine poetry. It was the best part of everyone's life. (Cohen [1963] 1994, 69–70)

ALIENATION

One would be hard-pressed to overestimate the role of the space here. The park is anthropomorphized ("nourished," "heart," "gave") and invites an escapism that is primarily figurative (the protagonist dreams a way out of everyday life), but can also be taken literally. There are indeed quite a few passages in which Breavman gets into the car with Krantz and heads off, into the big wide world. Chapter 12 of Book II is a case in point:

> Still Breavman and Krantz often used to drive through the whole night. They'd listen to pop tunes on the local stations or classics from the United States. They'd head north to the Laurentians or east to the Townships. [...] Moving at that speed they were not bound to anything. (Cohen [1963] 1994, 98)

Music, and art in general, also proves useful for disengaging from everyday reality. "The news is sad but it's in a song so it's not so bad," as Breavman says a few pages down in the same chapter. What is worth noting here is that space only has a positive impact on the characters when they are in a non-urban context; nature (Murray Hill Parc, the Laurentians, the Eastern Townships) is experienced as purer than the reality of the metropolis with its compressed social relations and the weight of history. The city gets under its residents' skin and will not let go:

> Some say that no one ever leaves Montreal, for that city, like Canada itself, is designed to preserve the past, a past that happened somewhere else. This past is not preserved in the buildings or monuments, which fall easily to profit, but in the minds of her citizens. The clothes they wear, the jobs they perform are only the disguises of fashion. (Cohen [1963] 1994, 122)[4]

The picture that Cohen paints of Montréal is not new, just like the distinction between city and countryside is a familiar trope in many literary traditions. It is an established theme in European literature, where nature is presented as a *locus amoenus*, an idealized place of purity and sincerity that forms a contrast with the city, where semblance and illusion prevail. At the same time, nature also has a prominent and long-standing tradition in the arts in Canada, where it not only reflects a moral purity but also a purity of national identity. The Québécois identity was seen to be at its best in the countryside, expressed, among other ways, in the use of local dialects—the language of "the savage that I was in the infancy of the tall grass," as Michel Garneau once wrote (cf. Brisset 2012). This identity discourse really came to the fore during the Quiet Revolution, in literature too, including in the work of poet Paul Chamberland, which prompted Annie Brisset to comment: "We see the formation of a vicious circle of nostalgia which, exclusive and inward-turning, rejects the Other and its culture. In this nostalgia for a return to nature, there is also a call for a return to a language which, if not lost, has yet to re-emerge" (2012, 294). *The Favourite Game*, however, is particularly interested in the former dichotomy, of seeming and being: the protagonist is looking for himself and wants to be free to undertake this search. As such, a francophone Canadian reviewer not only regarded the protagonist's alienation as the central motif of *The Favourite Game* but also as something that connected Cohen with his francophone colleagues in Quebec (Henault, in Cohen papers, 6). For Siemerling (1994, 29) as well as for Leduc-Cummings the city as a place of "inner exile" is a recurring theme in the "imaginary Québécois": "For a long time, the image of the city in the Quebec imagination was rather negative. Urban alienation and an anti-urban discourse have long haunted the literature" (Leduc-Cummings 1992, 9).

Ultimately, Breavman has no choice but to flee Montréal. Drawn to the "land of the free," he heads for New York. The end of the book's second part coincides with his arrival in America, where he looks for a place at a safe, strategic distance from the hustle and bustle of the city: in a tower, with an international (student) community, and with a view of the river. In other words, his new home offers a broader perspective in all kinds of ways, with a few mental and physical escape routes within reach. But this time he also experiences a sense of freedom *within* the city: "Everybody spoke a kind of English, no resentment, he could talk to people everywhere" (Cohen [1963] 1994, 125). The allusion to tense linguistic and ideological relations in Montréal is implied, but obvious. In the preceding pages, the Jewish identity of the two main characters was made painfully clear when they entered a dance hall and were confronted by a group of dancers, "Catholics, French-Canadian, anti-Semitic, anti-Anglais" (47). Their attempts at seducing a francophone girl lead to a tense situation that culminates in a scuffle with a group of French-speaking boys. "*Reste là, maudit juif*" (Cohen [1963] 1994, 50), one of them snarls at Breavman in French. This, and a similar scene in *Beautiful Losers*,[5] prompted Sherry Simon to argue that

> Cohen's take on the nationalism of francophone Montreal during the 1960s reflects the frictions of the divided city in which he grew up. Anglophones lived in the more privileged west, Francophones in the east—and, although there was little physical distance between the communities, the weight of historical inequalities made communion impossible. (Simon 2012, 144)

In a letter to his sister in 1963, Cohen summarized the relationship with the francophone community as follows: "We know nothing about these people. Hugh MacLennan said nothing in his book but everything in his title, TWO SOLITUDES" (Cohen papers, 11–12). Yet this is only the partial truth. During the same period, Cohen was to make several overtures in francophone (mostly artistic) circles, which are rarely if ever mentioned in the many biographies. Before Cohen turned his gaze almost exclusively onto the rest of the world in subsequent years, he assumed a role that, albeit on a much smaller scale, was comparable to the translation activities of poets like John Glassco, F. R. Scott, and D. G. Jones. The most eye-catching example is undoubtedly his collaboration with Québécois filmmaker Claude

Jutra. "I'm learning a whole new vocabulary" (Cohen papers, 10A-38), Cohen wrote to the poet Glassco in January 1964, the year he received Quebec's Literary Competition Prize for his first novel. In October of the previous year Cohen had met his colleague at the Foster Poetry Conference in the Eastern Townships. In his letter, he shares his experience of translating the French script of *À tout prendre*, a film directed by Jutra. The English version is remarkable: *Take It All*[6] combines the English subtitles for the French dialog (translated by Cohen) with the spoken English of the interior monologues as they appeared in the original version. In the same letter Cohen hints at another translation he was set to do for Jutra, but that never materialized. The English translation of *À tout prendre* is hard to come by today (with the exception of a few archives), which is astonishing given that both the filmmaker and the translator are celebrated artists in Quebec; and Cohen himself contacted the Academy of Motion Picture Arts and Sciences in Hollywood and tried to enter the film into the Oscars' foreign film category.[7]

While the specific references to Quebec and Canada are fairly common throughout the literary work, they disappear in the later music. There Cohen only rarely links the universal sense of alienation to his Canadian or family background. The reference to his parents in "Almost Like the Blues" is an exception. By the same token, few international readers and listeners are familiar with the Jewish-Canadian social and literary backdrop to Cohen's work. The evolution is clear when we compare texts that have appeared in different versions. The procedure is always the same: the "realia" in the first text are removed or replaced by a more general formulation in the second. In "Memories," a song from 1977, for example, Cohen paraphrases the passage from *The Favourite Game* about the confrontation between anglophone Jews and francophone Catholics, but leaves out any concrete reference to Montréal. The story is reduced to an exciting encounter between a boy and a girl, and the failed attempt at seduction that follows. Another example is "Light As the Breeze," which also has its place names taken out. While the lyric booklet still says "St. Lawrence River is starting to freeze," in the actual song Cohen sticks to "The river is starting to freeze." The same happened in "Take This Longing": in Cohen's version, which was released in 1974, the singer's plea to his beloved evokes universal heartache. Three years earlier, however, Buffy Sainte-Marie released a version that is much more specific in places. Sainte-Marie outlines the song's rationale in the very first line ("I'm writing you to say goodbye"—this is a farewell letter) and a little later the location is mentioned by name too ("in the midst of New York City"). Even Cohen's own reworking of his best-known song "Hallelujah," which has been released in a range of versions (see the chapter on religion), fits this pattern. In short, one could argue that the concrete vocabulary and tone in Cohen's literary work were raised to a more abstract level in his music.[8] The explanation for this may be obvious: unlike his novels and books of poetry, from the outset Cohen's music was aimed at a bigger audience, which did not necessarily have a connection with Canada. The way Skelton Grant (1977, 107) sees it is that, compared to the literary work, the listener has a greater role to play in the music, thanks to its heightened dialogical character: "The shift from the formal statement of the poems to the casual conversation of the songs can be seen as a sensitive response to the more personal, immediate relationship between singer and audience." In the music Cohen's imagination expresses itself through more general points of reference—a bridge, a river, a street (corner), a hotel, a room. Listeners can picture these, wherever they hail from.[9]

IN SEARCH OF A SURVIVAL STRATEGY
THE INTERMEDIATE SPACE

In 1967 Cohen articulated his vocation clearly in the declaration of intent that is "Sisters of Mercy": "You who must leave everything that you cannot control. / It begins with your family, but soon it comes round to your soul." In "Came So Far for Beauty" (1979) he was to renew his vow in near-identical terms, and twenty-five years later "Undertow" (2004) could be read as a psychological self-diagnosis in which the undertow functions as a metaphor for his vocation: "I set out one night / when the tide was low / there were signs in the sky / but I did not know / I'd be caught in the grip / of the undertow." The numerous biographies illustrate just how serious Cohen was about these declarations of intent. Likewise, the characters who inhabit his artistic universe have trouble committing to anyone. If they are not to betray their vocation, attachment simply is not an option. He regularly sees himself, or is seen by others, as a "traitor"—from *The Favourite Game* and his speech to the Jewish Public Library, in Montréal, in 1964 (see Fournier and Norris 1994, 143–153) to the track of that name on *Recent Songs*. The spatial metaphors Cohen likes to use express the idea of an estrangement very well. There are plenty of examples. In "You Know Who I Am" he puts it like this: "I cannot follow you my love, / you cannot follow me / I am the distance you put between / all of the moments that we will be." In "Winter Lady," chronicling the admiration for an unattainable woman, the singer labels himself as a "station on your way"; in "Never Any Good" he views himself as a tourist (someone passing through, that is) when he looks back on an earlier relationship; and even in "The Notebooks" from *The Flame* the same idea pops up: "take the woman / by my side / I can't have her, / where I'm going / I can't even / tell her why."

Are there ways of living with the distance and the solitude of one's existence without betraying one's vocation? The work offers a few fragmentary answers. First, strangely enough, what may initially feel like a problematic distance could offer an opportunity. It has a calming effect, since the position of artist does not come with any restrictions and obligations aside from artistic ones. In poems like "Travel" (from *The Spice-Box of Earth*) and "Death to This Book" (from *Death of a Lady's Man*), Cohen views the journey as an escape. He achieves a similar effect through the frequent use of irony: he deliberately introduces a mental distance that functions as a shield that keeps intimate feelings at bay. At the same time, irony lets him deliver an unpleasant message in a light-hearted way. As Siemerling (1994, 22) puts it: "An ironic assertion of multiple positions around the figure of negation indeed accommodates important aspects of Cohen's 'I's (that never say where we expect them to go)." From where the artist is standing, that place is not only experienced as a sanctuary but it can also serve as a potential observation post. The objective distance allows the artist to subject both himself and others to close scrutiny. His gaze gives him a clear view of things; the best insider is an outsider. In "Democracy," Cohen analyzes American society from the outside. He watches as the ship of democracy sets sail for the United States: "I love the country, but I can't stand the scene." Admiration and criticism go hand in hand. The importance of this strategic position was mentioned at the end of chapter 2, when we saw the artist nestle by the window, from where he can keep an eye on both the outside world and his own inner landscape.

The symbolism of the window is familiar and can be found in the works of, among others, Edouard Manet, Adolph von Menzel, and Edward Hopper, where windows and blowing curtains hint at access to another, intangible reality. In Cohen they play a role in "So Long, Marianne," "Light As The Breeze," "Tower of Song," and "Stories Of The Street," to name but a few. In the latter we hear: "I lean from my window sill in this old hotel I chose, yes one hand on my suicide, one hand on the rose." The tension lies in this in-between position. The artist must first efface himself before he can pick the flower of art. He has to eliminate the man, with all his longings and ambitions, in order to create. In his first book of poetry he was not yet capable of doing so. In "Had We Nothing to Prove" the young poet acknowledges that in principle he might have stood in front of his window all night long, but he actually succumbed to his love: "There were the formalities of passion; so we sealed the shutters and were expedient in the brevity of the night."

The balcony is a similar observation post. It epitomizes the Montréal urban landscape, and is a prominent feature not only in Cohen's work but in many scenes from Québécois literature:

> The balcony represents the little universe of the working-class neighbourhoods, but also a major element of the Montreal urban landscape and for many people a necessity, practical or psychological. The novel boasts innumerable balcony scenes. Watching people go by, see and be seen, taking part in its essentially Latin character: from his balcony on the front row, the Montrealer looks at and participates in the spectacle of life. (Leduc-Cummings 1992, 12)

There is no better example than the carefully scripted scene from the documentary *The Song of Leonard Cohen* (1980), which shows Cohen giving an interview on the balcony of his apartment near Boulevard Saint-Laurent. By now an internationally renowned singer-songwriter, he is filmed in a domestic setting. As in all other accounts of his life and work, Cohen here subtly draws on the neutral, informative framework of the documentary to help shape his artistic persona. The sequence is iconic for a number of reasons. The framework feels familiar: he is filmed on his balcony, he is dressed in black, and he plays a few chords on his guitar. Seated at an outdoor table he then plays a tape with a recording of "Un Canadien errant," which had been released the previous year. The balcony symbolizes the dual mediating role Cohen fulfills here. On the one hand, he translates the song live into English for the filmmaker and his audience while also commenting on the text; on the other, the viewer sees footage of the urban life taking place below, alternating with Cohen's watchful gaze, hidden behind flashy shades.

The sanctuary and the observation post meet in the experience of excess. This is where Cohen can escape himself: in the intoxication of alcohol or drugs or in the ecstasy of sexuality he is "outside himself." In "Crazy to Love You" he formulates the idea rather cryptically as

ALIENATION

"heading for the highway." In "A Thousand Kisses Deep" he lets it be known that extreme feelings suit him better than moderation: "I'm good at love, I'm good at hate / It's in between I freeze." In between lies a vacuum, an uncomfortable place where he does not know what to do with himself. At the same time he tries to find himself in the experience of excess, to see who he is and what inspires him. In the 1960s he told Sandra Djwa: "If only people get high, they can face the evil part" (Simmons 2012, 119). He put his money where his mouth was: much of *Beautiful Losers*, for example, was written under the influence of drugs, and during his first tours drug use was rife too.

Finally, every now and then Cohen tries to undo this alienating distance, or to at least partially bridge it, by going in search of some sort of intermediate space, a geographical space, or a mental state that is experienced as balanced and enduring. This quest is a constant in Cohen's life and work. The most literal way in which he seeks out this intermediate space is evinced by his choice of neighbourhood. He did not opt for his childhood home. Westmount was a well-to-do suburb of Montréal where, as an anglophone Jew, he and his family were literally in the

Outtakes from the documentary *The Song of Leonard Cohen* (1980)

margins of the dominant francophone and Catholic society. It was during his college years that he would first leave his home turf and spend shorter or longer periods of time in New York City (officially to study, in practice to immerse himself in the art scene without ever gaining full inclusion), London (where he wrote his first novel), Hydra (a Greek island and artists' colony, where he bought a house, met Marianne, and wrote *Beautiful Losers*), Nashville (to record his second and third albums), as well as other places. When he returned to Montréal in the early 1970s it was not to Westmount but to a house he bought in the center of town, near Boulevard Saint-Laurent. This was not a naive choice. The "Main" occupies a symbolic place in the urban landscape and has seen its role shifting over the years. The neighbourhood was once home to quite a few Jews, then it turned into a conflict zone and a legendary dividing line between east and west, before eventually evolving into a place where the different communities met. This evolution, which took place in the 1960s and 1970s, is described as follows by Pierre Anctil:

> Almost at the same time as the identity quest proliferates in all its diversity on the Main, great writers emerge in Montreal, many from this neighbourhood, who spread the climate of diffuse and unspeakable poetry that emerges from it. With them, the boulevard Saint-Laurent makes its entry into Québécois and Canadian, even world literature, as an unexpected meeting place of cultures and hybrid identity. A consciousness emerges: the old artery, which for decades had been the backbone of the city, is being transformed once more into a place conducive to creation, to social marginality, and to new ideas. (2002, 87)

By settling there, Cohen could couple his local attachment with an openness to other languages and cultural communities. In the next section, I will look more closely at the way in which the work ties a local inspiration to an international aspiration.

ALIENATION

Another example of an intermediate space is the hotel, for which Cohen has a special predilection. In *Ladies and Gentlemen... Mr. Leonard Cohen* (1965) he was filmed in a hotel. In the 1960s it was not unusual for artists to rent a hotel room for several weeks or even months. It made the hotel an alternative home. Later in his life, too, the hotel room was the ideal habitat for Cohen: when, at the start of this century, he left the Buddhist Mount Baldy Zen monastery and felt that his depression had lifted, he joked to his friend Harry Rasky that he had found "the perfect hotel room" ([2001] 2010, 136). The hotel is equally ubiquitous in his repertoire. Titles like "Chelsea Hotel" and "Paper Thin Hotel" show this unequivocally. In *The Favourite Game* the hotel even becomes a full-fledged character. In a reflection on Cohen's first novel, Michael Ondaatje (1970, 30) notes that Lawrence Breavman occasionally retreats into the enclosed space of his hotel room with his lover Tamara. When the shutters are closed, the separation from the outside world is complete. With its neutral, almost sterile decoration, the interior of their room has nothing whatsoever to do with what goes on outside. The room is cleaned every morning; all sins are washed away. The room is like a blank piece of paper, on which anything can still be written, without any constraints. However, the interior of Breavman's hotel room changes when he falls in love with someone else. His new lover, Shell, wants to decorate the room and make it more personal. So the room comes to reflect them after all, and the outside world sneaks in yet again. The *locus amoenus* that Tamara was able to create is no more. This idea has been touched on in interviews, with Cohen indicating that he chooses his living space carefully: "It's nice to have an exterior that is somewhat ordered when the inside is somewhat disordered" (Rasky [2001] 2010, 68).

The neutral interior on the cover of *Songs from a Room* (bed, table, chair, woman) testifies to this. There is even something timeless about the title of this album, unlike that of others, which often contain references to either the past or the future (*Recent Songs, New Skin for the Old Ceremony, The Future, Ten New Songs, Old Ideas, Popular*

Problems). In *I Am a Hotel*, the only film Cohen worked on both in front of and behind the camera, he even seems to identify with the hotel. The short music film is a collection of five scenes based on just as many songs (and no dialogue): "The Guests," "Memories," "The Gypsy's Wife," "Chelsea Hotel #2," and "Suzanne." Cohen takes on the role of a resident who watches in amusement or takes part in the action while he sings. The atmosphere is a strange one: the artificial character of the hotel is conveyed by a fairy-tale world in which characters attract or repel each other. They do not simply walk, but strut or dance instead. French music journalist and writer Gilles Tordjman (2006, 139) labelled the intermediate space of the hotel room as "an itinerant exile" and interpreted the title of the short film as follows: "Being a hotel: accepting the vacancy, the availability, which allows the ghosts to put down their light suitcases. Welcoming those who are no longer travelling, but who keep turning up. Being a hotel *where things happen*" (140).

Alongside the hotel, the café can also serve as a temporary halting place. "From my deep café I survey the quiet snowfields," it says in the poem "Cherry Orchards."[10] In *Death of a Lady's Man* the café is situated in the port of Piraeus, the place of arrival on and departure from his favourite island, Hydra. Likewise, the rented home can be a halting place. And although Cohen evokes this image less often, the "Tower of Song" is certainly one of the most symbolic places for the artist. It is the house of Music—with a capital "M"—where Cohen can only linger briefly, and where he must pay his rent every day.[11] Even in this tower of art, he is never fully at home. This not only stems from the tension between domesticity and alienation but also from his position in the artistic field: in his capacity as a singer he is sometimes regarded with suspicion because he is also a poet, whereas literary critics are of the opinion that his place is in the music world. At times this ambiguous position is a hindrance to him, at others a benefit. In 2014 in "Almost Like the Blues" he referred to "all my bad reviews," which haunted him his whole life.

ALIENATION

COHEN'S ARTISTIC PRACTICE AS A PENDULUM BETWEEN LOCAL INSPIRATION AND UNIVERSAL ASPIRATION

The search for an intermediate space in Cohen's artistic practice can also be interpreted in a more abstract way: quite a few literary and musical traditions converge in his imagination. He takes his inspiration from an extremely wide range of sources. He looks well beyond Canadian borders, as is suggested by the many references in interviews, mottos, and titles to Canadian artists (e.g., Irving Layton, A. M. Klein, Mordecai Richler, Georges Dor), as well as American (e.g., Ray Charles, Herman Melville, George Jones, Frederick Knight), European (e.g., W. B. Yeats, Albert Camus, Byron, Lorca) and Asian (e.g., Rumi, Hafiz). Every now and then these connections are made explicit in the texts themselves—for example in the adaptations and translations he has done of Lorca, Byron, Rumi, and others. Yet not all of the planned projects have come to fruition. Cohen repeatedly said that he intended to translate Edith Piaf's work into English. It would have been a fitting choice, considering that his music has more affinity with European traditions than American ones. He never made a secret of his love of American country music either, and he injected quite a few bluesy elements into the songs on his last albums, possibly because the connection between words and music is strong in the blues. This idiosyncratic combination of styles and materials means that Cohen sometimes walks along, but usually just outside, the lines of music and literary history.[12]

Cohen does not cite his references to these different traditions the way a scholar would, but often subtly blends them in the artistic process. The exception here is his first book of poetry, *Let Us Compare Mythologies*, in which he did disentangle the individual components for his readers. In "Ballad," for example, the poet turns into a kind of Frankenstein, cutting and pasting as he tries to describe his beloved. The poem begins with the statement that his beloved is dead, and has been found mutilated. Seeing her only through the eyes of writers and artists, he evokes her appearance with a sequence of familiar images: "Everyone knew my lady / from the movies and the art-galleries, / Body from Goldwyn. Botticelli had drawn her long limbs. / Rossetti the full mouth. / Ingres had coloured her skin. / She should not have walked so bravely through the streets." The outcome is ambiguous. To what extent can the poet still speak of "*my* lady"? She is known to anybody and nobody.

Given this eclecticism, there are many different approaches to his work.[13] It can be looked at in relation to his roots, to the rest of the world, or to anything that transcends this. He covers specific topics (the US political system in "Democracy," the 1992 race riots in Los Angeles on "The Future," the September 11 attacks on "On That Day" and on "A Street," the devastating impact of AIDS on "Ain't No Cure for Love," Hurricane Katrina on "Samson in New Orleans"), while also wanting to lift them to a more abstract level (What is democracy? How can we live with others? Is love destructive or constructive? Is there such a thing as individuality?). Cohen steers a deft course between a local embeddedness and an international, at times even universal, aspiration. "Your most particular answer will be your most universal one," he confided to Jennifer Warnes in the 1990s (Burger 2014, 264). "I live within that polarity," he said a few years earlier in an interview in which he talked about his relationship with Montréal (Benazon 1986, 50).

On that issue, he differs from a number of other writers from Montréal. For example, Mordecai Richler portrays an urbane geography in his work, "closely allied to the life of the Jewish community in Montreal" (Biron et al. [2007] 2010, 478), whereas Cohen's universal aspiration situates him closer to A. M. Klein: Klein "*came out* of the Jewish community of Montreal, but [he] [...] had a perspective on it and on the country, and on the province. He made a step outside the community. He was no longer protected by it" (Benazon 1986, 45). In view of this variety of influences, some critics have reproached him for neglecting his home country. In 1972 his compatriot Malcolm Reid sneered that he was more interested in "America, Europe, talking to My Generation, joining the Robert Graveses and the Lawrence Durells in their sunny, non-national Parnassi," before concluding rather bitterly: "[T]here is something tragic in our quest for universal engagements when we haven't come to grips with a situation in which we are ourselves implicated" (Reid, cited in Simon 2006, 38).

For Reid, Sherry Simon argues, rootedness is "necessary to a certain stage of struggle toward social goals" (Simon 2006, 38). Reid's views must be read within the context of the tense socio-political situation of the 1960s and 1970s and the Quiet Revolution. His remarks were not exceptional. In a Bourdieuan study about the role of translation and identity in Francophone theatre in Quebec during this period, Annie Brisset notes that these theatre productions harnessed their themes and style to "distinguish" themselves from the socially and artistically dominant other. The result was an artistic production and an accompanying discourse that promoted a Québécois identity that was as pure and homogenous as possible. As a counter example, she cites the poetry of writer and translator Michel Garneau, who played a significant and distinctive role in Quebec's artistic identity politics with his idiosyncratic Québécois translations of Shakespeare: "His apologia for cross-breeding uses poetic language to reveal and acclaim the mixed background of the Québécois identity: 'J'ai tout le sang mêlé / les ancêtres sont mes étrangers / un peu d'hurabénaquois / un peu d'irlancossais'" (My blood is all mixed up / my ancestors are strangers / a bit of Hurabénaquois / a bit of Irish-Scots (Brisset 2012, 290). In this excerpt from a 1974 poem, Garneau draws on both lexicon and syntax to represent the hybrid Québécois identity. The Québécois's receptiveness to the Other is not a silent threat here, but a manifest quality. Some forty years later, in 2011 in the poem "Les regards," he once again praised the heterogeneity that some artists—among them his brother Sylvain Garneau, as well as Leonard Cohen—have brought to bear on their life and work.

In and around Cohen's work, "here" and "elsewhere" are interdependent. As such his artistic self-representation does not consist of an unanchored cosmopolitanism that could conceivably culminate in the unreserved embrace of another home country. A case in point is this fragment from the "note to the Chinese reader," included in the Chinese translation of *Beautiful Losers*, in which the author does not align himself with a single place or tradition:

> Dear Reader,
> Thank you for coming to this book. [...] I sincerely appreciate the efforts of the translator and the publishers in bringing this curious work to your attention. [...] When I was young, my friends and I read and admired the old Chinese poets. [...] So you can understand, Dear Reader, how privileged I feel to be able to graze, even for a moment, and with such meager credentials, on the outskirts of your tradition. [...] This book was written [...] on Hydra, an island in the Aegean Sea. (Cohen 2000, s.p.)

By placing the reader's perspective alongside the author's, Cohen underlines the spatiality and mobility of his work, made possible in part by the publisher and the translator: the reader "comes" to the book that was written in another space and time while the author, in the process of writing, is "grazing" on the "outskirts" of a cultural tradition that is alien to him.

Even today, few Montrealers would see Cohen as an uprooted cosmopolitan, even if he is sometimes presented as one on the international stage. The dual French translations of his work, including that of *Book of Longing* (2006), suggest as much. The French edition (from 2008) emphasizes the universal dimension of Cohen's oeuvre. The back cover reads: "The Anglophone Québécois from Montreal is first and foremost a *universal* poet" (my italics). He is also described as the author of a number of "*succès planétaires*" (global successes), while the theme of *Le livre du Désir* is summarized as "*traces des voyages*" (travel impressions) and *"explorations spirituelles"* (spiritual explorations). A short glossary was included at the back of the book with a few Canadian and Asian references, but the local, rooted dimension is overshadowed by the image of Cohen as a universal poet. The blurb of *Livre du constant désir* (the Québécois version from 2007) on the other hand is much more restrained. Only Montréal and California are mentioned. Nonetheless, translator Michel Garneau does not mince his words in the press. To him Cohen is a Montréal poet before all else, someone who "has been particularly marked" (Garneau, in Montpetit 2007) by his hometown.

Cohen has never made a secret of this attachment to his hometown. In an unpublished article from 1963 he stated: "I think it is dangerous for a writer to cut himself off from his origins. Mine are in Montréal. I love the city. I love what is happening there. It will always be the scene of my personal mythology, and it will always nourish me" (Cohen papers, 10A-34). Twenty-five years later his views had not changed. On Norwegian television he confessed: "I really feel a Montrealler. I don't even know if it's Montreal; it's a certain street in Montreal where I have a little house, that's what I guess I call 'home.'" He would do so up until the end of his life. Perhaps Cohen was able to keep referencing Montréal both in and outside of his work all this time because he always looked for—and found?—perspectives *within* his hometown that could open up a window on the world. "In Montreal," Cohen writes in his personal notes, "many languages are spoken and every language is familiar" (Cohen papers, 1-18). Ian Rae is right in saying that as early as *Let Us Compare Mythologies* Cohen

> is starting to address the complexities of writing in a multicultural space, where traditions overlap and cultural ciphers bear multiple connotations. [...] Cohen addresses English Canadian, Jewish Canadian, Québécois, and American cultures in *The Favorite Game*, and then adds Iroquois to this grouping in *Beautiful Losers*. (Rae 2008, 52-56)

How exceptional is it that Cohen cannot be subsumed under a single literary or musical tradition, but tends to move between or alongside them? Although this claim could apply to many artists who are keen to sidestep any form of categorization, this hybridity is really rather pronounced in Cohen. There are plenty of tracks to illustrate this. Take the aforementioned "Un Canadien errant," for example. In 1979, shortly after the electoral victory of the separatist Parti Québécois in Quebec, Cohen recorded his own version of this classic of the Canadian repertoire. Its writer, Antoine Gérin-Lajoie, wrote the lyrics around the time of the Lower Canada Rebellion of 1837. In response to attempted land reforms, armed uprisings broke out, which were violently quashed by the British. Several French-Canadian rebels were sentenced to death or forced into exile. Although "Un Canadien errant" may thus be considered as a typical Canadian song, one should add that even the original version looks outward. The schism between "here" and "elsewhere" is central to the text. In his adaptation, Cohen has magnified this aspect, in part by using a Mexican mariachi band. It was a deliberate choice: "I thought the resonances that were developed through that kind of treatment were quite interesting, and humorous, because you have a Jew singing a French-Canadian song with a Mexican band so it really does become a statement of exile" (O'Riordan and Meyer 1982, 118). Although "Un Canadien errant" is an outlier in Cohen's discography—an existing song he recorded entirely in French—he was to remake it in 2004 by using its melody for "The Faith," a song released on *Dear Heather*.

A second example on the same album, *Recent Songs,* is "Ballad of the Absent Mare," in which he really runs with the parallels between different traditions. The track is an adaptation of "Ten Bulls," a Buddhist parable about the discovery of the self in ten stages. This incremental spiritual quest was originally presented through the figure of a boy who goes in search of a lost bull. In the end it transpires that the bull too is merely a false image, used to visualize the self, and that it must be transcended if true self-knowledge is to be attained. The parable is a consistent refusal to tie the self to a particular place or to accord it an unambiguous meaning. Cohen's reworking is fairly radical: he transposes the story to an American setting and focuses on a cowboy in search of the mare he thought was lost. Even the music feels American. The loud trumpet conjures a vast and warm landscape that is reminiscent of the open plain in *McCabe & Mrs. Miller*. Cohen adds a third frame of reference when, at the end, the cowboy addresses his found mare with a quote (clearly indicated as such in the booklet with quotations marks) from the book of Ruth: "And he leans on her neck / and he whispers low / 'Whither thou goest I will go.'"

It is no coincidence that "Un Canadien errant" and "Ballad of the Absent Mare" were included on the same album. Roscoe Beck, the bass player who made his first appearance on *Recent Songs* and has since joined almost every tour as "musical director," remembers the 1979 band producing a kind of world music *avant la lettre*, featuring American, Canadian, Russian, and Armenian musicians. "It really was a mixing of different worlds," Beck (2012, 1) explains. This is why, right up until the final tours, Cohen viewed the backing band on *Recent Songs* as his yardstick.[14] It was producer John Lissauer, keen to inject some Ethiopian and Middle Eastern notes on *New Skin for the Old Ceremony*, who provided the initial impetus for this cosmopolitanism. During rehearsals for the *Old Ideas* tour, in August 2012, Cohen revealed that he had hit the right tone on both *Recent Songs* and the *Field Commander Cohen* tour of the same year, and therefore advised his musicians to play the live album every now and then to get a sense of the musical style he had in mind. It also explains the instrument swap in 2012, when Dino Soldo's wind instruments made way for Alexandru Bublitchi's violin. The violin had been prominent in the 1979 backing band. Roscoe Beck (2012, 4) is clear on this: "Dino [Soldo] was in a way a substitute for the violinist we couldn't find in 2008. We were trying to recapture that sound and we heard several different violinists that we tried in the group. They were all fine musicians but no one quite captured that spirit that we had heard before with Raffi [Hakopian, the violinist who worked with Cohen in 1979]."

COHEN COMES HOME
A CONTEMPORARY PERSPECTIVE ON HIS WORK

The evolution of Cohen's writing, as outlined above, in tandem with the growing international appeal of his work over the years make him the type of contemporary artist whose productions can function in all kinds of different contexts. Both his musical and literary works illustrate what David Damrosch, following Goethe, has termed "world literature." In his monograph *What Is World Literature?* he covers the concept at length:

> I take world literature to encompass all literary works that circulate beyond their culture of origin, either in translation or in their original language. [...] [A] work only has an *effective* life as world literature whenever, and wherever, it is actively present within a literary system beyond that of its original culture. (2003, 4)

Damrosch stresses that works that are considered world literature are characterized by a high level of "variability," which is "one of its constitutive features—one of its greatest strengths when the work is well presented and read well, and its greatest vulnerability when it is mishandled or misappropriated by its newfound foreign friends" (5).

This is indeed what happens when a work circulates internationally. It is inevitably subject to transformations when it is read or listened to by a new audience. Damrosch argues that these transformations are shaped by the interaction between three textual dimensions, which varies depending on the reception context: likeness, unlikeness, and an in-between, alienating "like-but-unlike." The preceding pages have shown that Cohen makes these three dimensions the subject of his work, both in the complex web of intertextual references and in the appropriation of various artistic traditions. The resonance with a familiar European "repertoire" (Even-Zohar[15])—musically the French "chansonnier," in literature the Anglo-French tradition of "dark romanticism" / "*romantisme noir*"—helped his work find acceptance with a European audience, while the Canadian context of his work remained largely unknown in Europe. Although this changed with the publication of a series of biographies, it remains to be seen to what extent these have truly impacted the reception of the work. That mix of like and unlike also manifested itself in his artistic persona. With his mysterious artistic universe and his enigmatic stage presence, Cohen managed to intrigue an audience that certainly got a sense of who he was and what he was talking about, but could never quite get to the bottom of it. For many this was the magic of his music, even for his best-known biographer, Sylvie Simmons:

> I remember hearing his voice for the first time on a compilation album CBS released in the UK in 1968—he was singing "Sisters of Mercy." I can clearly remember it lifting me up and pinning me to the wall. At that time I didn't stop to analyse why it should have had such a powerful effect, but thinking about it since, I believe it had to do with that mix of intimacy and authority in Leonard's voice and the sense that this wasn't just some regular guy, this was a man who knew something, who understood, and who had come alone to you, personally, to explain the mystery. *His songs were so very mysterious, but somehow familiar.* (Arjatsalo 2012, s.p.; my italics)

One of the most remarkable chapters in Damrosch's book addresses the changes in the international reception of Franz Kafka—"Kafka Comes Home." Damrosch argues that in recent years the author, who is known the world over for an oeuvre in which he expresses a *universal* feeling of alienation, is increasingly being read through the *specific* ethnic and cultural context in which he wrote. Authors like Kafka and Joyce "are more and more being invited home again, reconnected to roots they may not have severed so fully as had been thought" (Damrosch 2003, 187). What about Cohen? Of course Cohen's writing occupies a completely different status than Kafka's, but there are a few interesting parallels, such as the multilingual and multicultural society in which both worked; the bizarre tension between melancholy and the comic unreliability of certain narrators and protagonists; the mysterious aura created around the person of the artist at the point of reception, encouraged by the authors themselves; and of course the theme of societal and existential alienation in their work. The renewed interest for and from the context of creation is comparable too: today Cohen is indeed ubiquitous in Montréal. It is of course the place where he is buried: "Cohen's grave always has footsteps leading to it, no matter how high the snow," according to Zelermyer (Bilefsky 2018, 1). And shortly after his death two towering murals were painted downtown, both featuring the well-known and quasi-identical image of the wise old man with the fedora. Cohen himself had a hand in this return. For the opening track on *You Want It Darker* he headed to the Shaar Hashomayim synagogue, where he had his bar mitzvah as a boy, and collaborated with cantor Gideon Zelermyer and his choir. In the light of Cohen's earlier career, this return, also evident in the academic interest generated by his work, cannot be taken for granted. Twenty-five years ago, Ira Nadel marveled at "the enigma" of Cohen's reception: "excessive in Europe, tempered in North America and limited in Canada; London raves, New York questions, and Toronto tries to understand" (Nadel 1993, 108–121). It is all in the game.

The blurb of the French *Le livre du désir*, quoted above, captures the way Cohen was read and received in his final decade quite well. In virtually every review of the close to ten-year tour he was portrayed as an international artist with a universal message. That said, more local readings are possible too. Prior to his international breakthrough in the mid-1960s, Cohen's work was linked in (mostly Canadian) academic circles to local Jewish, Montréal, and Canadian traditions, and recent years have also seen an upsurge in alternative interpretations of his work, which have led to retranslations in Quebec, among other things. In addition to the aforementioned *Book of Longing* (2006) there has been a dual French translation of *Stranger Music* (1993): one for France (*Musique d'ailleurs*, a publication also intended for the rest of the world), the other for Quebec (*Étrange musique étrangère*). Michel Garneau, a renowned writer and translator as well as a personal friend of Cohen's, was responsible for the Canadian version. The two translations of *Book of Longing* expose a subtle but significant difference in their reception, which is tied to two areas of tension in Cohen's work: the interaction between a local/universal frame of reference on the one hand, and the interplay between vulgar/elevated language on the other. Although strictly speaking independent, the two conceptual pairs can influence each other and have a reinforcing or dissipating effect. The former dichotomy was illustrated earlier with reference to the presence or absence of realia (culture-specific items). An example of the latter can be found in the short poem "The Moon" (which, incidentally, is reminiscent of Philip Larkin's "Sad Steps," from 1974). The first line, hinting at the magnificence of the moon, contrasts with the following two, about the moon and about himself, in which the tone coarsens:

> The moon is outside
> I saw the great uncomplicated thing
> when I went to take a leak just now
> (Cohen 2006, 46)

At other times Cohen plays on the double meaning of words, leaving it up to the reader and translator to decide. The poem "Collapse of Zen," also from *Book of Longing*, is an often-quoted example, because Garneau himself has commented on the text and its two different French translations in an interview:

> When I can wedge my face
> into the place

and struggle with my breathing
as she brings her eager fingers down

French translators Jacques Vassal and Jean-Dominique Brierre rendered "the place" as "le lieu des lieux" (a paraphrase of "le saint des saints") while Garneau opted for the less marked "la bonne place." According to Garneau, the French translation lacked the sexual ambivalence of "the place." "I have nothing against it," Garneau said, "but it's not smutty. And Leonard, he's smutty!" (Cormier 2008). The trend toward a more elevated translation in the French version is not just reflected in a higher language register but also manifests itself in formal choices: a more frequent use of capitals, more literary verb tenses (the *passé simple*, or simple past, instead of the *imparfait*, or past imperfect, tense), a more faithful reproduction of rhyme schemes, for example. A comparison of the titles alone is telling, and shows that Garneau's translation is more explicit and audacious than Vassal-Briere's:

Cohen	Translation for France	Translation for Quebec
Stranger Music	*Musique d'ailleurs* (J. Guiloineau)	*Étrange musique étrangère* (M. Garneau)
Book of Longing	*Le livre du désir* (J. Vassal and J. D. Brierre)	*Livre du constant désir* (M. Garneau)

The two French translations sound fairly neutral, thanks to their formal and lexical equivalence, whereas by adding a word to both ("étrange" and "constant") Garneau makes the titles much more explicit. The addition of the definite article "le" in Vassal and Brierre's translation lends the book a definitive status of sorts. In interviews Cohen had argued that he had deliberately omitted the article precisely to avoid this association; the earlier *Book of Mercy* went without an article for the same reason (cf. also Tanasescu and Alberti [2016] and Mus [2017]).

ALIENATION

Although the two conceptual pairs local/universal | vulgar/elevated are not synonymous, there is every indication that a "universalizing" reading is conducive to an elevated interpretation, which may go some way to explaining certain of Vassal and Brierre's translation choices. Conversely, it seems that the local writing, as we saw in the first books, may go hand in hand with a vulgar language register. *Beautiful Losers* is a case in point: the novel is not just defined by its local dimension (see Simon 2012, 144–145), but also by its transgressive style. While hard to read, it was the content that caused particular offence to many readers. Above all, Cohen was criticized for the novel's (perceived) misogyny (see also Intermezzo 2).

Both the local and the vulgar dimensions of Cohen's oeuvre are much less prominent in Europe, and it is doubtful whether today, a few years after his passing, they are still being highlighted on the other side of the pond. At first sight, the picture seems as uniform there as it is in Europe. The weeks and months after November 2016 saw the publication of quite a few texts that paid fulsome tribute to Cohen. The *New York Times* carried an article with the suggestive title "Is Leonard Cohen the New Secular Saint of Montreal?" (Bilefsky 2018); a CTV news headline quoted music experts describing Cohen's legacy as "a national treasure" (MacLeod 2016); and two years later Derek Webster was full of praise in the Canadian journal *The Walrus*:

> Cohen never repudiated his hometown. In return, francophones and anglophones alike always treated him like the prodigal son, weeping joyful tears every time he returned—especially the last and final time. Everything he needed was elsewhere, but Leonard Cohen came back. Could there be any deeper tribute to the resonance of home? (Webster 2018)

But there are some other voices too. Myra Bloom, a lecturer in the English department at Concordia University, produced a more critical piece about what she referred to as "the darker side of Leonard

Cohen": "I think it worth considering how the posthumous focus on the 'later' Cohen [...] obscures a more complex understanding of a man who, before he became divine, was obsessed with the flesh, and not always in ways that are palatable today" (Bloom 2018). Bloom alludes here to what Martin Jay earlier termed the "aesthetic alibi," and which I looked at from the artist's perspective at the start of this chapter: the total surrender to the artistic vocation, which ought to justify all sacrifices and liberties. The idea that a woman should also make herself subservient to this artistic vocation would, as Bloom points out, frequently be abused under the cloak of art's demands. "In terms of the objectification of woman, Cohen's songs [...] are nowhere near as extreme as his fiction," she states, and concludes by asking whether *Beautiful Losers* can retain its unassailable status in the Canadian canon today (Bloom 2018). It is difficult to assess whether this status is under genuine threat, but it is noteworthy that the extended run of tributes is now occasionally interspersed with more critical pieces, which have drawn fans and critics into polemics. William Logan, for instance, wrote a scathing review of *The Flame* for the *New York Times* (2019), while film critic Amy Taubin challenged Cohen's reputation as a gentleman in an article for *Artforum*, entitled "Not My Man" (2019), in response to Nick Broomfield's documentary *Marianne and Leonard: Words of Love* (2019). The farewell letter Cohen had written to Marianne shortly before her death, and which was made public afterwards by the CBC, and eagerly shared and read on all kinds of (leading) media, was the subject of another critical piece in December 2018. On theconversation.com, Tanya Dalziell and Paul Genoni argued that the farewell letter in question, which had previously been disseminated as an authentic document, was a paraphrase made by Jan Christian Mollestad in a CBC Radio interview and later published in edited form on the CBC website. Both authors consider Mollestad's version to be "a little more pleasing" (Dalziell and Genoni 2018) than the original—entirely in line with the image we have of the late-era Leonard Cohen.

To what extent are these readings shaped by recent events—from the rehabilitation of female writers in literary studies to the many "Me Too" scandals that are reverberating around all echelons of society? The academic study of Leonard Cohen will be given a fresh impetus once the dust of fifteen years of buzz and excitement around the man and the artist has settled. A key factor in this will be the opening up of the archives.[16] But looking at the resources available to us now, one thing is certain: the interplay of local embeddedness, global exile, and universal aspirations, which comes to the fore both in the life and in the works as a deliberate choice, an unescapable necessity, or a genuine desire, should not be seen as fixed but rather as a guarantee of new readings and interpretations in the years to come.

NOTES

1. I will look at this in more detail at the beginning of the next chapter.
2. In 1994 the original foreword, from 1970, was replaced by one written by Paul Quarrington.
3. In some foreign-language editions, the poem was left out, as if it was not considered to be a part of the actual text. This was the case in both the Dutch and French translations. In other languages this varied depending on the edition. In the United States the poem was not included in the editions of 1963 (Viking Press), 1965 (Avon), 1970 (Avon), or 1971 (Bantam Books), but it was printed in the 2003 edition (Vintage Books). In England, the poem was not included in the editions of 1971 (Jonathan Cape), 1974 (Panther Books), and 2001 (Penguin Books), but did appear in that of 2009 (Blue Door). In Germany it was left out of the 1977 (Märzverlag) and 1983 (Rowohlt) editions, but was included in that of 2011 (BTB). In Spain it was not a part of the 2011 edition (Espiral), but was in 2017 (Penguin Random House Grupo Editorial). In Italy (2013, Minimum Fax) and Romania (2003, Polirom) the poem was included (in translation), and in Canada, too, the poem was printed (in every edition). My thanks to Dominique Boile for this information.
4. In a letter from the same year he writes about his book: "It has a Montreal spirit about it, something which exists no longer in the city, at least for me, and maybe you, too." (The letter is addressed to a certain "Maria and Barrie") (Cohen papers, 11-11). Later, in 1979, he indicated that diversity is coming under increasing pressure (Rasky [2001] 2010, 72).

5   "The protagonist [of *Beautiful Losers*] once again finds himself in the middle of a crowd that confuses dancing, fighting, politics and sex. This time the event is a nationalist rally, and in the excitement of mingled bodies he bursts into the chanting of anti-English slogans, even though he knows that the anti-colonialist rhetoric of 'Our Turn!' is aimed at people like himself" (Simon 2011, 144).

6   Others, including Leach (1999, 67), have remarked that the French title might have been better translated as *All Things Considered* or *When All's Said and Done*.

7   The Cinémathèque québécoise has saved a transcript of the remarkable telephone conversation between Cohen and the lady on the other end of the line in Hollywood. A copy can be found in the appendix. It is doubtful whether the transcript is authentic, but it certainly illustrates the ironic game Cohen often played when speaking in public. It also shows that the Canadian situation was primarily a domestic affair, which did not translate well to Hollywood.

8   Christophe Lebold (2013, 620) identifies a similar kind of broadening within a single album: "Organized according to a perfect geometry, *Ten New Songs* opens with the confession of a renegade of matters of the heart who cheats, lies, and smiles when he is angry ('In My Secret Life') and closes with a universal prayer that should comfort the world ('The Land of Plenty')."

9   This vagueness is a deliberate and effective textual strategy, as a look at some adaptations of Cohen's work testifies. First, there is different reception of "Hallelujah" and John Lennon's "Imagine," two songs that have been covered countless times. But while Cohen's biggest hit leaves plenty of room for interpretation, certain lines in "Imagine" betray a very specific stance. Yoko Ono has said that she has to constantly turn down artists' requests for small changes in "their" version of the song because they cannot identify with certain lines (Light 2013, 133–134). Another example is the so-called Mennel affair. The curious incident took place on the French version of the popular talent show *The Voice*. Singer Mennel Ibtissem sang an Arab-English version of "Hallelujah," but instead of a literal translation of Cohen's text, the Arab text featured a verse rewritten by the Kuwaity poet Mohamed Elhessiane, in which the erotic dimension was toned down and the religious aspect of the lyrics was far more explicit. Although Mennel was initially a crowd favorite, she was subsequently vilified. The explanations for the resulting outrage vary: she had hoodwinked listeners by singing a different version; the new lyrics were (too) religious; she had Arab roots; she had allegedly made light of the attack on the Promenade des Anglais in Nice in 2016 on her Facebook page.

10 Journalist, essayist, and poet Malcolm Reid (2010) has collected his memories of the Montréal scene of the 1960s in a book titled *Deep café*. This café represents the anglophone bohemian milieu in which Cohen found his voice during the early years of his (then literary) career.

11 Cohen's son, Adam, has also appropriated the image of the "Tower of Song." On the release of his album *Like a Man* (2012) he spoke in nearly every interview of

having finally found his room and having earned his place in what he called the "family business."

12 This may be a point on which he differs from Bob Dylan, whose artistic trajectory long resonated with the context in which the songs originated or in which they were performed, both socially (many of his tracks are protest songs, allowing Dylan to inscribe himself into the zeitgeist) and musically. While Dylan was a major figure on the American folk-music scene, he also renewed the genre from within in 1965 by not only playing acoustically but also going electric (most notably on the album *Bringing It All Back Home* and later at the Newport Folk Festival), and even producing a rock sound on the single "Like a Rolling Stone." Cohen's artistic roots are also in folk, yet he never fully allied himself with this or any other artistic tradition. Some particularities of the social and artistic context filter through in his work, but never very emphatically.

13 And, accordingly, quite a few different disciplines in which it is studied: Canadian literature, comparative literature, translation studies, cultural studies, popular-music studies, theology, philosophy, and so on.

14 All in all, this is remarkable, to say the least: the album release in 1979 went largely unnoticed, and later too its reception was muted. In a keynote lecture in 1993 Stephen Scobie admitted, "I confess it is not an album I go back to often" (Scobie 1993).

15 For Itamar Even-Zohar (1990, 17) the repertoire is a category situated between the specificity of the text and the generality of the (literary or cultural) system: "Repertoire is conceived of here as the aggregate of laws and elements (either single, bound, or total models) that govern the production of texts."

16 In the documentary *Leonard Cohen: Portrait Intime* by Armelle Brusq ([1996] 2009) Cohen gives a tour of his house in Los Angeles, and shows the documentary maker several filing boxes. "These boxes are manuscripts that have never been published," he explains. "This is the real work. All of this is my real work. So I keep adding to this heap of blackened pages." Today, only a fraction of Cohen's archives is available in the Thomas Fisher Rare Book Library at the University of Toronto. Manuscripts, draft versions, letters, notes—absolutely everything has been saved and neatly organized, often by Cohen himself. "He sorts and labels his own material before he sends it to us," says librarian Jennifer Toews (2011). The rest of the archive material is being inventoried by Alexandra Pleshoyano (the academic ambassador for the Leonard Cohen Estate and Archive) in close collaboration with Robert Kory. The aim of the Leonard Cohen Family Trust is that the "placement of the Archive, in the near future, will provide an anchor for the study of Leonard Cohen's work in Canada and around the world for generations to come" (Pleshoyano 2019).

INTERMEZZO 1

"ANOTHER VOCABULARY"
A WRITER IN SEARCH OF HIS LANGUAGE (1)

CASE STUDY OF AN UNPUBLISHED SHORT STORY

The untitled short story discussed here can be found in the archive of the Thomas Fisher Rare Book Library at the University of Toronto.[1] Although the text is undated, it seems safe to assume that it dates back to the earliest period of Cohen's career, in the mid-1950s.[2] It is a fascinating historical document for a number of reasons, but *not* because it is one of Cohen's best literary works. On the contrary: it shows a writer still searching for his style, composing a one-dimensional story and depicting stereotypical characters rather than realistic, complex, or contradictory figures. The story's value lies in the fact that some of the core issues and main themes that are crystallized in the later oeuvre are already present at this early stage. This is the first instance Cohen uses the Biblical story of David and Bathsheba, an intertext that would prove crucial for the composition of "Hallelujah" thirty years later. He also voiced a clear artistic ambition through his protagonist, and although the phrasing is a little rudimentary, it does contain the nucleus of what would be elaborated in various ways in subsequent texts. Finally, this document can be considered unique because, compared to the other short stories that Cohen wrote at the start of his career (which appeared in literary magazines or were unpublished), it is one of the longer pieces and has never been published or discussed before.

The plot is relatively straightforward. Protagonist and first-person narrator Roger Solicer describes an encounter with a French-Canadian couple, Pierre Dupuis and Rachelle Leveque. Midway through the story, this culminates in an amorous moment between Roger and Rachelle. After saying goodbye to the pair, Roger spends time with Lucy, a female friend. While he is with her, he looks back on the encounter with Rachelle and on earlier relationships to get some insight into love, beauty, suffering, and communication. From the outset, the spatio-temporal frame is made explicit: the story is set in and around a boathouse in Quebec, on the shore of Lake Masson, not far from Sainte-Marguerite in the Laurentians. It is summer, and the events take place shortly after the death of Solicer's father. The reader is instantly reminded of the passing of Cohen's own father in 1944—a theme that returns in various other (published and unpublished) short stories from the first archival box and of course later in *The Favourite Game*. As with Lawrence Breavman, the autobiographical affinity between author and protagonist is obvious. Solicer is a student at McGill University, who spends his leisure time out in the country in Quebec, in this case to finish a thesis. And similar to the literary works from the first part of Cohen's career (and especially in his first two novels), the setting is not an abstract universe but a very clearly defined space. Even the relationship between Pierre and Roger is framed with reference to the broader relations between the anglophone and francophone sections of society. Dupuis is a French-speaking nationalist—"blood, soil and family"—while Solicer is an English-speaking freethinker.

While we are still far from the anonymized and mythologized world of Suzanne, the relationships between the characters are depicted using typically Cohenesque themes that return in the opening track of the first album: love, lust, power, and knowledge. In what follows, I will start by roughly outlining the plot and identifying the characters' motives before analyzing some of the themes that preoccupy the protagonist in closer detail: love, suffering, and beauty. I will end by exploring whether this text says anything about the power of language and literature and can therefore be read as a metanarrative.

The story can be divided into three parts. The first part revolves around the Roger-Pierre-Rachelle triangle. The relationships between them seem clear (two men and one woman; a couple and a stranger), but soon blur. Given their relatively distant behaviour toward each other, Roger doubts whether Pierre and Rachelle are actually a couple. And while the difference between Pierre, who incarnates a classic masculine principle (intransigence, paternalism, authority), and Rachelle, who displays more feminine traits (tenderness, empathy), may be clear-cut, Roger's position is much more ambiguous. His empathetic nature resembles Rachelle's, yet many of his actions are governed by the principle of masculine lust.

The second part features a nocturnal, sensuous encounter between Rachelle and Roger. He spies on her as she bathes half-naked in the river, and then walks over to her. Again, lust takes centre stage here: although they do not have intercourse, the atmosphere is erotically charged, and Roger has the opportunity to look at her body. He himself labels his use of language, which is performative, as "a trick": "the speech was spoken to impress her," he concludes afterward. When he talks to Rachelle, Roger is focused on what his words can achieve and sees language first and foremost as a way of winning over women, just like Cohen does in the opening poem of *Let Us Compare Mythologies*. However, we gradually learn that Roger is not just driven by lust, but also by a longing to *understand* the scene and the wish to effectively *articulate* his experience. He is so impressed with Rachelle's mysterious beauty that language proves inadequate: "I did not know what to say." At that point he resorts to existing reference points, and he tries to interpret the experience he just had with the help of an ancient Biblical story:

> I did not want to speak my own words. I could only think of that hot night in Jerusalem and David. I hoped my voice would not frighten her or frighten me, and I spoke very softly.
> "And it came to pass in an eveningtide, that David arose from off his bed, and walked upon the roof of the king's house: and from the roof he saw a woman washing herself; and the woman was very beautiful to look upon."

Put differently, world literature has the requisite power of expression to help him both understand and talk about the experience. On the next page, Roger reinterprets the entire scene, this time through a quote from Gerard Manley Hopkins. As I argued in chapter 3 on alienation, this is a method Cohen applied throughout his career. To begin with, like here, he did so very explicitly—the quotation marks are the author's own—but over time the allusions became more and more implicit (in chapter 4, on religion, I touch on the evolution of "Hallelujah," in which the Biblical references became less evident in successive versions). At any rate, it is remarkable to see Cohen quote this passage in one of his very first texts only to integrate it many years later in what is arguably his best-known song.

In the story's third part, the couple say goodbye, leaving Roger behind, alone. He decides to return to civilization and to have a drink in a nearby bar, where he knows the waitress Lucy. The two begin to talk and discuss Roger's ex-girlfriend Lenore, among other topics. In the end, Roger and Lucy go back to the boathouse, where they make love. After this episode, the three women's names—Rachelle, Lucy, and Lenore—keep going through Roger's mind. Each of them represents a specific type of woman or relationship: Lenore is attractive, and she is his ex-lover; Rachelle is attractive too, but not an ex-lover; Lucy, finally, is someone he does not find attractive, but does have sex with. The final paragraphs are clearly less action-driven and more introspective: Roger's train of thought shows that he is not all that interested (and perhaps never was) in the women's feelings or in a romantic relationship, but that he *compares* them—like his author would shortly afterwards compare mythologies—and uses them to gain knowledge. Drawing on the three different relationships, he tries to formulate an answer to some crucial questions. What is love? What is beauty? What is suffering? And how can all this be expressed in language?

Let us start with the first question, which has preoccupied Roger for a long time. When he and Lenore were a couple, it emerged that instead of commitment it was absolute independence that was the ideal worth striving for in a romantic relationship. The split came after both concluded that a degree of dependence had crept into the relationship: "you armed with need, and I with lust." The importance of (in)dependence was already alluded to by the narrator in the first few pages of the story. In a descriptive passage Roger finds himself in harmony with nature; he observes the behaviour of swallows, describing it in terms reminiscent of what Cohen would articulate in 1961 in "A Kite Is a Victim": images of both the subtle game between the bird and the wind and the dangerous relationship between the fish and the hook are used here already. What has the experience with Rachelle and Pierre taught him about love? If there is such a thing as love or, more broadly, a true connection between people, it is invariably short-lived. During the time that Pierre, Rachel, and Roger spend together (the greater part of the story), three distinct moments of harmony and bonding can be discerned. The first takes place during a picnic together—"the three of us bound, I think, at least for moments, by a sort of love for each other." There is a connection, albeit a fragile one, as attested by the writer's doubt and the brevity of the moment when something akin to love is experienced. There is another moment of harmonic union when the three characters are sitting around the campfire at night:

> The moon climbed above the mountains and bled across the water. The light and shadows did wonderful things to Rachelle's face. We watched our fire burn itself away. We watched the embers and they told stories to us. To me they seemed like the unburied corpses of passionate animals. What they were to Rachelle or Pierre I will never know for the night demanded silence and none of us dared talk. And when the embers too gave no light, leaving all the night's glory to the moon, Pierre stood up and made his way towards the tent. Rachelle followed him. When they were in the tent I urinated on the embers to completely extinguish them.

Like the brevity of their first encounter, the image of the embers aptly expresses the transience of their togetherness, and it also evokes the mist, the falling leaf, and the smoke that Cohen uses in later texts (see also chapter 6, "Encounter"). Although there is a certain energy about the moment ("they told stories to us"—language is generated spontaneously and facilitates direct communication), the experience remains drenched in a kind of unknowability and ineffability. This momentary idyll, which is captured so effectively in the descriptive passage at the start of the fragment, is ultimately disrupted by Roger himself. His choice of words is striking: "I *urinated* on the embers" (my italics). The enchanting atmosphere and the poetic language contrast with the mundane action and the choice of the sterile-vulgar "urinate." This pattern returns in the third encounter, between Roger and Rachelle: again, a symbiotic feeling is evoked through the beauty and power of nature, again the moment is ephemeral, and again there is a contrast between the harmonic intensity of the moment and its abrupt and vulgar end:

> Suddenly I realized that I was angry. The beauty of the episode, the boy and girl meeting on the silver shore, the embryonic kiss—all of this disappeared before a sense of outrage which overtook me. The bitch. The cock-teaser. [...] We should have rolled by the water and she should have told me that she was alone and a virgin and I was the first man who had taken her. *That would have been beauty.* (my italics)

The final sentence is telling. It emerges that Roger is not driven by a longing for love, but for *beauty* and the desire to understand it.

Put like this, the story can also be read like a metanarrative, with the intrigue serving a broader reflection on the meaning of literature and the power of language in general. Aside from the examples quoted above, there are several other passages that revolve around the success or failure of human communication. The subject is first raised in the opening pages, where the narrator takes a fairly literal approach: Pierre speaks French and Roger English. After Pierre introduces himself in French, Roger replies: "'I'm sorry,' I began (in English), 'my French is very poor. I didn't understand your last question. Do you speak English?'" But this lack of understanding also manifests itself in the characters' ways of thinking, which are so different that Rachelle has to assume the role of interpreter to clarify both Pierre's other language (French) and his other ideas:

> Then Rachelle, speaking English with only a hint of a French accent, said, "You mustn't mind what Pierre says. His love of this land is sometimes quite a beautiful thing. He believes in blood and soil and family, you know, things which people hardly ever think about today. He has resentments but no hates. And when he feels he can trust you he will even speak English. You'll see."

Both the rivalry between Pierre and Roger and the intransigence of their convictions stand in sharp contrast with Rachelle's easy-going attitude; as well as interpreting, she can be seen singing and dancing. Her clarifications foster greater understanding between the men. Their conversations also frequently draw attention to language itself. We see an example of the repeated allusions to the universal language of the Bible when Roger responds to Pierre's request not to throw any garbage into the woods: "Nonsense. [...] The animals love me for it. They call me Teacher and sometimes Brother human." Pierre instantly recognizes the religious reference ("Thank you St. Francis"), and concludes: "At least, my English friend, you have been reading the right books." In the paragraph that follows they each speak their own language, but they communicate seamlessly. Pierre and Roger throw some food to a squirrel: "'Here, here,' I called to him. 'Ici, ici,' Pierre called to him." The squirrel ignores the gesture, and it looks as if this time it is the animal that fails to understand. Taking on the role of mediator yet again, Rachelle finds that the little creature is happy to snatch the food from her hand. The ironic undertone, which had accompanied the encounter with Pierre and Rachelle from the outset, becomes more and more explicit toward the end of the scene, especially when Roger again resorts to very conspicuous religious language ("Mother Earth") and Rachelle replies: "You're as bad as Pierre, [...] with all your symbolic interpretations."

The erstwhile relationship between Roger and Lenore was similarly marred by a communication problem. Toward the end of the text we get to read a letter from her (a text-within-a-text), in which she addresses the issue: "My dearest Roger, I know how these letters must annoy you but I must communicate with you in some way." Lenore's letter can be understood here in relation to the broader question raised at the end of the story, when Roger draws on his experiences with the three women to ponder love, suffering, beauty, and language. For Roger the relationship crisis has its origins in a "betrayal"—not by the lovers themselves, because they might have cheated on each other, but by language which, in Roger's view, had raised expectations for Lenore that he did not have:

Love ends. We had our love together. Now it's over. Why is that a betrayal? Just because you think it is, that's why. Just because the songs under the window and the stolen flowers should mean something. They must mean something.

The comparison of the three relationships leads first to a realization, which then culminates in a linguistic crisis. Insomuch as language makes itself subservient to reality by wanting to clarify it, it is always doomed to fail. To avoid misunderstandings and incorrect interpretations language must play a more active role: it must generate meanings and thereby help to create and shape the world. Before Roger tries to lose himself in alcohol and sex with Lucy, he formulates an urgent task, which could easily be a description of the artistic project of Leonard Cohen the author in the years to follow:

Suffering. Beauty. Suffering. Beauty. It seemed I had no other words to think with. [...] When would I learn to think in other words? I did not mean suffering. I did not mean beauty. I thought desperately: I must find other words. Suffering. Beauty. Did they mean the same thing to me? I needed another vocabulary. There were rocks I didn't know the names of. There were machines I didn't know the names of. I had to learn to speak in names.

"Another vocabulary" can be taken literally here. Having been confronted with other languages in Montréal, Cohen understood early on that each language is capable of creating a distinct worldview. With his translation of *À tout prendre* in the early 1960s—as he wrote to John Glassco, "I'm learning a whole new vocabulary"—he was to experience this for himself. Even the phrases in archaic English, which are scattered throughout the short story, can be viewed as part of such a quest. As I will argue in the second intermezzo, multilingualism also plays a prominent role in *Beautiful Losers*, where it functions as a means of discovering and demonstrating what language is capable of. However, the outcome of this literary experiment flies in the face of the short story's calls for a more active role for language.

NOTES

1   Unfortunately the document is incomplete. At present the text comprises twenty-two pages that are hand-numbered (possibly by Cohen himself); pages 3, 4, and 18 are missing, but this does not make the story any less intelligible. There is also an error in the numbering: there is no page 11, but two (different) pages numbered 10.
2   The text can be found in the first box of the (incomplete, but chronologically ordered) archive, which is described as follows in the library catalog: "unpublished prose fragments, unpublished short stories, *The Ballet of Lepers*—unpublished novel." Considering its place in the archive collection—alongside "The Ballet of Lepers," which we know Cohen was working on during the second half of the 1950s—and given the author's style in this story, the text must have been written roughly around the same time.

INTERMEZZO 2

"DON'T FOLLOW THE STORY, FOLLOW THE EMOTION"
A WRITER IN SEARCH OF HIS LANGUAGE (2)

THE INTERNATIONAL RECEPTION OF *BEAUTIFUL LOSERS*

1.

Anyone perusing the many reviews and critiques of *Beautiful Losers* will find that the book had a rather ambivalent reception, and that is putting it mildly. Within a Canadian and an academic context, it is without doubt the most widely discussed work in the whole of Cohen's career. After an extremely mixed reception upon its publication in 1966—the novel was both extolled and vilified by literary critics—it eventually secured a firm place in the Canadian literary canon as "*the quintessential Canadian postmodern novel*"—as Sylvia Söderlind (1991, 41) described the book, following Linda Hutcheon (1984, 1988). Yet the novel did not find as much favour with a general and international readership. In 1974 Hutcheon wrote that "[f]or a Canadian work it has received considerable international attention, yet few literary critics have dared take it seriously" (42), and nearly fifty years later we can conclude that while *Beautiful Losers* has been translated around the world,[1] it has rarely been a serious topic of literary debate outside of its North American home.

Viewed from a Canadian perspective, the translations were something of a confirmation and consolidation of the writer's domestic consecration, whereas internationally they were more of a tribute to the *singer* Leonard Cohen. As soon as he attracted an audience large enough for both his discography and his bibliography to guarantee sales, quite a few literary publishers went ahead and had his novels and poetry collections translated. This is obvious from the publication dates. The first translations of *Beautiful Losers* appeared in the early 1970s—in other words, by the time Cohen had already released two (or in some cases three or more) albums. In France, for example, where the singer has always been very successful, the translation of the first two novels got underway in 1971, and subsequently each new publication would be translated around the same time. But the poetry that predates 1971 (*Let Us Compare Mythologies*, *The Spice-Box of Earth*, *Flowers for Hitler*, and *Parasites of Heaven*) never appeared in translation in France. Unlike other of Cohen's literary works, which did attract a greater readership abroad, either because they were far more accessible or because they were more in tune with the musical work (the anthology *Stranger Music* as well as the recent poetry collections *Book of Longing* and *The Flame* all contain a selection of both poetic and musical work), *Beautiful Losers* has always remained something of a collectors' item for foreign readers. By contrast, in Canada it has long been a fixture in university curricula,[2] and the book is now seen as a cult classic.

Why this distinction between a "literary," "profound" interpretation and an "acoustic," "lazy" reading that sees the novel being read in the light of the early (or later) musical work? On the face of it, the explanation is fairly simple. For foreign readers, the chronology had been reversed: Cohen came to them first as a singer and only later as a writer, so it made sense to interpret the literary work through a musical lens. Besides, with its intrinsic melodic sensibility and the visible or audible presence of its singer (see chapter 2), Cohen's music could speak more directly to its audience than the literature could. Never more so than in the case of *Beautiful Losers*, an uncompromising literary experiment that demands a lot from its readers, and is therefore anything but a conventional book that is easy to identify with. "Whatever plot is here, its interest is minimal," says Hutcheon (1974, 42). Likewise, Scobie (1978, 96) rejects the term "plot," speaking instead of a "narrative situation" shaped by four main characters—Edith, Catherine Tekakwitha, F., and the unnamed protagonist *I*.

The second reason also ties in with the nature of artistic communication. The likes of Margaret Atwood (1972) and Peter Wilkins (2000) read *Beautiful Losers* as an allegory of Canadian society and national identity. This reading is consolidated in the more recent *Encyclopedia of Literature in Canada*, in which Ira B. Nadel, in his entry on Cohen, describes the novel as a "rewrite of Canadian history" (New 2002, 218), while Gittings and Slemon touch on *Beautiful Losers* in their entry on "allegory":

> Leonard Cohen's *Beautiful Losers* (1966) also allegorizes colonial Canada as a female body subject to sexual/imperial exploitation: here the rape of Edith, a First Nations woman, by the descendants of the original French colonists in an American-owned quarry is intended to allegorize the Catholic Church's violation of First Nations culture in Canada and the US neo-imperialist "rape" of Canadian resources. (New 2002, 17)

Although Cohen's early musical work, like "Story of Isaac" (see the chapter on religion), was also often allegorical in nature, his writing style became more direct over time. Besides, a marked difference with the early musical allegories is that the Biblical intertext of the Isaac story is much more widely known than the Canadian intertext of Cohen's second novel.[3]

In short, as well as the allegorical, indirect reading itself, the referent of the allegory also appears to get in the way of the international reception. Put differently, the novel is too explicitly tied to one specific place. What was obvious to many Canadian critics did not receive much attention in the international media. This local embeddedness is rarely mentioned in the paratexts surrounding the translations. Perhaps the allegorical dimension was not all that clear. Although the novel "is unambiguously tied to francophone Montreal of the 1960s" (Davey 2000, 13), Canada and Quebec are not that frequently mentioned, or at least far less often than in *The Favourite Game*. Or perhaps the novel's experimental character was far more conspicuous to the critics than the local inspiration: any spatial framework alluded to in the paratexts is not Canadian, that is a social intertext, but North American, being the artistic intertext of the Beat Poets and American popular culture in general. In the wake of Pierre Nepveu, Pleshoyano (2016, 227) likewise identifies a distinct American dimension in the novel, but links it to the identity of the Québécois: "the Americanness of today's Québécois is one of the main strands of their quest for an identity." An important exception to the widespread underrating of the local inspiration is the fragmented "translation"—note the scare quotes—by Michel Garneau. Although there is no specific version of *Beautiful Losers* for Quebec, Garneau produced a short translation on sight. He did so during a radio broadcast in Quebec when asked to read an excerpt from the existing French translation. Garneau deemed it a failure because too many culture-specific items had been incorrectly translated: "la Main" for "Boulevard Saint-Laurent," "marrons" for "hot-dogs," for example.[4] It was a clear statement.

A fourth factor that threatened to complicate the international reception is the fact that *Beautiful Losers* seems very much of its time. This is best illustrated by Solecki's description in the *Oxford Companion to Canadian Literature*: "the novel, which is neither as shocking nor as disturbing now as it was when it first appeared, seems to express the spirit of a very particular time" (Solecki, in Toye 1983, 586; Solecki, in Benson and Toye 1997, 831) This same sentiment is reflected in the many translations, with their paratexts describing the book as "a novel of the sixties" (Canada, 1991, McClelland & Stewart), "a literary representation of the age" (Hungary, 2006, Jonatan Press Bt.), "one of the craziest and most dazzling books of the sixties" (France, 2002, Christian Bourgois), and drawing analogies between the author and Allen Ginsberg (France, 1973, Christian Bourgois), Walt Whitman (France, 1973, Christian Bourgois), Henry Miller (the Netherlands, 1971, De Bezige Bij; the United States, 1967, Bantam Books), Kurt Vonnegut, Thomas Pynchon, Bob Dylan, and Marilyn Monroe (Spain, 2017, Lumen). In the foreword to the Canadian edition of 1991, Stan Dragland acknowledges that the book is of its time, while simultaneously stressing its lasting value. This tension between transience and longevity is touched upon in quite a few forewords and afterwords. It would appear that one of the unspoken aims of these introductions and conclusions is to furnish the commercial motives behind a translation or reissue in later years with a defence of the book's literary value, with the challenge being to define *Beautiful Losers* not (only) as a document of historical interest but (also) as a literary work that has stood the test of time. Dragland writes:

> *Beautiful Losers* is no longer considered a holy book by guru-seeking readers, but it isn't dated. Because it broke so successfully with traditional form, showing outrageous new possibilities for fiction to a rather staid Canadian scene, it is one of the most important novels written in this country. (1991, 269)

The introduction to the edition in the United Kingdom (Blue Door, 2009) boasts a similar argument, with its author using two spatial metaphors that capture the transience and the longevity quite well: "[*Beautiful Losers*] both *encapsulates* and *transcends* the era in which it was written" (17; my italics). The introductions and conclusions to other translations situate the transcendent or lasting value of the novel in both its form and its content. The form is primarily considered within a literary framework, with reference to the postmodern, experimental writing in the line of James Joyce (US), which has not lost any of its "power of expression" (Germany) or "freshness" (Canada). The content is linked to a long literary tradition ("classic erotic tragedy" (UK), "humanism" (UK), "Dionysian aspects of life associated with Antiquity" (Hungary), "melancholic prophets of that great era" (Hungary), as well as Cohen's own musical career. While that career did not yet exist in 1966, critics nevertheless identify common themes (love, eroticism, religion), and some see the book as foreshadowing songs like "Hallelujah" (the combination of a sacred and a profane register, UK) and "Famous Blue Raincoat" (the dynamic of a love triangle, Spain). The Spanish version even speaks of *"levadura"*: *Beautiful Losers* as the "leaven" of the later work.

2.

Even though *Beautiful Losers* is anchored in a specific time and place, it can also be read as a work with near-universal aspirations.[5] If so, the deluge of names and references is merely a ladder the reader must climb to gain access to the book's underlying, universal-human themes. Frank Davey states that when he taught at York University in 1973, students asked him to include the book in the syllabus: "They had identified with the self-transcending ideology of *Beautiful Losers*, aspired to the history-effacing world in his lyrics, where 'the mist' of human action 'leaves no scar' of consequence, where differences between nations, ethnicities, religions and races are erased by sacramental love" (Davey 1994, 17).[6] In his monograph on the making of a Canadian literary tradition, Marshall (1980, 142) refers to *Beautiful*

Losers precisely because the book "yields up fascinating insights into the nature of Canada," and that of "modern confused man" in general. Marshall discusses the politically most explicit passages—"The English did to us what we did to the Indians, and the Americans did to the English what the English did to us" is a line that many critics have commented on—but adds that since the character of F. calls for "*universal* revenge" (my italics) the author made a statement that went beyond the national sounding board. In doing so, Cohen distanced himself from poet-peers like A. M. Klein: Cohen's "awareness of the historical fate of Indians and Québécois is here extended and intensified to include English-Canadians and those victims of all groups of men: plants and animals" (Marshall 1980, 141).

Stephen Scobie likewise expresses his reservations about an exclusively political-allegorical reading of the book (1978, 113), identifying instead a more general thrust—he speaks of "the central 'signal'" in *Beautiful Losers*: "Systems in themselves are useless unless they are broken, but once they are broken the 'stem' appears" (101). The destruction of systems is the method, while the book's central project can be summarized as an attempt "to escape the bounds of time; to destroy history; to move beyond individual personality; to become Magic; to enter what Dave Godfrey calls the 'overworld'; to transcend the limitations of reason, of humanity, of mortality itself" (99). To illustrate his position, Scobie identifies and discusses the main systems: religion, sexuality, politics, history and the "banal" (a term he borrows from Godfrey, and that mainly applies to pop songs, movies, and machinery). The analysis is detailed and extremely convincing, but remarkably there is one system Scobie does not address: language. In subsequent publications, quite possibly driven by new directions in comparative literature, he did write at length about the destructive and deconstructing power of language, albeit mainly in Cohen's later oeuvre (see Scobie 1993).

Others, like Siemerling (1994), Davey (2000), and Hofmann (2010), looked in detail at the power(lessness) of language in *Beautiful Losers*.

The theme is introduced in the book's opening lines. A seemingly banal question—"Catherine Tekakwitha, who are you?"—soon reveals that language creates a distance between the subject and the world. The book's prime concern is epistemological: Who is this woman and how can we get to know her? The scholarly language of the unnamed historian *I* proves to be more of a hindrance than a help in his efforts to understand the world. "You live in a world of names" is the reproach F. hurls at his friend *I*. He could have been addressing Roger Solicer, the main character of the short story discussed earlier. In the years separating the two narratives, Cohen's ideas about language have clearly evolved: in the other chapters of *Beautiful Losers* the destructive force of language is illustrated in a range of different ways. Within the narrative set-up, English acquires a specific connotation as "the colonizing symbolic language of the Catholic church" (Siemerling, in Hofmann 2010, 191). It is also via the book's form, with its experimental syntax and bold lexical variations, that language as system also loses its power to communicate. Two alternatives present themselves. There is the existing language of the Iroquois, which serves as a kind of idealized protolanguage with an intrinsic relationship between words and things, while the narrator also makes several attempts "[to] invent [...] a minor use of the major language," as Hofmann (2010, 196) put it in the wake of Deleuze and Guattari. What at first glance appears to be a destructive distortion of English is really supposed to be a productive attempt to reintroduce the materiality of reality in and through language. The method: translation. The outcome: scream, stutter, stammer, murmur.

3.

There is something to be said for the claim that *Beautiful Losers* struggled to reach an international readership because it was an "untranslatable" novel. But what makes a novel untranslatable? In Antoine Berman's hermeneutic approach to translation *every* translation activity is marked by a series of *"déformations."* In addition to this there may be other, more specific problems. While Berman thinks it is possible to replace one standard language with another (English with Dutch, or with French, for instance), this becomes less straightforward when translating colloquial language varieties. Multilingual texts, in which languages are superimposed on one another for a specific effect, are similarly hard to translate. Both elements appear to play a crucial role in *Beautiful Losers*. While pushing the boundaries of English, inside and outside of the existing language variants, the novel is also informed by an elaborate multilingual game. As the two main languages in Quebec, French and English play a prominent but not exclusive role. Since these languages are in a diglossic relationship, converting the social meanings of the two and the relationships between them to another one is not all that straightforward.

In the Dutch translation, the English-French construction is replaced by Dutch-French. For Flemish readers some of the original diglossia will filter through, as French was long the sole official language in Belgium, and socially superior to Dutch. But the specific social connotations are different of course—Belgium is not Canada—all the more so for readers from the Netherlands, who have little familiarity and therefore less affinity with French. It becomes even more complicated in the French translation, for example in the passage in which a French quote has been inserted into the English text (chapter 6, Book 1 offers one of many examples): this linguistic contrast vanishes in the translation and is replaced by a formal difference (roman vs. italics). Another example can be found in Book 3 of the novel ("An Epilogue in the Third Person"—the most conventional part), where the penultimate paragraph features a few more French quotes, this time followed by an English translation. It appears to make sense to see the translation in the source text as helping the anglophone reader understand the French text. The French version, however, prints the exact same text in the exact same order—first the French quote, followed by the English translation. Although the source text has been directly imported into the "translation," this construction could have the wrong effect on the reader who understands the French and does not need the English addition. Then again, these kinds of passages, in which the form of the text is retained but some of the content is altered, also offer an opportunity for the translator to give French readers a glimpse of the linguistic (and spatio-temporal) framework of the novel. Whether intentionally or not, a "foreignizing" (Venuti) translation strategy is deployed here, which shows that the text was not originally written in French. A similar mix of preservation and adaptation of the multilingualism can be seen in chapter 44, Book 1, where Cohen had three advertisements printed in and among the main body of the text: a free book coupon, an ad for shapely legs, and another for holy water. Because all three of the advertisements are framed, each appears as a stand-alone segment, as a separate "document," although only the last one contains an image and the first two use text only. In the French version, the first two ads were translated and placed *within* the main body of the text—while it remains clear that these are quotes, this is less obvious from the form and the translator has also significantly shortened the second quote. The third advertisement, by contrast, was reproduced in full and appears in English. (For the sake of completeness, in the Dutch version all three ads were translated and placed in the main body of the text in a smaller font size.)

This brief summary shows just how hard it is to retain the referential function of language in a translation. But how important is this function? What is the status of the spatio-temporal framework, and how does it relate to the novel's "universal" aspirations? To what extent does the author draw on the referential function in the first place? The multilingualism is aimed as much at deconstructing the language system as such as at evoking a particular socio-discursive reality. In a long essay Frank Davey argues that quite a few of the characters are actually francophone, even though Cohen relays their words in English. For example,

"DON'T FOLLOW THE STORY, FOLLOW THE EMOTION"

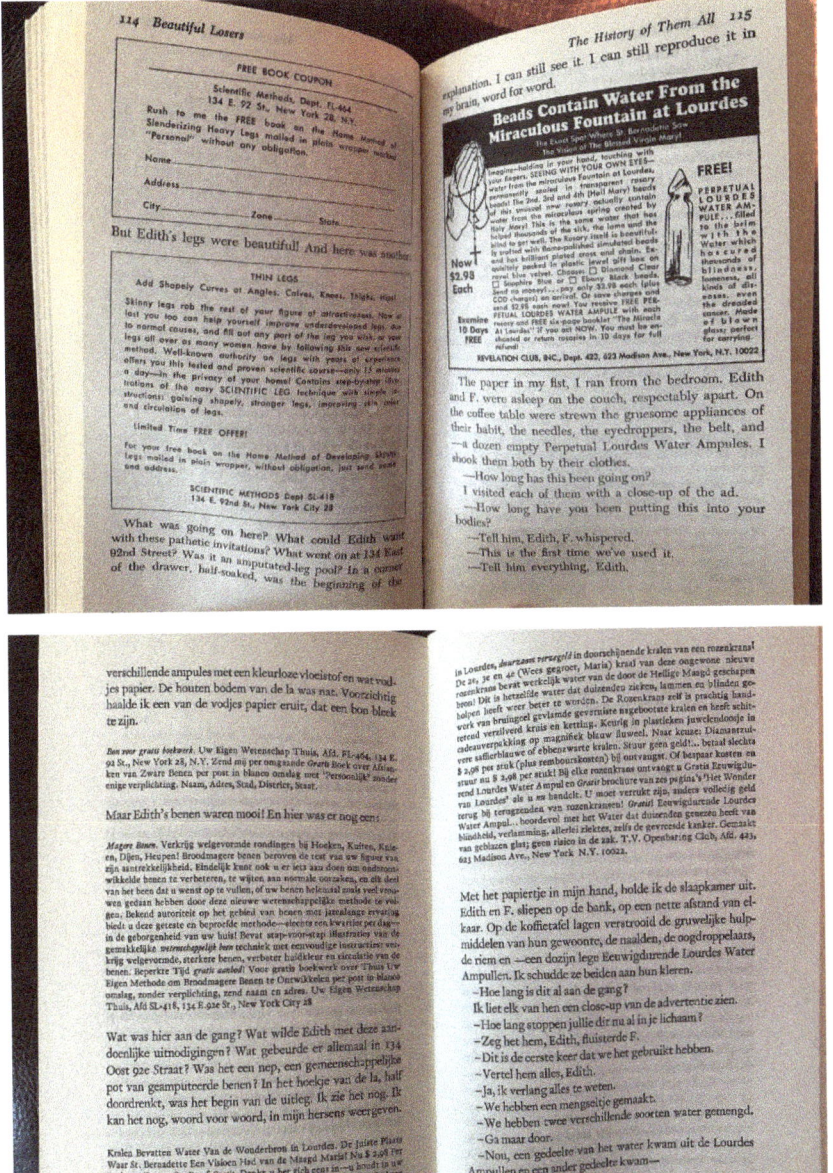

TOP: *Beautiful Losers*, Canadian version (McClelland & Stewart), BOTTOM: *Glorieuze verliezers*, Dutch version (De Bezige Bij, tr. John Vandenbergh)

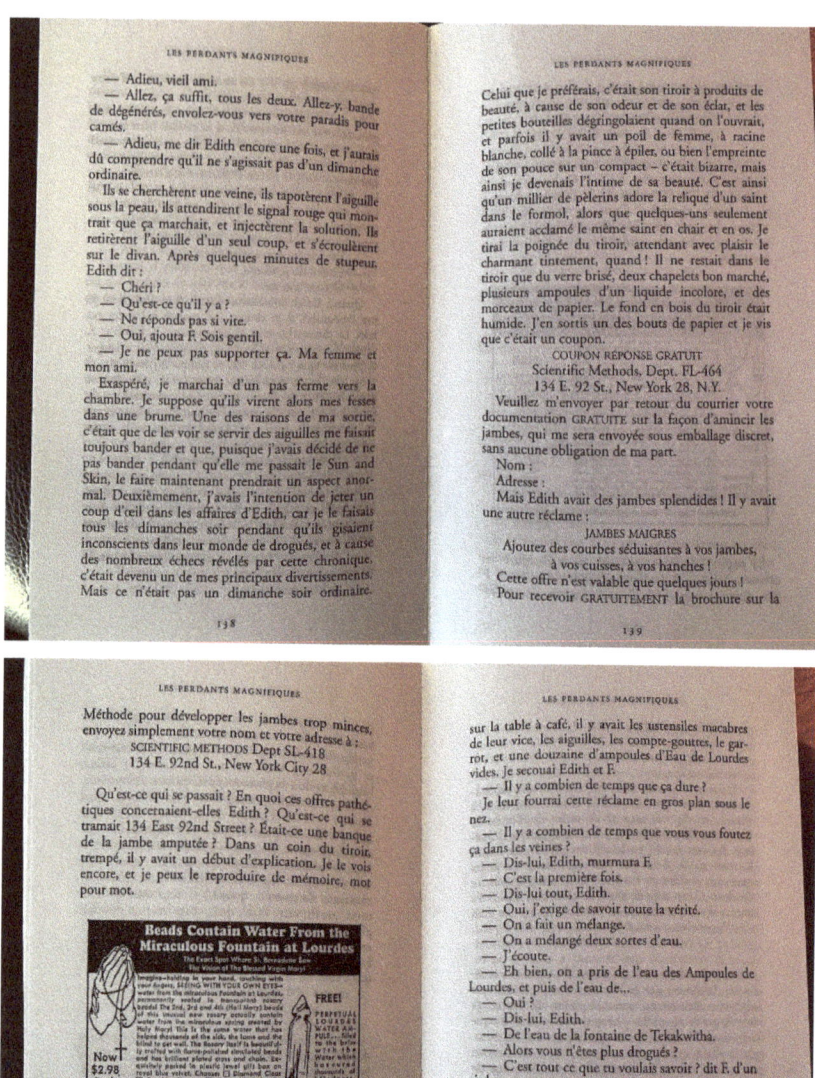

Les Perdants Magnifiques, French version (Christian Bourgois éditeur, tr. Michel Doury)

"DON'T FOLLOW THE STORY, FOLLOW THE EMOTION"

> "A long letter from F." [...], part 2 of the novel, is readable as a French text, one that is presented to the reader in English through the same novelistic convention that presents the Aboriginal speech of Catherine's aunts in English. There is overwhelming evidence in the novel that F. is francophone. (Davey 2000, 14)

In one of the manuscripts of *Beautiful Losers*, Cohen jotted in the margins: "[D]on't follow the story, follow the emotion" (Cohen papers, 9). If we were to take the author's advice—obviously there are other, equally legitimate reading methods—the referentiality of the language is no longer the primary goal of the reading experience (although it can influence it). Cohen's remark does not mean one is free to let go of the text. On the contrary. The reader is asked to go in search of the emotion—the imperative "follow" places the reader in a subordinate position and situates the emotion in the text itself, where it is represented and evoked through form and content. At the same time, this exhortation is rather vague: What does it mean to follow the emotion? How is it supposed to be done? By stressing the importance of the form (and downplaying the significance of the plot), Cohen appears to suggest the possibility of a non-linear reading. In other words, it is far from certain that the line of emotion coincides with the sequence of paragraphs and pages. In Cohen's previously cited "note to the Chinese reader," written in 2000 to mark the Chinese translation of *Beautiful Losers*, he sees his second novel "more [as] a sunstroke than a book" and suggests such a non-linear reading himself:

> May I suggest that you skip over the parts you don't like? Dip into it here and there. Perhaps there will be a passage, or even a page, that resonates with your curiosity. After a while, if you are sufficiently bored or unemployed, you may want to read it from cover to cover.

Behind the customary half-ironic, half-modest rhetorical flourishes, Cohen formulates a reading method in which the plot is secondary but the emotion all the more salient—as are, this time around, the reader's own sensibilities.

"Follow the emotion": Could this also be a guideline for the translators of *Beautiful Losers*, offering them a potential method for converting this "untranslatable" text into another language? Could it also explain why the novel did not work in some translations? Let us take the Dutch translation as an example. Despite Cohen's popularity, there were very few in-depth critiques of *Beautiful Losers* in the Netherlands and Flanders. There was the odd brief review: Dutch newspaper *Het Parool* questioned the quality of the translation and was scathing about the book because the story is "minimal" and the rest of the novel gives "the impression of being mere filler" (Van Stiphout 1971, 9); *Trouw*, another quality paper, echoed this sentiment: "the book is a failure," writes J. van Doorne (1971, 19); and the journalist in local daily *Leeuwarder courant* assumes that the translator, "who also translated Henry Miller [...] must have been less than impressed with Cohen's prose" (Anon. 1971, 5). The sole exception to these brief evaluations is the review by Gerrit Komrij—a Dutch writer, critic, translator, and, as Wikipedia puts it, "fearsome polemicist"—who differs from other reviewers in terms of length (a full fives pages), but not judgment. His conclusion both summarizes and surpasses the other reviews: "imagination *nil*, structure *nil*, originality *nil*, style *nil*, self-control *nil*, premise *nil*" (1974, 194). He takes offence at the formal experiment as such, irrespective of any distortion by or in the translation. "Drivel" (190), "unnatural dialogue," and "Cohenisms" (192) are clearly not descriptions of an experimental poetics but explicit reproaches aimed at illustrating that Cohen "does not write but *expresses himself*" (190; italics Komrij's) and uses punctuation "that does not punctuate anything" (193).

Yet despite the novel's experimental character, the idea of transfer is also a common thread running through the text. Characters and readers are often directly addressed, and attention drawn to the success or failure of the communicative actions. The concept of translation is ubiquitous in the book: alongside various forms of intralingual, interlingual, and intersemiotic translation, translation also serves "as a master trope for any manner of inter-experiential relations that have a transformative effect on the subject and his or her way of being-in-the-world," says Stacey (2014, 173).[7]

We all know that reflections on translation frequently draw on metaphors and tropes to define the activity, even though these can sometimes prompt (even more) semantic confusion. The same is true for all manner of affiliated concepts, such as the idea of "untranslatability," which, according to Chesterman (2016, 6), forms part of what he labels "supermemes," "ideas of such pervasive influence that they come up again and again in the history of the subject, albeit sometimes in slightly different guises." In the course of the history of translation studies, two arguments have been defended: one that translation is impossible—at any time or any place, or in specific, say literary cases—and the second that translation is definitely possible. Chesterman (2016, 7) notes that "from the linguistic angle, the untranslatability idea looks like a restriction of language to *langue* only, to language as system; it seems to deny the role played by *parole*, by what people can do in their actual use of language." As explained above, in a sense this is what Cohen himself does in the source text. He breaks open the language system in order to make speech-as-translation work. It is not surprising, therefore, that alongside traditional interlingual translations of *Beautiful Losers* there have also been some intersemiotic, fragmentary translations or variants. Sarah Perkins and Ian Jackson created a series of colourful illustrations to accompany the well-known passage "God is alive, magic is afoot" (a paragraph from the book featuring numerous variations on this phrase, like a kind of mantra), which is presented like a poem, chopped into pieces and in varying font sizes. Singer Buffy Sainte-Marie was inspired by the same passage, which she put to music on her album *Illuminations* (1969). In view of recent developments in translation studies and practice, with translators enjoying both greater visibility and freedom, there might well be room for more alternative translations of *Beautiful Losers*.

It is tempting to think that after writing *Beautiful Losers* its maker, Leonard Cohen, had to redefine his own approach to language. As early as 1978 Stephen Scobie argued that this novel constituted a kind of end point, and while it did not rule out Cohen writing more novels in the future, he would certainly do so in a different way. We can now safely say that *Beautiful Losers* was his final novel, and we can repeat Scobie's conclusion from 1978: henceforth, language would be more and more often accompanied by music. It is perhaps no coincidence that one year after *Beautiful Losers* the first studio album was released.

NOTES

1 Between 1970 and 1973 the novel was published in no fewer than seven languages: Japanese, Swedish, Dutch, Italian, German, French, and Danish. The comprehensive fan website leonardcohenfiles.com lists some sixty different editions, published in over twenty languages.

2 In 1991, Stan Dragland wrote that at that time Cohen was read a little less than before. He cited three reasons: the novel being a product of its time, Cohen's departure from the Canadian literary scene, and the self-referentiality of his later work, which readers were not always enamored with (Dragland 1991, 261).

3 This does not detract from the fact that *Beautiful Losers* has a very strong religious intertext as well, but one that does not necessarily function as an allegory. Hutcheon (1980, 15) notes that the crux of Cohen's work in general, and of his second novel especially, "is to force the reader to invert, to ironize, the intertexts," which makes a clear-cut interpretation harder if not impossible. As an example, she cites *Beautiful Losers*, which "can be read [...] as a parody or as an ironic inversion of the Bible, both in its overall structure and in its functional images" (15).

4 There are some remarkable formal differences too: in the French version, chapters 41 and 42 (Book 1) were combined.

5 I am particularly interested here in the dichotomy between local versus international (or universal), aware that this excludes other interpretations, including the fascinating discussion by Ravvin (1993), who views *Beautiful Losers* as "an examination of the role of the Holocaust in contemporary culture, and as a call to heed the lessons learned from the Nazi victimization of the Jews" (22).

6 It goes without saying that other interpretations are possible too, often determined by the time in which they are read. Davey immediately adds that the students he taught two years later were of a different opinion, and "regarded Cohen's writing as escapist and irrelevant to their career concerns" (1994, 17). Brian Trehearne notes that today's generation of students "often aren't prepared for some of the shocking work Cohen put forward as a young writer and some leave his class liking him less than when they enrolled" (Enos 2017). And, as indicated in the previous chapter, others, including Myra Bloom, have questioned the compatibility of *Beautiful Losers* with current literary debates and social sensibilities regarding feminist and post-colonial issues.

7 A little later he explains this idea: "It is precisely a relationship to the absolutely outside, the totally alien, with which *Beautiful Losers* is engaged via its interest in translation; at stake is a delineation of the constraints of modern consciousness itself" (Stacey 2014, 179).

FOUR

RELIGION
HOW THE PRIEST, PROPHET, AND BELIEVER SERVE ARTISTIC EXPRESSION

The stranger is not the only daimon furnishing Leonard Cohen with an interesting narrative for his life and work; the framework of religion has likewise offered some personas that Cohen has been able to identify with, either partially or fully, and depending on the moment.

Earlier I wrote of the fine line between semblance and reality in Cohen's work, and this is certainly true in a religious context. His religious references are invariably linked to eroticism, sex, and power. The exemplary role of the saints in *Beautiful Losers*, for instance, is anything but traditional given that the unnamed first-person narrator who dominates the novel aspires to "fuck" or "go down on" a saint. And who are the *Sisters of Mercy* in the song of the same name? Divine beings who seduce the singer? "They lay down beside me, I made my confession to them," Cohen sings. It is up to the listener to deduce what this confession entails. Much is implied, but little is made explicit, except that religion, sex, and artistic inspiration reinforce one another. In the line that follows, "They touched both my eyes," the allusion to Christ healing two blind men through touch can be seen as a metaphor for the inspiration of the muses. The jar of oil from the less well-known poem "I Have Two Bars of Soap" (from *The Spice-Box of Earth*) is similarly ambiguous. Is this anointing oil or massage oil for the poet's lover? And in "Celebration," from the same book, the allusion to oral sex is not overt, but obvious enough: "Kneel, love, a thousand feet below me, / So far I can barely see your mouth and hands / Perform the ceremony." Next up, in a rather overblown metaphor, the orgasm is compared to the destruction of the Temple by Samson. Conversely, in "Light As the Breeze" the man's servility to the woman he adores is described as worship: "It don't matter how you worship, as long as you're down on your knees." The conflation of the deified woman and the deity portrayed as a woman is a common technique in Cohen's texts. Obviously, the coupling of spirituality and eroticism is not exactly new. It is a central idea in various religious texts and traditions. "I often confuse women with God," was the headline of an interview from 1985 (de Waard 1985). One fine illustration can be found in *Book of Longing*, in which Cohen follows the Jewish tradition by writing "God" as the ineffable "G-d," but also turns "sex" into "s-x."

What is the place of religion in the work of a man who hails from a Jewish family, became acquainted with Catholicism through his parents' Irish-Catholic housekeeper, encountered Buddhism in his thirties, and took inspiration from the Islamic tradition in some of his more recent titles? Each one of these religions occupies a distinct place in Cohen's life and work, although he has always made it absolutely clear that he is a Jew above all else. In "Not a Jew," a short poem from *Book of Longing*, he brings matters to a head: "Anyone who says / I'm not a Jew / is not a Jew / I'm very sorry / but this decision / is final." Fourteen years earlier, on *The Future*, he stated firmly but no less flippantly: "I'm the little Jew who wrote the Bible." These assertions are so bold that the reader may well doubt their veracity. After all, they are merely the words of one of the author's many artistic personas. But it cannot be denied that this Jewish identity is pervasive. Cohen did not hesitate to reschedule gigs when they happened to clash with a major Jewish holiday.[1] In "Almost Like the Blues" he sings unequivocally: "My father says I'm chosen," alluding to the priestly vocation inherent in his name. A similar thought can be found in the notebooks section of *The Flame*: "As a child I had the dream that I might speak in the highest name" (Cohen 2018, 168). That said, this Jewish identity is not unambiguous: as a young artist Cohen distanced himself from Montréal's Jewish community, in which his family had been long-standing members. He did so in 1964, during a reading at the Jewish Public Library, which caused quite an uproar in the local press. Drawing on the "priest" versus "prophet" dichotomy, he positioned himself as a poet in relation to the Jewish community. While the priest occupies a place within the community and claims to be its representative, the prophet acts from a more autonomous position. Either knowingly or unknowingly, Cohen took up a distinction first developed by Max Weber and reformulated his artistic position as a liminal figure in religious terms. The tragedy of poet A. M. Klein, Cohen's older colleague, was that he could not separate the two: "Klein chose to be a priest though it was as a prophet that we needed him, as a prophet he needed us and he needed himself… And now we have his silence" (Cohen, in Siemerling 1994, 32). To Cohen, Klein's fate was nothing less than a warning, summed up by Siemerling as follows:

> Having thus read Klein's predicament, Cohen constructs, in his text from 1964, the possibility of poetic speech as the emphatic acceptance of an outsider position. This marginality nevertheless has a

close connection with a community that is still *its* other, and which indirectly evokes its forgotten origin by the exclusion of a once-central position. The outsidedness of exile, for Cohen, signifies a paradoxically central possibility. [...] The poet clearly follows in the footsteps of the prophet, yet will ultimately try to have it both ways: to be a priest comprehended by its community *and* a prophet able to break the communal rule, and thus to combine the communication with an unknown other with the address of the priest to the community. He will claim a place on both sides, the powerful outside of secure knowledge and community and the different role inside the circle in which the priest, however, is but a *primus inter pares*. From this intersection between two perspectives, Cohen would like to speak. (32–34)

When, three years after his reading, Cohen made his debut as a singer-songwriter, he had to make another decision on his ambivalent position as an insider or outsider: was he going to be a "believer among believers," or someone who is above or beyond the crowd. In the introduction and in chapter 2, I already exposed the lie inherent in the idea of a homogenous musical community formed by the singer and his audience. The singer is always—both literally and figuratively—above the people, be it as a priest or as a prophet. This became clear during a performance in Tel Aviv in 2009. At the end of the evening, Cohen raised his hands over the audience and spoke the priestly blessing in Hebrew (a clip of this extraordinary finale circulates online).[2] The benediction, which forms part of the Jewish liturgy, is traditionally given by the "kohanim"—that is to say, by the descendants of the Jewish priest class, to which Leonard Cohen belongs. This was not the first time he addressed his audience with such pastoral words. He used to regularly finish gigs with the brief parting song "Whither Thou Goest," which has a Biblical message too.[3]

Cohen's positioning has a lot to do with a longing for power, which is far more evident in the early work than in the later oeuvre. In 1961 he notes in *The Spice-Box of Earth*: "I played with the idea that I was the Messiah"—the Messiah having been described as both prophet *and* king. It should come as no surprise, then, that in the later works (ranging from *Book of Mercy* to *The Flame*) the figure of the leader occasionally made way for that of the humble believer. Around the time when Cohen released "Hallelujah," Bob Dylan concluded that his Canadian colleague's lyrics were beginning to resemble humble prayers. Likewise, in the title track of the otherwise rather virile *The Future* the singer is more modest than he appears to be on the face of it: the compelling order "Repent!" in the title track does not originate with him. He takes a more detached view of things: "When *they* said 'repent,' I wonder what *they* meant" (my italics). In an interview Cohen commented on this phrase with his former perspective in mind: "I don't want to sit here and sound like I'm speaking from the point of view of a prophet [...]. I don't presume to say what we should repent for—or even if we should. I am making this comment simply as somebody who believes that something massive has happened to us" (Gilmore 2008, 362). This evolution is confirmed in the opening poem of *The Flame*, one of the collection's best, which sees him taking stock and acknowledging that there were times when his ego was too dominant. He turns to his younger self with a modicum of irony: "Go tell the young messiah / What happens to the heart."

But it was Cohen himself who labelled his final tours as spiritual experiments, taking it in turns to assume the role of priest and believer. At times he would speak and sing in a self-assured voice, at others he would humbly kneel, bow his head, and thank his fellow musicians and the listeners with his hand on his heart. And at the start of each gig, as the band members mounted the stage together, they would engage in a little ritual and sing "Pauper ego sum," a Latin song in the round. This double role suggests awareness of the ambiguous position they occupy on stage. It was not long before Cohen conquered the hearts of thousands of listeners worldwide with it, to the extent that Brian Trehearne, in the foreword to this book (a first version of which was written in 2015), concludes that Cohen had become a "secular saint," a description Dan Bilefsky (2018) was to repeat three years later in the *New York Times* and which has gone on to influence many a reviewer and author since. The sizable monograph *Leonard Cohen: L'homme qui voyait tomber les anges* (Leonard Cohen: The man who saw the angels fall, 2013) by Christophe Lebold is a case in point. It depicts Cohen as a spiritual master and a guide for his many readers and listeners (including the author). As such, the conclusion does not come as a surprise: "Leonard Cohen saves us" (Lebold 2013, 675).

RELIGION AS INSTITUTION, RITUAL PRACTICE, AND EXPERIMENT

Cohen's sometimes ambiguous approach to religion seems to suggest that it is at best mere ornamentation rather than a foundation for him: the religious vocabulary evokes a certain atmosphere, but does not originate in genuine feeling. This is Bart Meuleman's hypothesis in the introduction to an essay on Cohen's music (Meuleman 2009, 50). However, he reconsiders his opinion when he detects a cathartic dimension in Cohen's attempts at getting a grip on the destructive force of lust via music:

> On the one hand there is the lust, on the other the bitter regret at the havoc it wreaks or—on later records—the cathartic effect of the attempts at getting it under control. Perhaps Cohen's work is more religious than I thought. (55)

This correction not only says something about Cohen's craft, but also about the word "religion" itself. The concept evokes so many different associations that they cannot possibly all be lumped together.

First, one way of determining Cohen's attitude toward religion is to look at his relationship with the institution of religion. In his capacity as a prophet he tends to stand outside it, while as a priest he is an inextricable part of it, but in either case he has no choice but to keep defining his position *in relation to* the institution. His mistrust of the church—and by extension of all ideologies and institutions—is extremely strong because in his view it offers nothing but a simplified representation of reality, just as it is often distorted by its representatives' lust for power. This view holds true for various contexts, but for Cohen it grew out of the Quiet Revolution in Quebec, during which, in addition to calls for a distinct Québécois identity, efforts were made to achieve the absolute separation of (Catholic) church and state. Up until that point the Catholic Church had had a strong presence in Quebec's cultural and political life. We must see Cohen's venomous attack on the church in *Beautiful Losers* (1966) in the spirit of those times. The tone is so exaggerated that it all but obscures the ultimate aim of his critique. Here is a brief excerpt from the long string of accusations:

> I would like to accuse the Church. I accuse the Roman Catholic Church of Quebec of ruining my sex life and of shoving my member up a relic box meant for a finger, I accuse the R.C.C. of Q. of making me commit queer horrible acts with F., another victim of the system, I accuse the Church of killing Indians, I accuse the Church of refusing to let Edith go down on me properly. (Cohen [1966] 1991, 50)

In this passage, religion is explicitly tied to a concrete here and now. But Cohen's oeuvre throws up many other associations. Perhaps religion is first and foremost a ritual practice in his work. After all, one does not try to explain a belief system to a child; instead one teaches it religious practices, which then gradually evolve into habits. The documentary *I'm Your Man* (Lunson 2005) shows a photo of a young Cohen in the synagogue. He comments on the remarkable contrast between the loaded religious attributes and ritual texts on the one hand, and his childlike wonder on the other. The photo reveals the beginning of an initiation process, which does not really get underway through learning but by way of an unconscious and often involuntary immersion in what is initially an alienating world. The realm of religion, which manifested itself in the synagogue and was continued at home, was strongly embedded in everyday life. For many traditional Jewish families that world helped shape their lives. In *Jews and Words* Amos Oz and Fania Oz-Salzberger (2014, 41) argue that "this piece of social history is [...] the single most important fact about the survival of the Jews. At the youngest age, when words can be magical and stories spellbinding, a unique vocabulary came along with the sweet and savory Sabbath-meal offerings." And so it was for the Cohen family, which had played an important role in Montréal's institutional religious life. Cohen's paternal great-grandfather, Lazarus, had a synagogue built in the city, and his brother, Zvi Hirsh Cohen, became the city's chief rabbi. Cohen's grandfather, Lyon Cohen, was the founder and chairman of the Canadian Jewish Congress and helped set up *The Jewish Times*, the first Anglo-Jewish newspaper in Canada. His maternal grandfather, Solomon Klinistky-Klein, was a rabbi too. And yet for the young Leonard the world of religion became more and more removed from his daily life, as if the link between the rituals and life itself had been severed. Although these rituals had originally welled up from life, they were now gradually becoming detached from it. One of the few things that still connected the two worlds was music, which directly impacts one's mood and thus carries religion spontaneously into life. Music's enchanting effect also works the other way around: it carries the listener away and takes him or her from an undefined outside (the chaos of life) to an enclosed inside (the reliable world of religion).

 The seductive power of religious music is unmistakable on "Who by Fire," a track from 1974. The lengthy instrumental intro by Javier Mas during the final concert tours really brought its hypnotic power to the fore. "Who by Fire" is based on a well-known Jewish prayer, the *Unetanneh Tokef*,[4] which is sung on Yom Kippur (Day of Atonement) and Rosh Hashanah (Jewish New Year), at the opened ark with the Torah scrolls. The text contains a reference to a Book of Life, which also makes an appearance in the Biblical story of the golden calf. After Moses asks for his people to be forgiven for making an idol, God responds as follows: "Whoever has sinned against me I will blot out of my book" (Exodus 32:33). Superimposed on this and other allusions in the Hebrew Bible is the rabbinic tradition, as recorded in the Talmud, which stipulated that during Jewish New Year three books would be opened: one for wholly righteous people (whose names would be added to the Book of Life), one for the thoroughly wicked (who would go straight into the Book of Death), and finally a book for the in-between cases (whose final judgment would be postponed for ten days until the Day of Atonement). The traditional version of the prayer raises issues that ultimately boil down to one and the same fundamental question: Who will be there in the end? The answer is this: the King, the living God. In his version, Cohen retains the form of the prayer as well as its melody, psalmodic tone, and repetitive questioning structure: "And who by fire, who by water, / who in the sunshine, who in the night time, / who by high ordeal, who by common trial, / who in your merry merry month of May, / who by very slow decay." The repetition of both lyrics and melody lend the song a certain intensity. It is the ancient principle of music as a bearer and enhancer of the word, which comes clearly into focus in the singing of psalms and, in the Christian tradition, in Gregorian chanting. On "The Faith" and especially on "Villanelle for Our Time" (based on a poem written by F. R. Scott), both from 2004, Cohen takes this trenchant repetition to extremes.

On "Who by Fire" Cohen completes the movement from outside (chaos, insecurity) to inside (order, reassurance). The music can achieve something that words cannot. At the same time "Who by Fire" differs substantially from traditional religious music on a few counts. Cohen offers a more contemporary take: "who by powder" could be a reference to the dangers of drug use, for example. But the most radical change is the answer at the end of each verse, which is not a reassurance but an urgent and unanswered counter question: "Who shall I say is calling?" The comfort of an extant God is openly called into question. Although such fundamental doubts about the existence of God are also raised in the Bible, the silence that follows the question in Cohen's songs is far more emphatic than that in, say, the psalms. Religious certainties were similarly challenged in the title of Cohen's second book of poetry, *The Spice-Box of Earth*. The titular spice box refers to the traditional wooden container used to signal the end of the Jewish Sabbath. Each dinner guest is invited to smell the wonderful aromas as a reminder of the wealth of creation and thus greet the new week with renewed vigor. In Cohen's book, however, the box does not contain fragrant spices, but earth. Yet despite the implicit or explicit doubts that Cohen weaves into his texts, despite the complex relationship with religion that lies at the heart of this, his songs are frequently sung at religious celebrations. In 2009 Ruth Gan Kagan, a rabbi in Jerusalem, introduced "Hallelujah" at a Yom Kippur service. She acknowledged that "Hallelujah" is not a hymn for the firm believer, but for the one who has doubts or who has stopped believing altogether.

> [T]he song is an opportunity to bring that heretical part in—not just the one who is ready for repenting, but the part that is doubting. [...] Yom Kippur is not an easy day. That confusion is good, and it works better to admit that. Maybe I'm not sure I want to ask forgiveness—and who from, anyway? We should bring the poems that reflect this more complex relationship with God into the service. (Light 2013, 182–183)

In Cohen's version of "Who by Fire" something has changed. That the religious system insinuates itself into daily life is something that can no longer be taken for granted. Childlike naïveté has made way for a critical question, which was raised as early as Cohen's first book of poetry. At the age of twenty-two he regarded the world from a distance, yet still accorded religion a prominent place. What is more, in the title *Let Us Compare Mythologies* he lends his artistic work an almost scientific allure and a letter from the same year reveals a similar ambition:

> I want to continue experimenting with the myth applying it to contemporary life, and isolating it in contemporary experience, thus making new myths and modifying old ones. I want to put mythic time into my poems, so they can be identified with every true fable ever sung, and still be concerned with our own time, and the poems hanging in our own skies. (December 27, 1956, in Nadel [1996] 2007, 46)

Gilles Tordjman (2006, 36) compares Cohen's first book of poetry with the construction of a laboratory, before going on to consider *The Spice-Box of Earth* as the moment when Cohen starts actively experimenting. Five years later it transpires that Cohen has not given up on this ambition. In a letter to a friend he mentions the theologian and writer William Kelly, someone who intrigues him:

> I'd like to see what he does next. I'd like to know how he treats the language men speak today, if he can make myths out of the buildings and machines we live in right now. Can he speak in a fresher language? Can he find a way to address jet bombers in the vocative? Can he stand alone with his subject without "thous" and "these"? Can he talk straight? I think he can. If he can preserve this sense of urgency in speech closer to speech he uses everyday then I think we'll have some poetry. (November 18, 1961, Cohen papers, 11–5)

In any case, from 1956 religion is placed in a broader perspective (especially that of Greek, Jewish, and Christian mythology), but the idea remains the same. The crux of the matter is distance, both in terms of the myths themselves (hailing from a different era, they must be assimilated into everyday life) and Cohen's own position (he wants to actually do something with the myth). From now on, religion is of interest primarily as form: he removes the connotations, images, atmosphere, and allusions from their context and inserts them into an everyday setting. The comparison consists of the combination of the mythical elements. Whereas religion once slipped into life imperceptibly, it now forms part of an experiment that is purposely planned and executed. The artist's craft lies in making the assimilation as seamless as possible, so that the listener or reader is immersed in a mythical universe without realizing it. So, just because the myth functions in an ordinary context does not mean it loses its magic. On the contrary: the reality of everyday life acquires something magical. A world opens up in which the reader or listener can lose himself. The invitation can come across as sincere, as well as preposterous. For example, a *New York Times* reviewer drew the following conclusion about the "spiritual ecstasy" in *Beautiful Losers*: "Because its author is no fraud, *Beautiful Losers* has a certain power. [...] It can be laughed off, or it can be undergone" (Fremont-Smith 1966, 45). And when, in turn, the divine is anthropomorphized, the result is likewise not a weakening but a deepening of its character. O'Neil believes this is what happens in "Suzanne," describing it as a dramatization:

> Cohen dramatizes Christ's dual nature as both human and divine by recreating the emotions he experienced during the crucifixion. "Broken/Long before the sky would open," the martyred god is "Forsaken/almost human." Jesus is omniscient and protecting, but, like modern man—and the artist—he feels abandoned and misunderstood by the world. (2015, 93)

RELIGION AND THE SEARCH FOR MEANING

Whatever the outcome, the experiment is no mere exercise. Granted, the religious imagery is exceedingly vague at times, but therein lies its power. Besides, this operation heralds a return to what religion really ought to be or what it once was: a practice inextricably linked to life. This fundamental connection between faith and life is reflected in the way (Jewish and Christian) believers read their sacred texts. They familiarize themselves with the stories and experiences that were recorded centuries ago through an actualizing reading. Their faith revolves around the idea that the suffering, the trials and tribulations, indeed the entire history of the Jewish people constitute the history of any believer. This finds concrete expression in praying in the first person. In that respect some of Cohen's tracks could be described as religious *through and through*. Certain passages from the uncompromising "Last Year's Man" can be read in this way. Other compelling examples include "If It Be Your Will," "The Law," and especially "Born in Chains," a track Cohen sang during his final tours and released in 2014 on *Popular Problems*. The opening lines are intriguing:

> I was born in chains
> But I was taken out of Egypt
> I was bound to a burden
> But the burden it was raised.
> I fled to the edge
> of the Mighty Sea of Sorrow
> Pursued by the riders
> Of a cruel and dark regime
> But the waters parted
> And my soul crossed over
> Out of Egypt
> Out of Pharaoh's dream.

The exodus from Egypt, to which this is an overt reference, tells the Old Testament story of the Israelite slaves who, led by Moses, escaped the pharaoh's tyranny. With God's help, Moses was able to part the sea, allowing his people to make the crossing to Canaan, the promised land. The story is central to Judaism and is commemorated every year during Passover. Cohen draws on it to articulate his own psychological exodus.

Religious language lends itself to being used creatively: its elusiveness endows it with a flexibility that can give concrete shape to unanswered existential questions, undefined desires, and vague states of mind.[5] The words furnish the experience—in this case Cohen's psychological torment—with a language and a framework that was not there before. And so the perfectly honed lyrics of "Born in Chains" have their origin in an indefinable feeling. What is put here very eloquently is in fact based on a vague sense of despair. This is a state of mind Cohen had previously put into words in "I Can't Forget," with opening lines that leave little to the imagination: "I stumbled out of bed / I got ready for the struggle / I smoked a cigarette / And I tightened up my gut." At first glance, the two tracks have nothing in common, but the singer has stated that they cover the same ground. Initially he considered "I Can't Forget" to be a more accurate reflection of his mood than "Born in Chains," a track he worked on for many years. So perhaps it is fair to speak of two versions: in one the tone is raw and realistic, in the other the same subject is considered in a broader context.

Religious language is blessed with great eloquence, the product of a familiar form and an unfamiliar and perhaps even unknowable content. Put differently, the passing on from generation to generation creates a sense of familiarity, while the content of the texts always transcends the individual, which is precisely where it derives its power of expression. In practice, Cohen sometimes uses specific religious terms, of which "Hallelujah" is undoubtedly the best-known example: the entire track is synthesized in one word. Likewise, Cohen's absolute surrender to death in the final albums is condensed in concepts that are lifted straight from a discourse in which they are already endowed with a meaning and emotional charge: "Amen" (on *Old Ideas*) for example, as well as "Jubilee" and "Hineini" (both on *You Want It Darker*). The latter title translates as "Here I am." It is what Abraham answered when God called him to sacrifice his son Isaac, and a prayer sung during Rosh Hashanah and Yom Kippur. Alongside specific concepts he also draws on particular religious figures (Jesus, Joan of Arc, Bernadette), narratives ("Story of Isaac," "Last Year's Man"), and musical structures ("Who by Fire") to anchor this intensity in his work. As I argued in chapter 3, this often culminates in distinctly polyphonic writing. In *Book of Mercy*, for example, the conceptual and formal intertextual dialog with the biblical book of Psalms and a wider mystical tradition, as well as with John Donne's *Devotions Upon Emergent Occasions* (1624) and the central Jewish prayer *Amidah,* or *Shemoneh Esreh,* is very pronounced indeed.

Religion offers a foothold, certainty. In "Night Comes On," one of his most autobiographical tracks, Cohen sings of clinging to religion at moments of despair: "I took to religion." He uses comparable terms to describe his lover Marianne's attachment to him: "You held on to me like I was a crucifix." But this structuring force has a downside too. Given its all-encompassing nature, religion can also evoke the wrong kind of associations with which the individual believer cannot always identify. In "The Genius," a poem from *The Spice-Box of Earth*, Cohen talks of his Jewish identity. He lists a series of stereotypes to which the poet is invariably reduced. "For you," he writes at the beginning of each stanza, "I will be a ghetto jew," followed in subsequent stanzas by "an apostolate jew," "a banker jew," "a Broadway jew," "a doctor jew," and "a Dachau jew." He appears to accept these labels, until the poem's final line when the tone changes: "For you / I will be a Dachau jew / and lie down in lime / with twisted limbs / and bloated pain / no mind can understand." However much the poet is reduced to clichés (either by others or by religion itself), his twisted limbs and constant pain somehow escape this fate and will never be understood by anyone. What is deep inside remains both untouched and unfathomable.

Remarkably, as Brian Trehearne (2013–2019) observed, many years later he was to write a song in which he followed a similar pattern. On

"I'm Your Man" (1988), Cohen is initially prepared to take on a series of roles: a lover, a partner, a boxer, a doctor (on the 1994 live album he even talks of "a Jewish doctor"), a driver, and so on. But in the chorus, he states in no uncertain terms that "the beast" within him will not go to sleep (in "Hunter's Lullaby" [1984] he already evoked the image of "the beast he cannot bind"). A bold statement, if ever there was one. Between 1961 and 1988 not much has changed in this respect: there is something uncompromising in his soul which will not be tamed, not by lovers, friends, or strangers, and not by religion or any other major systems. Neither "The Genius" nor "I'm Your Man" specify the person addressed. She may be a woman, but it is equally possible that Cohen here addresses his audience. Around the time of "I'm Your Man," the artist experienced mounting pressure from the audience to live up to his image. In that respect "the beast" acquires a positive connotation: whatever is expected of him, however much they try to reduce him to a single (religious or otherwise) identity, there will always be something that is impervious to change. In "Leaving the Table" (on *You Want It Darker*) this question of identity is simply no longer an issue. In a clear nod to "I'm Your Man," his conclusion here is that "the wretched beast is tame."

THE WORLD OF "SUZANNE" AS A RELIGIOUS EXPERIENCE

Cohen's approach to religion changed over the years. Religious naïveté made way for a critical self-examination that stoked his curiosity and encouraged him to experiment and explore the workings of religion. While he initially kept a tight grip on the reins, eventually the balance began to shift. The evolution of "Born in Chains" shows that Cohen had written a story over which he no longer had complete control. The net of the myth he had spun now closed itself around him and assimilated him in a new narrative, which was at once reassuring and alienating. But the transition is not always a gradual one.

RELIGION

Some of Cohen's characters suddenly find themselves facing a different world. The moment when a deeper dimension manifests itself in real life can be considered a religious experience or at least it is often interpreted in religious terms. It is that moment that Cohen tries to articulate in one of his most famous tracks. Even so, music journalist Serge Simonart once argued on Belgian radio that the song is about nothing, and in a sense he was right. Cohen himself described the very first track on his first album as "reportage," on the face of it no more than a tea party with a woman by the water. So, what really is at stake in "Suzanne"?

The true story behind this track has been told many times. It is usually noted that the woman in question is not Suzanne Elrod (the mother of Cohen's children Adam and Lorca), but Suzanne Verdal, the wife of his sculptor friend Armand Vaillancourt. Cohen, enchanted by her enigmatic personality, is said to have visited her numerous times. She lived near the St. Lawrence River, close to the harbour in Montréal's old town. The lyrics contain other concrete references to Montréal. When Cohen talks about the sun that "pours down like honey on our lady of the harbour," many Montrealers would recognize this as a clear allusion to the Notre-Dame-de-Bon-Secours, a large statue of the Virgin Mary on top of the Sailors' Church overlooking the harbour and the river. "She shows you where to look," he clarifies a little later on. All in all, it is not surprising that the city's inhabitants have claimed the song as their own, but that is not to say that this is what "Suzanne" means to most listeners. For Europeans, the allusions to Montréal are not all that obvious. In fact, the opposite is true: there are no concrete references. Only two proper names are mentioned, that of Suzanne and Jesus: both enigmatic figures who are never really furnished with a solid identity. Although Suzanne gives the song its title, it is still unclear who she really is, and what place she occupies in this timeless and nameless universe—no specific time is mentioned, there is only *a* place near *a* river. From the outset, an enchanting, fairy-tale atmosphere is evoked, which is maintained right through to the end. This is pretty much all we can infer from the widely known opening lines: "Suzanne takes you down to her place near the river / You can hear the boats go by / You can spend the night beside her." Only the form of address is noticeably direct: taking centre stage here is not the performer's first-hand account, but Suzanne's meeting with an unidentified "you." The listener perhaps?

The song's real subject is precisely this personal encounter, or the attempt at one. The image of Suzanne is more ambiguous than the overall atmosphere of the song which, at least for Cohen, is remarkably loving. Suzanne is fascinating, somewhat intimidating even: on the one hand she is half crazy and dressed in rags and feathers, while on the other she has a mysterious, almost oriental appeal. She moves among the filthy "garbage" and the beautiful "flowers." This duality reflects her position, on the border between two worlds. The real crux of the encounter is described in line five: "And just when you mean to tell her / that you have no love to give her / then she gets you on her wavelength / and she lets the river answer / that you've always been her lover." Unlike some other women in Cohen's artistic universe, Suzanne is an exceptionally powerful figure. She is the one who determines what happens. While at first you were on different "wavelengths" (the word is very apt in this maritime setting), Suzanne now drags you over to *her* world. That movement forms the heart of the song. Suzanne's world, which now opens up, is not so much another space, but a deeper dimension that manifests itself in the existing world. In his Dutch version, the artist Herman van Veen[6] managed to convey this idea quite well. He talks of a city—an autonomous and bustling microcosm—which appears to be dormant (but does exist) and then suddenly comes to life. With dreamy guitar sounds, enchanting vocabulary, and a gentle voice, both Cohen and Van Veen manage to make this sensation palpable.[7]

The consequences of Suzanne's "wavelength" are unfathomable. Not that anything happens in the sense that journalist Simonart was thinking of, but still: what changes is the way the world appears. The moment Suzanne shows her world, one realizes that, viewed from her perspective, one has always been her lover. Ultimately, she holds up a mirror to the listener and shows that the boundaries between the two worlds are not as absolute as one might have thought. All you can do is surrender to her truth. What that "world" or "truth" entails is not made explicit, but all the classic ingredients of the Cohenesque universe are here, presented in a two-tier structure: beauty and ugliness, the meek or broken man and an enlightened God figure, an unbalanced male-female relationship, a blend of carnality and religiosity. Seen in this way, the encounter is about much more than personal contact: each one of the above-mentioned binary oppositions is challenged. Rather than with dichotomies, "Suzanne" deals with mirror images. Even the different characters become interchangeable, as evinced by the pronouns that are swapped around in each last line of the chorus: "For you've touched her [Suzanne] perfect body with your mind / For he [Jesus] has touched your perfect body with his mind / For she [Suzanne] has touched your perfect body with her mind." After briefly revealing themselves, both worlds merge again. There is no explicit message floating on the surface, only a mood, a feeling, an impression, and it is this that constitutes the strength of the song.

FROM THE RELIGIOUS EXPERIENCE TO THE PRAYER

It may be easier to talk about religion from an outsider's perspective, that is to say, by positioning oneself *opposite* the institution, rather than through a testimony *from within* a connection to the faith, for instance in a prayer that directly addresses God. Still, Cohen's oeuvre contains several personal prayers. *Book of Mercy* (1984) is the best example: this book of psalms, prayers, and meditations shows the complexity of his religious identity. While the book may pay homage to his Jewish roots, Cohen was only able to write it after his Zen master, Roshi, taught him how to draw on the wealth of Jewish texts and prayers. In the early 1980s he applied himself to the study of the Talmud. Biographer Ira Nadel (1994, 123) notes that while writing *Book of Mercy* Cohen frequented the synagogue and became a "more devout Jew." Rabbi Mordechai Finley, who would encounter Cohen in the synagogue in Los Angeles, confirms that he does not view the Kabbalah (a Jewish mystical tradition) from a theological perspective; rather, he sees it as more of an applied spiritual psychology: "I think Leonard is actually the greatest liturgist alive today. I read his poems aloud at high holidays, from *Book of Mercy*. I think *Book of Mercy* should be in our prayer book" (315). Not every text is formulated in the first person, but that does not make the collection any less personal. While the technique of alternating narrative perspectives in the rest of Cohen's oeuvre often culminates in a postmodern, ironic game, in *Book of Mercy*, Pezzarello believes (1997, 14) it actually intensifies Cohen's sincerity, because these alternating perspectives are an accurate representation of the "division of the self" (16). In interviews to mark the book's publication, Cohen sounded remarkably down to earth: "I mean it as a prayerbook. It's not meant to be poetry. It's an address to God, specifically ... very much a prayerbook" (Cohen, cited in Halpern 1984, 7).

Another well-known prayer is "If It Be Your Will," a track released in the same year as *Book of Mercy*. Like on "Who by Fire," the lyrics are based on a Jewish liturgical text that is spoken on the eve of Yom Kippur. Cohen places his fate as an artist in the hands of a higher authority ("you"—the term God is not used) to whom he turns. He asks for permission to speak and does so humbly. "The Window" (from 1979) can also be read as a prayer. The images of the spear and the crown of thorns associated with Christ on the cross are used to describe the pain and suffering that accompany love. Just as Christ felt forsaken by God and was at the mercy of those in power, so love is at the mercy of beauty and pride, since they keep threatening to take its place: "Why do you stand by the window / abandoned to beauty and pride / the thorn of the night in your bosom / the spear of the age in your side."

Similar religious imagery is used on the track "Show Me the Place," particularly that of the stone rolled back from Christ's grave at his resurrection. Like "Who by Fire," it has a repetitive (prayer) structure:

> Show me the place where you want your slave to go
> Show me the place help me roll away the stone
> Show me the place I can't move this thing alone
> Show me the place where the Word became a man
> Show me the place where the suffering began.

In other words, there are signs of a clear evolution in Cohen's oeuvre. Whereas in earlier work the message was frequently wrapped in a frame or story, in later work the religious vocabulary fits in more seamlessly, and sometimes he even manages to get his message across directly. "Story of Isaac," from 1969, shows how Cohen drew rather ostentatiously on an existing Bible story to air his social critique.[8] That being said, he did have an original take on the narrative. It is Isaac who is speaking here. At one point, the Biblical figure from the past seems to address the contemporary listener: "You who build these altars now / To sacrifice these children, / You must not do it anymore." Given the social context in which the track came about, the "you" here could refer to the army commanders during the Vietnam war who, unlike Abraham, were not motivated by a higher calling (which suggests that Cohen condones Abraham's act) but by purely rational schemes in which life and death were weighed as part of a cold-blooded strategy. Abraham's "axe of gold" becomes a "blunt and bloody hatchet." Bram van der Hout arrives at a similar conclusion when he demonstrates, in a comparison of the Isaac motif in Cohen and Woody Allen, what it boils down to for the former:

> The almighty rulers who send their sons to war are playing God. They think they can shape history and think they can calculate the

costs and benefits of a war in advance and decide that the death of a previously estimated number of young people is a worthwhile sacrifice for the preservation of the capitalist ideal of global trade and freedom. The end justifies the means. (2003, 20)

Although there is no denying that the track resonates with social and current affairs, "Story of Isaac" cannot be classified as an outright protest song. In an interview with William Ruhlmann (1993, 16) Cohen remarked: "It's a song that couldn't stand specifically in the anti-war camp. It says, 'Man of peace, man of war, the peacock [spreads its fan].' It doesn't matter where you are, it's vanity that's running this show."

Be that as it may, such blatant intertextual "construction mechanisms" became far less obvious in later years. In "The Notebooks" of *The Flame*, Cohen puts it like this: "This is not a parable / It's but a human life" (2018, 251). Twenty years on from "Story of Isaac," Cohen described the album *I'm Your Man* as less "allegorical" than its predecessors (Adria 1990), and a little later still he had found his own religious language and a personal symbolism through which to express his intimate feelings. The evolution in the writing process of "Hallelujah" illustrates this very well. In interviews Cohen has spoken of the infinite number of edits he needed to arrive at a finished song. Two different versions have appeared on the official albums: the original four-verse song on the studio album *Various Positions* (1984) and a variation he started singing from 1988 onward and which appeared in 1994 on *Cohen Live*. The early versions of the song contained far more explicit Biblical references. Over time, Cohen scrapped them: "Finally I understood that it was not necessary to refer to the Bible anymore" (Light 2013, 18).

The intertwined hearts that frequently pop up in his work are another good example of an individual vocabulary. Cohen described his "order of the unified heart" as a variation on the yin and yang, as a symbol in which opposites are united and differences eliminated.

He himself wears his "unified hearts" on a ring, christened his band the "Unified Heart Touring Company" and made the symbol available to fans on T-shirts and other memorabilia. Similar examples are the Buddhist stamp of his Dharma name, Jikan, and the burning bush (a reference to the story in Exodus) that grace the front cover of *The Flame* but that had already popped up in previous publications. In "The Notebooks" from this most recent collection, these three symbols appear beside one of the numerous self-portraits with the telling message: "then let our own symbols speak for us, if we can't" (2018, 204). As argued here in chapter 1, these attributes have all helped create the mythical personality that Leonard Cohen has become—at least to some.

Perhaps this evolution from an indirect, narrative style to direct expression is characteristic of writers who have outgrown their early work. It makes sense, because those who want to express complex issues in a simple style need an extensive vocabulary to find the right words. There are plenty of examples of artists who have gone on to deploy a new, freer form of expression in their later work—in fact, Adorno (2002) identified a pattern that he labelled "late style." And while the question remains whether religion in Leonard Cohen's work is fundamental or ornamental, that does not alter the fact that the words often conceal something else, something original, a sense of connection with something higher or deeper, with something that can carry different names, or that can be ineffable: "G-d," for instance—the vowel-less transcription in the Jewish tradition[9] underlines the unimaginable nature of this higher force. The creation and expression of this connection is precarious and precious. Sometimes the singer or poet is overwhelmed by it, sometimes it is sought out spontaneously through prayer. It certainly needs a register, or a place even, within which it can exist and be perceived. One of the common threads running through Cohen's oeuvre is precisely the ongoing search for that place.

NOTES

1. This was the case in 2013, when gigs in Leeds and London clashed with Rosh Hashanah and Yom Kippur.
2. Cohen is not fluent in Hebrew, but knows the language from the Jewish rite. He once compared Hebrew and Yiddish and identified a difference in the scope of their communication: local for Yiddish, universal-Biblical for Hebrew (see Benazon 1986, 45). The fragment from 2009 can be found at http://www.youtube.com/watch?v=4imJ7wWB9FU.
3. Although the song was officially released on the album *Live in London* (2009), it first popped up in Cohen's repertoire in 1988. The brief track was written in 1954 by Guy Singer, who took his inspiration from a few Biblical verses from Ruth (1:16). Her message is quite different from that of the priestly blessing. Turning to her mother-in-law, Naomi, she speaks the words: "Don't urge me to leave you or to turn back from you. Where you go I will go, and where you stay I will stay. Your people will be my people and your God my God."
4. The text is ascribed to Rabbi Amnon—an otherwise unknown eleventh-century scholar from Mainz—but is actually a great deal older and may date as far back as the sixth or seventh century.
5. Perhaps it was the need to give religion a place in life that drove Cohen to Buddhism. He loved the structure and the discipline of life in the monastery on Mount Baldy: rising at three o'clock in the morning before committing to many hours of meditation.
6. With his 1969 cover version, Herman Van Veen made Cohen's song famous in the Dutch-speaking world. The translation was done by Rob Chrispijn, a Dutch producer and lyricist who also translated lyrics by Dylan.
7. It was undoubtedly this powerful mood that was taken as the basis for the Dutch version, which is lyrically rather different from the original. In 2018, I played the track to an audience in Montréal during a guest lecture at the School of Continuing Studies at McGill University. More than half of the listeners indicated that they had "understood" the song, even though they did not understand a word of the Dutch. The translation features some remarkable passages. For instance, Van Veen replaced the intriguing and mysterious tea ritual ("tea and oranges that come all the way from China") by "*pepermuntjes*," which alludes to the "mints" that worshipers at Dutch Protestant church services traditionally suck on during the sermon. Stef Bos, another Dutch singer, makes fun of it in his song "Pepermunt." The translated lyrics of Bos's song read: "When the sermon begins to pall / when you just cannot listen any more / Mints / It's the cocaine of the protestants / catnip for the Dutch reformed junk."

8   A biographical interpretation is possible too: the noteworthy addition "I was nine years old" at the start of the song could be a reference to Cohen's age when he lost his father. Such a loss can be seen as the moment Cohen's childhood was sacrificed.
9   In *Book of Longing* Cohen invariably writes "G-d." While in earlier poems he wrote "God," in the anthology *Stranger Music* he would occasionally replace it with "G-d" (for instance in the psalms taken from *Book of Mercy*). It would be interesting to look at the other changes in the poems and see if there is a pattern.

FIVE

POWER
ARTISTIC PERSONAS CAUGHT BETWEEN VULNERABILITY AND AUTHORITY

The evolution of Cohen's self-representation from (powerful) leader to (humble) believer—both in his lyrics and on stage—was one of the themes running through the previous chapter. How absolute is the distinction between these two positions? The way they manifest themselves varies from period to period, but a special interest in all things power-related has always pervaded Cohen's life and work. It epitomizes many if not all of his characters: defenseless and merciless women, meek followers and tyrannical masters, shy and self-assured artists, and so on. In the documentary *Ladies and Gentlemen... Mr. Leonard Cohen* we saw a fairly arrogant poet at work. "I believed I was among the great," Cohen has said, looking back on the 1950s (Simmons 2012, 39). What interested him most in those days was the power that might accrue to him as a writer, including easy access to sex with dozens of women. No wonder, then, that at one point his misogynist image began to put readers off. Brian Trehearne has said that at the end of his lecture series he felt compelled to draw up a memo entitled "What Is Good in Cohen?" But the hunger for power appears to significantly abate in the later work. Starting with *Book of Mercy* and subsequently on *Ten New Songs*, the tone becomes much milder. Is this the placidity of an aging man? Or could it be argued that Cohen no longer had to try so hard, because at this stage in his career he had acquired the power he had been seeking from the start? The world tours of his later years would certainly suggest as much. Picking up his guitar and playing the opening notes of "Suzanne" was all it took to elicit spontaneous applause from the thousands in the audience. He also enjoyed great respect from his backing band. I spoke with them all and was struck by the combination of admiration and reticence toward the singer. There was an invisible line they did not want to cross. They certainly did not presume to speak on his behalf, let alone interpret his art. Cohen was never more powerful than during the final phase of his career.

In his beautiful essay *The Curtain* ([2005] 2007) Milan Kundera distinguishes between an artist's "morning freedom" and "vesperal freedom." With reference to the changing styles of Picasso, Beethoven, and Fellini, Kundera outlines how "a young person's freedom and an old person's freedom are separate continents" (141). Whereas young, uncompromising artists are happy to join forces and to claim their artistic freedom in a youthful rage while still doing their best to seduce the audience, the older artist is free from this dependence on both his fellow artists and the public. This is why, in his final works, Fellini was able to savour what he described as "joyful irresponsibility" and Picasso and Beethoven could take delight in their vesperal freedom—which is "a miracle, an island," in Kundera's words (144).

Edward Said formulated a similar idea in *On Late Style: Music and Literature Against the Grain*. Although the book was published posthumously, it is a crystallization of ideas that Said had formulated in various articles and lectures in the late 1980s. The notion of "late style," borrowed from Adorno, is the style "of a kind of self-imposed exile from what is generally acceptable, coming after it, and surviving beyond it" (Said 2017, 10). Said develops the concept in greater detail than Kundera: what matters is that artistic lateness should *not* be seen "as harmony and resolution but as intransigence, difficulty and unresolved contradiction" (x). Said writes at length about the changing structure of many artists' later works and, taking inspiration from Adorno's writing on Beethoven, shows how the composer's final works communicate an impression of being unfinished. This claim is preceded by two assumptions:

> [F]irst, that when he was a young composer, Beethoven's work was vigorous and organically whole, whereas it has now become more wayward and eccentric; and second, that as an older man facing death, Beethoven realizes that his work proclaims, as Rose Subotnik puts it, that "no synthesis is conceivable (but is in effect) the remains of a synthesis, the vestige of an individual human subject sorely aware of the wholeness, and consequently the survival, that has eluded it forever." (6)

Likewise, the iconic, one-dimensional figure of the later Cohen conceals a poetic in which caesuras and discontinuity are the rule rather than the exception.[1] In 1994 Ken Norris wrote that "if there is any one thing that distinguishes the early Cohen [...] from the later Cohen [...], it is that the later works truly employ the book as the unit of composition. The early books are very much 'collections' of poetry, while the later works present themselves as unified wholes." But the collections of poetry that appeared after 1994—and which could be labeled "later Cohen" from our contemporary vantage point—actually miss that unifying structure. *Book of Longing* and *The Flame*, as well as a music album like *Dear Heather*, are conceived like collages of texts or songs that were written at different moments in time (dates were added to some of the poems in *Book of Longing*), that do not always show great thematic coherence, and that combine different musical styles or literary genres. Daniel Bougnoux (2013, 65) compares *Dear Heather* with the later Matisse: "the spoken word prevailed over the sung, while lyrics and music appeared to go their separate ways, like they did in the late Matisse in whose paintings form and color appeared to separate." The notebook facsimiles that were included in the inlay of *Old Ideas* and in the main body of the text of *The Flame* can also be read in this light. The poet-singer is no longer seeking to achieve some form of thematic synthesis. The opening track of *You Want It Darker* sets the tone: "If you are the dealer / I'm out of the game." Cohen states in no uncertain terms that the game has become meaningless to him, whereas in the past he often drew on the image of the (poker) game to describe his world (for example in "The Stranger Song," "Tonight Will Be Fine," "The Captain," and "In My Secret Life"). Similarly, in "Treaty," he no longer cares who leads and who follows: "I don't care who takes this bloody hill."

It was a very different story once. Relationships between virtually all the characters in Cohen's oeuvre are shaped by power mechanisms. These are rarely described in abstract terms, but invariably transposed to concrete situations, either via the expression of the lyrical speaker's longing, loss, dominance, or dependence in relation to a loved one, or via a more detached, third-person description of a given situation. For example, the title of the track "Democracy" seems to promise a philosophical reflection on a form of political governance, but it is first and foremost an enumeration of concrete examples. Democracy is "coming from the sorrow in the street, from the homicidal bitchin' that goes down in every kitchen to determine who will serve and who will eat." It is intriguing to see that Cohen also manages to embody these power structures in his artistic persona on stage, for instance in dialogue with his backing singers. The relationship is clear-cut and transparent. Most of the time, their role is to enhance certain passages or to support his voice, but every now and then they are brought into the universe of his songs as fully fledged characters. In "Diamonds In The Mine" he wants to inform his audience that his relationship can no longer be salvaged. "You tell them now," he sings in a commanding tone of voice, and to reinforce his message he has his backing singers repeat the verse. In "Ain't No Cure for Love" they are similarly tasked with getting the message across and are once again brought into the song. The singer gives the prompt ("I even heard the angels declare it from above") and his angelic helpers do the rest. The high-pitched tones they then produce should make things clear. Like in "Diamonds in the Mine" Cohen directly addresses his backing vocalists: "Tell them, angels" (various performances during the 1988 tour). And during the live version of "To Love Somebody" (a Bee Gees cover) in 1980 the backing group is challenged again: "You don't know what it's like ... to love somebody," he snarled at them. The dialogue with his audience is another arena in which Cohen asserts himself. As a rule, he wants to subtly draw his listeners into the music (even here he assumes a leading role), but at some gigs he is more brazen. In 1970, he provoked his audience in Germany by giving the Hitler salute, while later that same year he warned a few hotheads in Aix-en-Provence in the South of France that he was prepared to fight, and two years after that security staff at a turbulent gig in Israel were the target of his ire. The contrast with his final concerts, when he would thank both his band and the audience humbly and profusely, and give his musicians the necessary space for solos, is striking.

This all paints a vivid, at times downright hilarious, and certainly entertaining picture. But the question remains as to how these hierarchical relationships are played out. The interplay of lyrics, music, singer(s), and audience is more than just a game, although a shadow of doubt and ambiguity will always shroud the characters' relationships. In "Is This What You Wanted" the singer tries to describe his relationship with his lover in terms of a power struggle. The track is little more than a series of comparisons in the form of "You were ..., I was...." The only thing these different images have in common is the inequality they imply. In other lyrics the contrast between the two positions is not always quite so extreme. For many, the appeal of Cohen's work lies precisely in this strange mix of vulnerability and authority. At times his voice sounds determined, even arrogant, at others broken and miserable. In the apocalyptic prophecy of "The Future" authority has the upper hand, whereas in the mournful "Take This Longing" brokenness dominates. Sometimes these two aspects can be heard simultaneously. "Hallelujah" is one such multi-layered song in which "the holy" and "the broken" can be heard alongside and over each other.[2] It is precisely this ambivalence that is carried through on stage, both between the singer and his backing vocalists and in each of their individual performances. In 1992 Cohen elaborated on this extraordinary tension in the Dutch newspaper *De Telegraaf*:

> I have let cherubic voices twine around my bronze baritone. I have a strong preference for "southern belles," those Scarlet O'Hara's: frail and indestructible at the same time. I will never cease to be amazed about the typical logic of that type of woman: singing topless, so to speak, but at the same time afraid that they are going to the devil because I make them sing the word "damn." (Cohen, in Golsteijn 1992)

FROM THE WORLD OF APPARENT CERTAINTIES TO THE BUDDHIST IDEAL OF THE VARIOUS POSITIONS

It should be clear from this brief introduction that it is all but impossible to overestimate the significance of power, even though its meaning changed as Cohen grew older. I will be taking a thematic approach in the pages that follow, linking the issue of power to affiliated concepts such as certainty/uncertainty and freedom/constraint.

POWER

The longing for power manifests itself on different levels. First, there is Cohen's ongoing search for teachers and father figures, both in his professional and his private life. The dialectic of master and slave usually expresses itself in the relationship between teacher (or sometimes saint) and student, and of course also in the relationships between men and women. The best-known father figures in Cohen's life are Buddhist Zen master Kyozan Joshu Sasaki (Roshi for short, literally "old master"), fellow writer Irving Layton, and publisher Jack McClelland[3]—three figures who played a crucial role in Cohen's career and are frequently mentioned in poems and acknowledgements. The wish for father figures is actually a recurring theme in both the francophone and anglophone literature of Quebec, which is always at risk of being overshadowed by the two central bodies of literature (British/American and French) and thus finds itself pushed to the periphery.[4]

The theme of power is also occasionally rendered as a hankering for a certainty that is reflected in Cohen's musical choices, like his predilection for country music. He views *Songs from a Room* as his very own country album: "the sound is spare, much less ornamented than *Songs of Leonard Cohen*" (Simmons 2012, 206). Toward the end of the 1960s, country, folk, and the blues were considered forms of "pure music," charged with endowing the commercially eroded pop music of the moment with its original potency. Like folk music, country was deemed to be capable of expressing simple truths in a straightforward and sincere way. "The message is clear, the words are strong," according to Cohen; "three chords and the truth," as American country singer Harlan Howard once put it.[5] The quest for clearly defined structures also crystallizes in recurring themes, like the shelter of religion, the rigidity of the military, or the transparency of the law, which regularly serve as backdrops to Cohen's work.[6] Several of the literary titles illustrate as much, foregrounding hierarchical or institutionalized relationships and offering starring roles for losers, slaves, and ladies' men. Such reassuring certainty can even be found in the imposed discipline of prison: the "luxury" of discipline is a recurring paradox. So too in "Night Comes On": "I needed so much / to have nothing to touch / I've always been greedy that way." And in the opening lines of "The Old Revolution": "I finally broke into the prison, / I found my place in the chain." Cohen's formulations veer toward what is known in Zen Buddhism as a koan: a brief, pithy statement of an aspect of Buddhist doctrine. Discipline, hierarchy, militarism, and religion: these concepts were at odds with the freedom movement of the 1960s and 1970s. Cohen was no hippie, but no puritan either. His wish for fixed structures of power may be a reaction to excess, which is equally entrenched in his work. It is a subject I will explore in more detail later on in this chapter.

Cohen's fascination with power is known to biographers and critics alike. But few have noticed that the title of his first novel incorporates another hierarchy. This may not be all that evident in the English title, but it is clearly the case in one of the two French translations in circulation. The first French version, from 1971, retained *The Favourite Game*, but in a more recent reprint from 2002 the publisher opted for a pun: *Jeux de Dames*. Although this literally means "game of checkers," it can of course also refer to a game with women. The title is apposite, as it picks up on the ambiguity of the English, which has gone largely unnoticed by critics. The second meaning of "game" is "prey." This play on words was one of the reasons Cohen ultimately opted for *The Favourite Game* and cast aside working titles like *Beauty at Close Quarters* and *Stars for Neatness*. The title certainly reflects the content. The hunt (as a game) for female beauty (as prey) is a recurring theme in the book. The double meaning comes explicitly to the fore in chapter 16 of part 1, and further allusions to it are made later.

Chapter 16 contains a description of a game from the childhood years of the protagonist and his female friend Shell, who would adopt the roles of Soldier and Whore (capitalized—both characters are archetypes). They are presented as exemplars of the ideal man and the ideal woman. Life is delightfully simple for the young Breavman. The youthful heroism and hubris lend the text a humorous undertone, but what is really at stake here is power. The Whore is regarded as the man's object of lust while the Soldier forms part of a rigorous system of superiors and subordinates. In this brief chapter from *The Favourite Game* the veiled ritual of love, which appears to be difficult to articulate, is swapped for a simple financial transaction. It propels us into a world of clear-cut meanings, which leaves no room for ambiguity.[7]

But this is only half the story. The above does not alter the fact that the world of certainties is ultimately often a fiction. Pitted against this stable world in which everything has a fixed place is a landscape in which chaos is rife, certainties are undermined, and nothing lasts forever. A straightforward, neatly defined world with strict power relations might offer the advantage of clarity, but it will rarely reflect the continuously changing reality. In "The Future" Cohen predicts "Things are going to slide, slide in all directions. Won't be nothing, nothing you can measure anymore." Equally, experts cannot always be counted on to do their job properly. In "One of Us Cannot Be Wrong," the final track on *Songs of Leonard Cohen*, the singer turns to a doctor and a saint, who both fall short, while in "In My Secret Life" he shatters the illusion of the dealer, who "wants you thinking / that it's either black or white." The same idea comes back in a fragment from the notebooks (included in *The Flame*, and dated 1989) that reads like an early version of "In My Secret Life":

> I take the train
> but I do not dare
> to really look at anybody
> riding with me there
> some are poor some are rich
> some are black some are white
> but I don't know which is which
> in my secret life
> (2018, 205)

It is not always clear whether this ambiguity is a blessing or a curse. At times it seems to elicit despair, at others it is a source of good fortune: "Thank God it's not that simple / in my secret life," Cohen concludes in the opening track of *Ten New Songs*. And what to make of the occasionally hilarious "One of Us Cannot Be Wrong"? Thematically, there is little that ties the four verses together, although on a structural level a certain pattern emerges. A situation that initially appeared to be clear or manageable keeps changing and turning into an unwieldy mess. We are presented with, successively, the certainty of religious rituals versus the elusiveness of a swarm of mosquitoes; the authority of a doctor and the remedy he prescribes versus the decline of his practice; the omnipotence of the saint and his scholastic wisdom versus the death by drowning of his body and the meaningless lessons of his resurrected spirit; and, finally, the images captured on film versus a painful blizzard of ice. "Torture," "ruin," "drowned," "blizzard": the evolution always sounds demoralizing, yet the song still ends on a plea: "Oh please let me come into the storm."

To express the idea of change and constant movement, Cohen likes to draw on meteorological imagery: "the storm," "the blizzard of the world," "the flood," "the squalls of hate," and so on, all evoke the unpredictable and indiscriminate force of nature. A fine example is "The Flood," the closing poem in *Book of Longing*, which also illustrates that it is a subject that has long preoccupied Cohen. He wrote the poem in 1973, published it in 2006, and recited it on his tour in 2013. The last few lines go as far as to challenge even the speaker's position:

> The flood it is gathering
> Soon it will move
> Across every valley
> Against every roof
> The body will drown
> And the soul will break loose

> I write all this down
> But I don't have the proof.
> (2006, 229)

In short, the dualistic worldview that is a common feature in Cohen's work (male-female, rich-poor, good-evil, left-right, and the like) is often under pressure. That was the gist of *Flowers for Hitler*, which alludes to the contrast between a banal object and a famous figure from world history. In a letter to his publisher, Cohen explains his intentions: "The whole point of the title is that the word HITLER has to be set against a domestic background—and that's the point of the book too" (McMaster University—Cohen archive, 1963–1965).

Working titles like *Sunshine for Napoleon* and *Walls for Genghis Khan* show a similar pattern. The poet takes absolute evil, which readers tend to situate outside their own world, and transposes it to a familiar context in which human relationships are controlled by sometimes brutal power mechanisms. It prompted Trehearne to write: "Cohen's method ridicules, even explodes, the history of rhetoric, poetic forms, calls for sympathy or identification, and the very notion of evil; in the language of his later song 'The Captain,' it shows the impossibility of finding 'a decent place to stand / in a massacre'" (2013, 18). The overriding theme of this collection—which calls to mind Hannah Arendt's notion of the "banality of evil" (1963), which she outlined in *Eichmann in Jerusalem*—was a very sensitive issue. Cohen's generation was the first faced with coming to terms with the Holocaust.

The one-sided dualism makes way for an invitation to the reader or listener to surrender to this chaos, which Cohen does not see as a temporary situation, but as a non-stop, existential battle. This chaos is variously labelled. Besides meteorological imagery, he draws on religious terminology ("Babylon"), the suggestive "Boogie Street" (on *Ten New Songs*), and the metaphor of the searing heat of the furnace (on "The Old Revolution," among others, which is of course haunted by the spectre of the gas chambers of the concentration camps). Some descriptions are more lighthearted, like those where he talks about the fickleness of the human heart, "that cooks and sizzles like shish kebab in our breast, too hot, too hot for the body" (Guillot 2016).

One of the most common images is that of war. A common theme is the undeclared, hidden war that is not experienced as such precisely because of its prolonged and covert nature. In interviews Cohen has spoken of the "frontline of the inner life" (see for instance Kirk 1988). *New Skin for the Old Ceremony*, especially, contains quite a few bellicose songs. "There Is a War" is not a plea for tolerance but an overt call for the listener to brave the war and face reality: "Why don't you come on back to the war, that's right, get in it." *Death of a Lady's Man* features a sequence of poems in which war is used as a metaphor for the challenges of married life, a life choice he had described three years earlier as "the hottest furnace of the spirit today" (Burger 2014, 81). It goes without saying that the war can also be read as a direct reference to real historical conflicts, like the Second World War, the Vietnam war, or the September 11 attacks.

By occasionally reversing his characters' positions, Cohen seems to expose the artificial character of hierarchical relationships. Gilles Tordjman (2006, 94–95) identifies a parallel between the master who fails in his duty and the koan, in which the wisdom of student and master can coalesce—likewise a recurring theme in Jewish literature. In "Ballad of the Absent Mare," which I looked at earlier, it is not always clear whether it is the master who is in control of the horse or the other way around.[8] Sometimes lessons are learned and instantly debunked again, while at other moments the power relations remain in force, so that the situation described seems less grotesque and comes across as much more realistic. In "A Kite Is a Victim," the opening poem of *The Spice-Box of Earth*, Cohen hit upon a beautiful image to capture this precarious balance.[9] The piece revolves around the subtle interplay of dependence and control, which alternate in a natural and balanced way in the art of kite-flying. To begin with, we encounter the kite flier who is literally pulling the strings and the kite that is trying to escape by climbing on the wind. A little later, Cohen compares kite-flying with fishing, and also likens the image of the kite to his own work: the writer has no choice but to entrust his work to the wind until it is picked up by a reader or listener who does something with it. But there is also a suggestion that the struggle between the two parties has been decided in advance. At the end of the day the kite is a victim you can simply haul down and store in a drawer, the fish is destined to be caught (giving the fishing a sadistic edge: "you play him carefully and long"), and ultimately it is the writer who decides to send his creation out into the world. The structure in the first three stanzas contrasts with the final one, in which the kite-flier's dominance is broken. The cord snaps, the power is lost, and what remains is the moon, which is not tied to anything. The kite-flier feels detached and must face up to his insignificance. In the end all he can do is admire the kite, which literally rises above him. And with that, the distinction between a superior and an inferior position is simply erased.

At other moments Cohen tries to have a hand in the various positions he assumes. This Buddhist outlook on life is reflected in the title of *Various Positions*: a Zen practitioner will not be bound. His aim is to detach himself and to adapt, to the best of his ability, in a constantly changing (outside) world. But that is not to say that freedom can be absolute. On *Various Positions* Cohen explores the limits of that freedom:

> One possibility is that we were made to live a life of ecstasy. To be infinitely beautiful, wild, and intoxicated. Another option is that we were created to live our lives cowering in a rigid structure. Between these extremes we have a choice of an infinite number of nuances. The tracks on *Various Positions* deal with the choices that define our free will.[10] (De Bruyn 1985, 47)

THE POWER OF THE ARTIST

The many speakers in Cohen's universe are both hero and antihero, alternating positions that manifest in different ways: in the structure of albums like *Recent Songs* and *Various Positions*, in the lifelong game with artistic personas, in the formal experiment of *Death of a Lady's Man*, and also in the ambiguous status of the woman. At times the artist depends on her, at others he wants to dominate her. That tension is described with great subtlety in "So Long, Marianne." In the opening paragraphs of chapter 3, I asked who took whom under his or her wing in this song: "I used to think I was some kind of Gypsy boy / before I let you take me home." From the word go, it is unclear who made the crucial first move. On the one hand, the speaker gives Marianne permission, as suggested by "I let you"—the controlling "let" is a recurring word in Cohen's lexicon. On the other hand, *she* is the one performing the action and giving her lover's life a radical twist by transforming his nomadic existence into a domestic one. The positions within the relationship shift. Marianne's dependence was once absolute: "You held on to me like I was a crucifix," Cohen sings. But now, when he begs her for her "hidden love," the situation is completely different. It is merely one step in the process of accepting that the relationship is over. This process is also driven by the song itself, through which Cohen seals the parting: "So long, Marianne." The title is not merely a passive statement, but a performative act.

In response to biographer Sylvie Simmons' question about the emotional significance of this track (163), Cohen said: "I didn't think I was saying goodbye, but I guess I was." The biographer concludes that it was almost "as if the song made the decision for him" (163). This biographical confession is an accurate reflection of the self-image that the artist has created in his work. Although he occasionally gives in to his longing to settle with his lover, he is repeatedly forced to conclude that it prevents him from pursuing his art and that it sabotages his creativity. Again and again, he feels compelled to abandon her—the "artistic alibi" identified by Martin Jay. He takes this decision over and over, and it is in this that he ultimately shows his power. He can be an artist *in between* two lovers. This is the pattern we see with Shell, who is dumped by Breavman, and with Annie, in the short love poem from *The Spice-Box of Earth*:

> With Annie gone
> Whose eyes to compare
> with the morning sun?
> Not that I did compare,
> But I do compare
> Now that she's gone.

In other words, the poet only truly becomes a poet the moment his loved one is gone. The art of comparison that Cohen alludes to here is one of the writer's main responsibilities. Another example, also from *The Spice-Box of Earth*, is "Travel." The author seems to be apologizing for the fact that he has chosen poetry. He talks about a path, no doubt that of his vocation as a writer: "Lost in the fields of your hair I was never lost / Enough to lose a way I had to take." Later he reiterates the idea that he cannot be both artist and lover at once, for instance in "My Wife and I" (from *Death of a Lady's Man*). Once his wife is asleep there is room for art again: "I closed the light and left the room carefully and I came down here to you"—the reader.

Control, independence, and release are crucial, notwithstanding those moments when this control is deliberately relinquished. This happens mainly in the experience of excess, which I described in chapter 3 as a sanctuary and observation post combined. Excess may be regarded as a moment of catharsis when the artist or his characters can become aware of boundaries that would otherwise remain invisible. This awareness, the fleeting moment when one is no longer caught in the routine of everyday actions and frameworks and boundaries momentarily reveal themselves, generates a form of freedom—a feeling that is also engendered by the aesthetic experience itself. The experience of excess is typically physical and can manifest itself in an insatiable hunger for sex as creative energy, or in the intoxication of dance, drugs, or alcohol. In *Songs of Love and Hate*, and later in songs like "Diamonds in the Mine" and "Leaving Green Sleeves," that excess could even be heard in the voice.[11] It can also manifest itself in violence, on the principle that a little bit of war can sometimes get human relationships back on track. In interviews Cohen has repeatedly stated that he is not a pacifist and is more interested in a peaceful movement than in a peace movement (De Bruyn 1985, 47). That propensity for violence finds an echo in his style. *Flowers for Hitler* is no doubt the best example of this. The book reflects the romantic poet's metamorphosis into the committed writer who rejects any form of meaningless doggerel. This transformation comes to the fore in the poem "Style." Cohen does not mince his words and addresses his reader directly: "I will forget my style / I will have no style." It must have come as a blow to readers in 1964 when earlier he had shown himself to be the man capable of evoking beguiling images, seducing women with his words, and comparing mythologies.

Could it be that Cohen, triggered by the theme of the Holocaust, began to interpret the role of the artist differently? Is it possible that he recognized the limitations of beauty, realizing that it could sometimes obstruct truth? In *Flowers for Hitler* he appears to be turning away from the power he had acquired with his dazzling style and to be trying to break with the pattern. Straightaway, in the opening poem, "What I'm Doing Here," he brings matters to a head: he can no longer see any good in himself—neither as a man, nor as an artist. In subsequent books this trend continues. Cohen becomes an anti-poet. He writes poems that are at odds with many readers' idea of poetry, and that are closer to minimalist, bitter, and sometimes downright nasty statements. Their settings are no longer bucolic with a touch of the idyllic, but urbane with an undertone of disappointment, rooted in the history of the moment.

A year later rumours circulated that Cohen was planning to give it all up. "Cohen quits his musical interests," *Toronto Star* reported (February 15, 1973); "Singer quits in disgust," the *Lethbridge Herald* wrote (February 17, 1973). But not long after he declared in an interview: "I went through an anti-intellectual phase. It was an interesting experience—it purifies the language" (Kapica 1973, 37). Considering the crisis of content and form, it probably does not come as a surprise that the collections from this period (*Flowers for Hitler*, *The Energy of Slaves*, and *Parasites of Heaven*) were unavailable for a long time[12] and that their share in the *Stranger Music* anthology is limited. But Brian Trehearne believes that it is on the strength of these titles that Cohen absolutely merits his place in the Canadian literary canon. "For me, a number of poems in *Flowers for Hitler* will never lose their power to shock and will continue to open the eyes of those who do not reflect sufficiently on the events [of the Holocaust]," Trehearne says (2013–2019).

A tentative shift in mentality can be identified in some poems in *Death of a Lady's Man*. In "The Café," one of the collection's first, the poet declares that he has found a new will to speak: "I want to talk." This ambition is still rather modest and fragile, since he resumes: "I have taken a drug that makes me want to talk."[13] In the bundles and albums that follow the voice grows stronger and eventually produces the sound of the "vesperal freedom" of the final ten years of Cohen's career.

NOTES

1   Here and there the concept of "late style" has already been obliquely associated with Leonard Cohen. Brian Trehearne mentioned it in a contribution on the dualistic and absolute judgments in Irving Layton's later work, which Trehearne reads through the prism of (among others) Cohen's *Flowers for Hitler* (see Trehearne 2013). In turn, Ira B. Nadel used the concept in an article about Philip Roth in 2013, in which he also briefly mentions Leonard Cohen. Similarly, in 2018 Nadel made a comparison between *You Want It Darker* and *Blackstar*, David Bowie's final album (Nadel 2018).

2   In *The Holy or the Broken: Leonard Cohen, Jeff Buckley and the Unlikely Ascent of "Hallelujah,"* Alan Light (2013) reconstructs the genesis of Cohen's best known track. He also lists the main cover versions (including those by John Cale and Jeff Buckley) and tries to explain the song's immense popularity. Light concludes that "Hallelujah" is so versatile that each new version highlights yet another dimension. He variously labels these dimensions as "religion, sex, hope, despair, love, death" (Light 2013, 131) and even "irony, sex, confusion, experience" (206). The title of his book retains only the two extremes—the holy and the broken—in between which each interpretation seeks to position itself.

3   During the laborious writing process of *Death of a Lady's Man*, McClelland was just about the only one at the publishing company who kept in touch with Cohen. On the occasion of Cohen's sixtieth birthday, he revealed, "[t]here's one unique thing about our author-publisher relationship. Leonard did not like the formality of contracts. As a matter of consequence, although we would always send him a contract as a matter of form, inevitably he would not sign and return them. I chose to ignore this. I think over the many years that we published his poetry and his fiction he signed only one contract" (McClelland, in Fournier and Norris 1994, 112).

4   For Margaret Atwood, the victim is a stock character in Canadian literature. This is something she identifies in Cohen's second novel: "*Beautiful Losers* depicts not only the sufferings of the victim, but the mentality of the Canadian onlooker who needs to identify with the victims" (1972, 100).

5   Country music also pops up regularly in the second half of his musical career: on "The Captain" he has fun with the genre, on "Tower of Song" he namechecks Hank Williams, on *Dear Heather* he reserves a place for a "Tennessee Waltz," and at a few gigs in June 2013 he paid tribute to George Jones with a cover of "Choices."

6   Judges and defendants appear on, among others, "A Singer Must Die," "The Traitor," and "The Law," although by the time we get to *You Want it Darker* they have outstayed their welcome: "I don't need a lawyer" he concludes on "Leaving the Table."

7   In the extraordinary scene in which he tortures a frog (Book 2, chapter 1), Breavman takes visible and almost sadistic delight in the power he can wield over the small creature, which is virtually anthropomorphized: "the legs of the frog were like a lady's" (Cohen [1063] 1994, 64).

8   While this song deals with a mare, in quite a few other texts—by Cohen, as well as the likes of Lorca—the horse traditionally symbolizes the man, who may or may not be reined in by a woman, like in "Take This Longing." Cohen must have been fond of the image of the bridled horse, seeing as he also incorporated it into various tour posters, *Book of Longing*, and an illustration that was projected onto the backdrop during his final tour.

9   The text is also included in the selection *Stranger Music*, although not as its opening poem. My interpretation is based on Stephen Scobie's analysis (1978, 25-28). Note that the image of the kite also appears on "Stories of the Street."
10 Christophe Lebold (2013, 498-499) summarizes the idea behind *Various Positions* as follows: "As its title indicates, the disc will be a Kama Sutra: a compilation of positions and postures that we can adopt with our partners in love—with God, with a woman, with life. The Kama Sutra will, by turns, be erotic, intellectual, and spiritual, but it will ask the same questions for each partner: how to approach them? How to love them? How to abandon them? The (unrealizable) goal: to turn things around. To settle once and for all the question of love, but to take it to extremes, seeking not one anchor for love and one way of raising one's voice, but nine (the number of songs)." Cohen said something similar about the previous album, *Recent Songs*. The opening track "The Guests" elicited the following comment: "it defines the album. You see the guests arrive and then the rest of the album is each of the guests makes a statement about his own particular position. And that goes right down through the record to the next side, right down to the end. It's as if each guest tells his story" (Rasky [2001] 2010, 112). Both the listener and the artist face these choices.
11 In recent years, he no longer yelled during gigs, but lent his words all the more power by reciting pieces of text, repeating phrases, speaking them slowly and stressing every single syllable, and frequently going down on his knees in the process. Some music journalists drew a comparison with trip hop, a music style with a slow tempo and a nostalgic undertone that emerged in the 1990s.
12 Cohen's renewed popularity prompted the reissue of these collections, not during the recent tours but, ironically enough, only after his death—by which time they had been out of print for some fifty years.
13 Stephen Scobie (1993, 7-22) approaches the existential crisis that is expressed in *The Energy of Slaves*, *Death of a Lady's Man*, and *Book of Mercy* from a different perspective. He places what he describes as "the major trilogy of Cohen's self-destruction" within a postmodern, Derridean framework in which the poet's power of expression is fundamentally eroded. *The Energy of Slaves* sets the tone: "what Cohen is doing is carrying out [...] a deconstruction of the figure of the poet as a unified source of utterance and meaning." The composition of *Death of a Lady's Man* proves that "there is no source: as Derrida says, at the source there is only a supplement." Similarly, in *Book of Mercy* the author places himself in "a position from which any sense of self-centredness has been emptied out. In prayer, the speaker steps aside from himself; he defers himself, endlessly, to the Other."

INTERMEZZO 3

"EVERYONE MUST FALL"
FREEDOM AS CONSCIOUSNESS: ABOUT LONGING AND LOSS

In this third intermezzo I want to zoom in on two distinct themes that often surface in Cohen's work, and that are at odds with the ideal of freedom: longing and loss. Freedom, which many of his characters are looking for, lies not so much in the victory of the powerful over the subordinate but in an individual consciousness of boundaries. The preceding has shown that this consciousness can be explored through excess, to which the subject—be it the artist, reader, or listener—has the courage to surrender. Cohen would later find a profound strength in this position of powerlessness, ranging from the liberating detachment of the Zen practitioner to the opportunities offered by the imperfect. At the same time, by surrendering to art and detaching from the self it becomes possible to approach reality in all its different facets and manifestations. In psychoanalytic terms, detachment enables the "work" of dreaming or mourning. For Darian Leader the mechanism underlying this psychological labour is identical to what Cubists like Picasso and Braque did in their work: examining the figure of man from a range of different perspectives. Leader writes:

> This parallel between the artistic process and the work of mourning can be found in other practices beyond Cubism. Think, for example, of the very different art of De Chirico and Morandi. In De Chirico's work, we see the same collection of motifs—a fountain, a shadow, a train on the horizon—repeated again and again but in different configurations. The elements are often identical, but their arrangement changes. These paintings occupied him for at least fifty years, and were sometimes produced on a daily basis. [...] Like the work of mourning described by Freud, a set of representations is given a special value, focused on and reshuffled. (2008, 29)

Citing writer-psychiatrist Gordon Livingstone, Leader clarifies that this work certainly does not always result in a transformation of the initial situation. Livingstone describes his experiences following the loss of his six-year-old son: "Perhaps that's how it is with a permanent loss: you examine it from every angle you can think of and then just carry it like a weight" (Leader 2008, 30). Put differently, consciousness cannot always reverse, undo, or curb a loss or a longing, but it can expedite a process of acceptance. The fragmentary character of Cohen's recent works, as well as the prominence of the many self-portraits in the final books of poetry and even the life-long obsession with the same recurring themes, can be seen as the "work" that is done in the artistic process. Roscoe Beck (Mas 2013, 5) even identifies an "uplifting power" in Cohen's oeuvre, while for Irving Layton this "state of exaltation" is what his songs are really about (Rasky [2001] 2010, 40).

What role can music play in this process of attaining consciousness? Many songs revolve around the confrontation between the *unavoidability* of feelings and the attitude the singer (and by extension the listener) can adopt to them. In the first place, music is capable of expressing this indefinable sense of unavoidability and rendering it audible. Obviously, this is not only true for Cohen: the musical translation of meanings and narratives is central to many classical music traditions. A banal anecdote about Mozart illustrates this. When his father played the do-re-mi-fa-sol-la-ti scale on the piano and suddenly paused, he is said to have run over to the instrument to finish the sequence and to play the "do" that brings resolution. The incident is interesting because in Cohen such "musical inevitability" often echoes what he sings about—the inescapability of a loss or the irresistibility of a longing.

The formal representation of such feelings usually occurs in a tacit interaction between language and music. On the one hand subjects like longing and loss are expressed in language through powerful metaphors—a fall being one of them. The falling motion is characterized by its inevitability: a fall cannot be stopped. And then there are the technical aspects of the music. The choice of a particular rhythm, timbre, or melody is matched—be it consciously or unconsciously—to the subjects addressed. A fall can be represented by a descending melody, a sense of melancholy by a prominent violin part, a dance by a waltz rhythm. But this should not be taken for granted: musical director Roscoe Beck (2012) told me that the band does not pursue any musical "effects" as such (like modulation, for example, a practice commonly used in pop music to achieve an uplifting effect), although the fusion of words and music always feels very natural. The link between form and content was made explicit on only one occasion, and it is no coincidence that this happened in Cohen's best-known song. On "Hallelujah" he speaks of a "secret chord" played by the Biblical King David: "it goes like this, the fourth, the fifth, the minor fall, the major lift" is a literal description of the musical sequence he is singing at that point. In the lyrics Cohen alludes to the books of Samuel, in which the power of music is a central theme. It is the only remedy that can deliver King Saul from the torment of an evil spirit.

David, "someone who is skillful in playing the lyre" (1 Samuel 16:16), is the right man for the job. Indeed, as I wrote in the chapter on artistry, the seductive power of music can remove the listener from his ordinary world and give birth to new insights.

The moment a longing or loss arises rarely coincides with the moment of perception. It germinates at an unguarded moment, and from thereon in grows until it can no longer be denied and subsequently erupts. Only then does the shift become visible and is it experienced as such. The opening lines of "Alexandra Leaving" describe such a sudden sensation, specifically the insight that love is over: "Suddenly the night has grown colder / The God of love preparing to depart." Cohen's song is a loose interpretation of a poem by Constantine P. Cavafy,[1] "The God Abandons Antony" (1911). As it was in the Biblical reference in "Hallelujah," the music here acts as a trigger. Cavafy was inspired by the story of Plutarch, who described how Mark Antony, under siege in Alexandria, heard the music and voices of a procession before losing consciousness in the realization that he had been abandoned by his patron god, Bacchus. Cavafy makes it clear that it takes courage to face up to such a loss. This awareness is at the centre of both Cavafy's version and Cohen's, in which the protagonist is not a city but a woman who must be surrendered. Both plead for an acceptance of this truth. As it does so often, the window serves as an observation post:

> go firmly to the window
> and listen with deep emotion,
> but not with the whining, the pleas of a coward:
> listen—your final pleasure—to the voices,
> to the exquisite music of that strange procession,
> to say goodbye to her, to the Alexandria you are losing.
> (Cavafy)
>
> Go firmly to the window, drink it in
> Exquisite music Alexandra laughing [...]

> Do not choose a coward's explanation
> that hides behind the cause and the effect [...]
> Say goodbye to Alexandra leaving
> Then say goodbye to Alexandra lost
> (Cohen)

Put differently, the moment when the insight is born is distinct from the course that the feelings take. The movement itself is independent of its experience. Without the singer realizing, the god of love prepared to depart. This departure continues unabated and culminates in the loss of the beloved Alexandra. The entire process is captured simply but effectively in the two lines of the chorus, from "leaving" to "lost": "Say goodbye to Alexandra leaving / Then say goodbye to Alexandra lost." Although it does not necessarily alter the course of the movement, this moment of attaining consciousness is certainly relevant. The shock of it forces the speaker to adopt a position. The singer must find a way of dealing with the ongoing process, which has now become an integral part of his life. There is not much he can do. It is a process of resignation, and at best he can watch, keep his distance, and "say goodbye." On "Here It Is" the singer arrives at the same conclusion: "Hello, my love, / and my love, Goodbye." Not coincidentally, both tracks feature on *Ten New Songs*, which shows Cohen at his most detached. "The longing persists, but the slavery is over," author and critic Leon Wieseltier (2005) wrote about this album.

Another image that foregrounds the inviolability of certain feelings is Cohen's comparison between love and a rampant growth in "Ain't No Cure for Love." The track is rumoured to have been written in reaction to the AIDS crisis in the mid-1980s. This is not mentioned directly, but the imagery is striking. Once again, we do not get to see the moment the growth first develops: the ailment is not diagnosed until the disease has reached an advanced stage. Love is not presented as a positive, healing power, but as a ruthless affliction that leaves one paralyzed and for which there is no remedy. The medical reference in Cohen's title is retained throughout the rest of the track. Doctors put in an appearance, love is described as a wound, and yearning as a painful longing. This medicalization of love reveals something else too. The inevitability of certain feelings is often perceived negatively. Because the subject has too little control over them (all anyone can do, when confronted with them, is surrender), they form a sharp contrast with the ideal of maximum self-determination. Thanks to the so-called masters of suspicion (Freud, Marx, and Nietzsche) it has become a cliché that this ideal is an illusion. Cohen appears to fully endorse this critique. It was his Buddhist background, among other things, that prompted him to cast serious doubt on the autonomy of the "self": "I am not the one who loves / It's love that seizes me," he sings humbly on "You Have Loved Enough"; and "I don't trust my inner feelings / Inner feelings come and go" on "That Don't Make It Junk"—both from *Ten New Songs*.

At the same time, such inevitability need not necessarily be perceived as negative. Might it not be reassuring if something irrevocably *good* were headed our way or if we were confronted with something that releases us from our social and human responsibility? Put in more positive terms: Might it not be healing to blithely feel part of a bigger movement? "Democracy" is such a track. It charts an abstract form of governance coming to the United States. To give voice to that movement, Cohen initially needed some sixty verses, of which five eventually made it onto the version that appeared on *The Future*.[2] The originality of the track lies in the stress on the movement itself (the form), combined with the concrete representation of the democracy (the content). Right from the start, the listener is led to the crux of the matter: "It's coming." It is not until the end of the first verse that the actual subject of this movement is named: "Democracy is coming to the USA." Much like a mantra, the message is repeated no fewer than six times. Gradually, the focus shifts to the democracy as such and finally to the effect it has on the singer. In the intermezzo, the description of the movement changes into a direct address in which the form of government is represented as an imposing ship that is setting course for America: "Sail on, Sail on / O mighty Ship of State." Despite the military marching music and the self-assurance in Cohen's voice, the entire track is suffused with powerlessness: as he addresses the powerful democracy, the singer finds himself in a humble position. Democracy is not only forcibly imposed, but it also enters through cracks and gaps, via a "*crack* in the wall," a "*hole* in the air," a "*silence*," a "*staggering* account," the "*sorrow* in the street*," the "wells of *disappointment*." The tone is cautiously optimistic though: Cohen denounces the sacrifices and the pain that the introduction of democracy as a form of governance entails,[3] but he ultimately remains hopeful amid a sense of despair: "I'm junk but I'm still holding up this little wild bouquet."

THE FALL
FROM DENIAL TO ACCEPTANCE

Cohen is not only interested in *what* is inevitable—the object of the longing or loss is seldom specified—but also in *how* this increasingly emphatic presence manifests itself in those who live through it. How is this process experienced? How is it handled? Is it possible to deal with it at all? And how does Cohen manage to convey this abstract experience to his listeners? In what follows, I will try to formulate an answer to these questions through the metaphor of the fall. Whereas alienation was still somewhat manageable (temporary solutions were available, including the intermediate space), it seems that nothing can be done about longing and loss, which is why the metaphor of the fall is so apt.

In "Gravity," a poem from *Book of Longing*, Cohen writes: "Love is strong as gravity / and everyone *must* fall." And on "That Don't Make It Junk": "you put me in a place where I *must* fall." In principle it is impossible to interrupt the flow, if only momentarily, and it is precisely this that Cohen's characters sometimes try, for instance on "The Smokey Life": "I held you till you learned to walk on air. So don't look down the ground is gone, there's no one waiting anyway." With perseverance and the help of others, a temporary pause, during which reality is momentarily denied, may be possible. Other characters, too, are looking for ways to prevent or break their fall. This is what happens in "True Love Leaves No Traces"[4] (1977), the musical adaptation of the poem "As the Mist Leaves No Scar" (1961):

> True love leaves no traces
> If you and I are one
> It's lost in our embraces
> Like stars against the sun
>
> As a falling leaf may rest
> a moment in the air
> so your head upon my breast
> so my hand upon your hair

A leaf whirls down so slowly that a still image can be discerned in that fall, which then continues unabated. "The Smokey Life" features the exact same image. Cohen labels this condition "true love"—a *transient* love that leaves no traces or scars, that does not infect the lovers (like it does in "Ain't No Cure for Love"). Like the idea of the intermediate space, this view of love as a still image does not promise a sustainable balance.

Another way of "stopping" the fall consists of denying it for as long as possible. So when Cohen's characters fall they keep looking up, that is to say, they look away from the here and now. When confronting a lost love, for example, they simply deny the split for as long as they can. In "So Long, Marianne" the singer finds himself caught between past and present, in a non-existent position, somewhere between being together and being separated: "I'm standing on a ledge and your fine spider web / is fastening my ankle to a stone."

He can see himself hovering above the abyss and looking into the depths to see the outcome of the fall (although the image of the ledge can also hint at suicide). With one leg in the web of the past, the singer is incapable or unwilling to free himself from his relationship with Marianne, yet at the same time he refuses to see what is in the ravine and explicitly demands the impossible, her hidden love. A similar yearning for the past can be heard on "Tower of Song." The lost lover has positioned herself on the opposite bank. She and the singer are separated by the unbridgeable river of their parting. The loss of the loved one is irreversible, but only manifests itself bit by bit, the way a river naturally widens:

> I see you standing on the other side
> I don't know how the river got so wide
> I loved you baby, way back when
> And all the bridges are burning that we might have crossed
> But I feel so close to everything that we lost

What is stressed here is the discrepancy between experience ("I feel so close") and reality ("everything that we lost"). Like so often, the "you" remains undefined: we are probably dealing with a lost lover, but the song could just as easily be a reflection on the singer's artistry. Looking at it from this angle, "Tower of Song" is nothing other than the retrospective of a man forced to leave everything behind to remain faithful to his artistic vocation. What he sees on the other side of the river is his former family life.

At times, Cohen's songs are little more than a melancholic evocation of his state of mind, reminiscent of the Portuguese sentiment known as *saudade*, which is expressed in fado music. "The Gypsy's Wife" revolves around this feeling too. The melody, instrumentation, and the persistent longing—formulated as a recurring question "Where is my Gypsy wife tonight?"—create a powerfully nostalgic atmosphere. It propels us right back into his personal past, which suddenly intrudes upon the listening experience. This past is simultaneously vivid (it makes itself sharply felt) and paralyzing (the realization that it is over hits hard); the experience is at once joyful and sad. This ambivalence makes it elusive, not unlike the "Gypsy's wife," who only appears as a fleeting shadow.

As well as denying the fall, Cohen's characters can also direct their gaze at the actual movement. It is no exaggeration to say that much of his work can be defined as an attempt to face up to this fall and to learn to live with it. "A manual for living with defeat," he summed up his career on "Going Home," and he concluded a gig in Austin (2009) with a blessing for the listeners: "May you fall on the side of luck." Some lyrics take the movement as their subject proper: the titles of "Coming Back to You" and "Slowly I Married Her" are telling. The former track, dealing with the longing to return after a split, can be read as addressing both a God and a woman. The singer concludes that everything he did and does can ultimately be traced back to the person being addressed: "I looked for you in everyone (...) I lived alone but I was only / coming back to you." Although he has no choice but to accept the "sentence" of the split, he realizes that the past retains its hold:

> They're handing down my sentence now
> And I know what I must do
> Another mile of silence[5] while I'm
> Coming back to you

The music likewise plays a significant role in conveying the movement. The powerful and compelling melody part shapes it, reinforced by long-held syllables in some live versions, by the electric guitar glissando in the accompaniment, and by the backing vocalists who sing a neatly descending melody.

"Slowly I Married Her" also focuses on a process—more so than the outcome. In this poem from *Death of a Lady's Man* the poet looks back on his marriage, which he views as the opposite of a public covenant, a process that unfolds suddenly and in complete silence. The title alone is telling. The procedural character of "slowly" and of the repetition of "came to" stands out against the momentary nature of the traditional marriage vows. Like in "Alexandra Leaving," in which the essence was encapsulated somewhere between "leaving" and "lost," this poem centres on the process of marrying ("I married her") that eventually culminates in marriage as a done deal ("we wed"). From the outset of his career, Cohen was interested in exploring the themes of marriage and adultery in his work[6] (see Nadel [1996] 2007, 46). In 1956 he wrote about *Let Us Compare Mythologies*: "Marriage and adultery will be a major theme in my book, for I believe this to be a central problem in our day. It is obvious that our concept of marriage is changing very quickly: the poet might perform a real service to his community by exploring the transition" (Cohen papers, 11–27). In *Death of a Lady's Man* Cohen moves beyond the cliché that marriage is not a short-term decision, but a process of commitment. The experience of this movement of conciliation is described in very ambivalent terms: "slowly and bitterly," "in boredom and joy," "slow and resentfully," and the like. Again, the image of a downward move is deployed, not just to express inevitability but above all to convey subjection:

> Slowly I kneeled
> and now we are wounded
> so deep and so well
> that no one can hurt us
> except Death itself

The outcome is ambiguous: "wounded so deep and so well." The characters gain access to love only in loneliness and complete despondency. It is an idea that haunts many of Cohen's texts. In "Anthem" love is no longer a matter for separate characters but for de-individualized hearts instead: "Every heart to love will *come*" (it is a movement, a process) "but like a refugee" (in complete helplessness). In "Light as the Breeze" it no longer matters how the loving is done, "as long as you're down on your knees." In "Hallelujah" love is "not some kind of victory march" but "a cold and very broken Hallelujah." And in "Take This Longing" beauty is "broken down," and Cohen the broken man: "I stand in ruins behind you."

The idea of imperfection has been mentioned on a few occasions. The characters that populate Cohen's universe are often broken figures. The examples are endless: the broken Jesus figure on "Suzanne," the broken man from "You Know Who I Am," the broken poet in "How We Used to Approach the Book of Changes: 1966" (from *The Energy of Slaves*), the broken banjo from the song of the same name, the lover with a broken limb from "Diamonds in the Mine," the broken sandal straps from "Take This Longing," the broken hearts of "The Guests" and "He Was Beautiful When He Sat Alone" (from *Parasites of Heaven*), the broken hill on "If It Be Your Will," the broken "Hallelujah," the broken knee in the tenth psalm from *Book of Mercy*, the scars in *The Favourite Game*. From *Let Us Compare Mythologies* to *The Flame*, brokenness is everywhere. Yet it is undergoing a drastic re-evaluation. Whereas initially all that was broken was seen in a negative light as something imperfect, from the late 1970s onwards it starts to be experienced as an opportunity, as a prerequisite even, for human interaction. The song "Anthem" is a kind of credo: this new notion is most cogently expressed in the well-known lines "there is a crack in everything, that's how the light gets in." The message appears to strike a chord with listeners. While "Anthem" may not be Cohen's best-known track, that one line is perhaps the most frequently cited of his entire oeuvre, and one that has inspired other poets too.[7] On *You Want It Darker* Cohen himself comes back to it when he slips an echo of the "crack in everything" into the serene but unsettling conclusion to "Treaty": "The poison enters into everything." The danger with such frequently cited lines is that they are taken out of context and reduced to one-dimensional slogans. Although there is certainly a noticeable change in the appreciation of all that is broken, it is not as if one perspective is simply swapped for another. The later work continues to reveal this tension between acceptance and resistance, between perfection and imperfection, between hope and despair, between good and evil, which is articulated very powerfully in oxymorons like "wounded so deep and so well," or later, on *Ten New Songs*, in the "invincible defeat" and the "formless circumstance," for example. "By the Rivers Dark" captures this ambiguity very well with reference to life in the Biblical city of Babylon:

> It is where we are without any real possibility of escaping from it. And many of the songs on the album [*Ten New Songs*] speak about this, of the reconciliation between these two ways of life, because finally, it may very well be that this holy city of Jerusalem sits right in the middle of the kingdom of sins, and we are prisoners of these two kingdoms and can never be in one forever. (Fitzgerald 2002)

The same idea is floated in "Two Worlds," one of the many adaptations of "A Thousand Kisses Deep," which was used for a Sony commercial. Cohen added a few lines to this version that illustrate this tension. Although the text opens with an unmistakable tribute to eternal love ("I love you when you opened / like a lily to the heat / And I love you when it closes / A thousand kisses deep"), the subsequent lines suggest that lies and deceit form an integral part of this union of love. What is more, Cohen situates the origins of this evil in what is ostensibly the most loving relationship of all, that between a parent and child. He does so through two "close-ups," two iconic pictures of innocence:

> I know you had to lie to me
> I know you had to cheat
> You learned it on your father's knee
> And at your mother's feet

Although Cohen wrote the poem in or around the year 2000, it is certainly not a sign of a sedate attempt at reconciliation: in vesperal freedom, nothing remains unsaid.

NOTES

1. The Greek poet Konstantinos Petrou Kavafis (1863–1933) was educated in English and often wrote his name as Cavafy. It was under this anglicized name that he became best known.
2. A few verses that did not make the cut are quoted in Zollo (1997). According to Maurice Ratcliff (2012, 51), there were as many as eighty originally, of which Cohen recited a few during the 1993 tour.
3. Remarkably, Cohen already used "ship of state" in the enumeration of a series of disasters in *Beautiful Losers*: "Sail on, sail on, O Ship of State, auto-accidents, births, Berlin, cures for cancer!" ([1996] 1991, 12). "Democracy" is by no means an uncritical paean to democracy.
4. In 2006, Anjani Thomas released her own musical version of the poem: "The Mist" appeared on the album *Blue Alert*, which was co-produced by Cohen. She used Cohen's original 1961 poem for the lyrics.
5. In some live versions, this becomes "a thousand miles of silence," which underlines the intensity. The inadequacy of language is exchanged for silence, as it is in "If It Be Your Will" (also on *Various Positions*): "If it be your will that I speak no more [...] I shall abide until / I am spoken for."
6. This has not escaped Bob Dylan's attention either. In Montréal in 1975, he performed the track "Isis," which also deals with a marriage and a divorce. He introduced it as follows: "This is a song about marriage. This is for Leonard, if he's still here."
7. Leonard Nolens' poem "Barst" (which translates as "Crack") was inspired by Cohen's "Anthem." For the Flemish poet, the crack is not a painful wound either, but a "nourishing soul," as the opening stanza suggests:

Er zit een barst in ieder ding, er loopt	There is a crack in every thing a a foreign
Een lichapamsvreemde nerf door alle vlees.	Marbling running through the flesh.
Die nerf, Cohen, die kerf is ook de kern,	That vein, dear Cohen, that grain is what we are
De voedzame ziel, het oneetbaar binnenste	The nourishing soul, the inedible inside

Van onze bek, de brakke	Of our mouth, the brackish
dwarsdoorsnede	vivisection
Van ons beest, de spleet in onze bast.	Of our beast, the slit within our skin.

(from the collection *Zeg aan de kinderen dat wij niet deugen* [Tell the children we're no good], 2011)

SIX

ENCOUNTER
"THE ONLY SONG I EVER HAD"

*Do not decode
these cries of mine—
They are the road,
and not the sign.*

*[...]
Undeciphered
let my song
rewire circuits
wired wrong,*

*and with my jingle
in your brain,
allow the Bridge
to arch again.*

The stanzas above were plucked from Leonard Cohen's *Book of Longing* ("All My News"). They sound like a warning to all those who would venture onto the paths of his sixty-year oeuvre. Those paths are strewn with songs, as well as poetry and prose, film and graphic work, with melancholic and light-hearted texts, North American, European, and oriental references, with poses and with silences. The author's message is clear: we should not look to that oeuvre for meaning, let alone an ultimate truth. Cohen compares his work with a road we should merely travel down. That road stands alone, and there is no signpost to point us to something else. The warning is reminiscent of Michel Foucault's observation about the disciplinary power of commentary in 1971: "it must—according to a paradox which it always displaces but from which it never escapes—say, for the first time, what has already been said, and repeat tirelessly what was, nevertheless, never said" (Foucault, Morris, and Patton, 1979). Cohen himself does not like to talk about the meaning of his texts. In 1980 he remarked:

> All your questions activate certain parts of your brain, but at the moment of experience that's all completely useless. [...] When a song "works" it has a power of its own and a truth of its own. What I mean by this is that it is a truth entirely different from the intellectual truth, it is a truth you experience. (De Bruyn 1980, 31)

More recently, at the press launch of *Old Ideas* in London, he offered another modest reply—or perhaps more of a quip to avoid answering the interviewer's question:[1] "We've got to be careful analysing these sacred mechanics because somebody will throw a monkey wrench into the thing and neither of us will ever write a line again." He appears to recall the warning given by Hugh MacLennan, one of Cohen's mentors at McGill University, who addressed his young pupil in 1955 by saying: "The trouble with approaching writing with a critic's mind is that you never do anything real because you become self-conscious" (Cohen papers, 10A-55).

These words may sound vague or hollow, but for Cohen the distinction between understanding and experiencing must have been a genuine concern, especially at the start of his career, when he distanced himself from a modernist and almost academic sounding poetry and later also from the beatniks' poetry, and instead embraced the direct expression of folk music. It is also a common theme in his work. It appears to be the most important lesson that the character of F. in *Beautiful Losers* wants to teach the unnamed narrator. In the opening pages, he asserts: "We've got to learn to stop bravely at the surface. We've got to learn to love appearances" ([1966] 1991, 4). A little later he is even more explicit: "Connect nothing: F. shouted. Place things side by side on your arborite table, if you must, but connect nothing!" (18). A few years prior to the publication of *Beautiful Losers* Dutch writer Harry Mulisch stated in a totally different context that "It is best to deepen the mystery."[2] In other words, art cannot solve the mystery of life, only make it tangible in heightened form. Could this be what Cohen meant with the above poem from *Book of Longing*? If so, it is no easy task to say something about Cohen's work, and certainly not anything conclusive, except to establish that since 2008, when he kicked off his world tour, quite a few new and different "circuits" have formed. There is no denying that the success of the gigs far exceeded expectations, of both young fans and the old guard, and both in his home country Canada and beyond, but the question remains how this response can be linked to his oeuvre. How can we speak of Leonard Cohen?

Cohen critics often leap from a biographical to a traditional scholarly perspective, and in doing so miss an essential point. On the one hand, the biographies read the work through his life, giving the interpretation a one-sided, limited reach. This is precisely what Cohen complained about in a letter to his sister, dated September 17, 1963, shortly after the publication of *The Favourite Game*. From Greece he grumbled: "For my friends and relatives I will always stand between them and my work" (Cohen papers, 11–13). The work, according to Cohen, is precisely the place where the biographical person can be transcended.

Then again, a classic scholarly approach often falls short too. What is a scholar to do with the inexplicable rapture that Cohen's music induces, which is hard to place in an analysis but that made just about every reviewer of the past 470 gigs wax lyrical? Admittedly, an academic study can deepen the experience of both text and music, while the analyst's incisive yet cold gaze threatens to erode the initial, overwhelming experience of reading or listening. Rather than intensifying, it can have a paralyzing effect. This may be inevitable. In his famous book *L'auberge du lointain*, Antoine Berman argued that "it is possible that *destruction is one of our relationships to a work* (in writing)" (1991, 67; Berman's italics). He made the assertion in a reflection on translation, but immediately added that "there are other ways of destroying a work: parody, pastiche, imitation and—above all—criticism." The artwork is analyzed "to the bone" and does not tolerate such stripping very well.

In recent years, the already rather extensive Cohen library has been supplemented with a few publications that offer an implicit answer to this. Various approaches were literally placed side by side, resulting in a heterogeneous but intriguing collection of testimonial, biographical, essayistic, journalistic, academic, and other voices. Think of the collection *Les révolutions de Leonard Cohen* (Ringuet and Rabinovitch 2016), as well as the Leonard Cohen—A Crack in Everything Symposium, organized by the Musée d'art contemporain de Montréal (2018), or the earlier book *Intricate Preparations, Writing Leonard Cohen* (Scobie 2000). In his introduction Scobie explicitly states:

> My intention in editing this book (and the special issue of *Essays on Canadian Writing*) has been to represent the varied and paradoxical nature of Cohen's reputation and reception. Thus, the book has its fair share of academic essays, along with the kind of discussion, less formal but no less intelligent, that goes on in non-academic circles, and includes personal reminiscences and the work of several writers who pay tribute to Cohen in poems that "translate" his work into new idioms. (3)

It therefore made sense to me not to view Leonard Cohen's career as a reflection of his biography, nor as a series of sterile texts, but as an organically grown oeuvre in which the artist tries to express himself in a unique way. I have wanted to foreground this voice so it can be heard as clearly and distinctly as possible—hence the many quotations interspersed with my own argument, and the emphasis on the musical work, in which the voice is audible and the interaction at gigs clearly visible. At the same time the voice corresponds with a single man and with the multitude of personas or daimons he assumes. Besides, this book is a spontaneous synthesis of a European outlook (that is to say, an interpretation of a "reterritorialized" [Deleuze] oeuvre) and a Canadian perspective (which I have appropriated through readings and interviews). In that sense my own voice as a reader and listener is audible too. I am aware of this, and I see this presence as inevitable (both limiting and broadening) and essential (because the person who is addressed is a crucial factor in Cohen's work).

"ALLOW THE BRIDGE TO ARCH AGAIN"
THE ENCOUNTER

In the poem quoted at the beginning of this chapter, Cohen does not elaborate on exactly how his poetry can or should function. Apparently a certain connection has to be made, but whether or not this succeeds is not wholly dependent on the reader or listener. All he or she can do is open up and "allow the Bridge / to arch again." But what is to be connected with what? What does this Bridge represent? Why has it been capitalized? Is Cohen trying to say something about the power of art in general—why art, more than other forms of communication, moves *and* enlightens? He does not seem to really know what this mystery entails either. When, in the same *Old Ideas* interview in London, he was asked for the umpteenth time about his fondness for Lorca, he offered no grand explanations, but merely acknowledged that the Spaniard's words, when he first read them, "spoke to me directly so that I understood"—in other words, a spontaneous connection had been established. What new bridges have been built since 2008, for example, for listeners who saw Cohen live for the first time or for those who rediscovered him? Were any bridges burnt for those who heard a Cohen who was different from the one they knew in the 1970s and 1980s? And if his songs were no more than classics can we speak of bridge building at all? Would a book about Leonard Cohen not be redundant in that case?

"Let my song rewire circuits wired wrong": Cohen expresses the explicit wish that his songs keep wiring new circuits not just because new readers and listeners discover the work, but also because the work itself invites different readings. By leaving the chronology out of consideration, at least partially, we can take a more thematic approach, so it looks as if the work consists of just a single book or a single song. This may well reflect the experience of the new fans, who only discovered Cohen's oeuvre after 2008, but maybe also that of the long-term faithful, who rediscovered and revisited the well-known albums and books. This new, mass reception is perhaps best defined as a form of "synchronic" reading, a way of reading that François Ricard described in a fine essay on Milan Kundera. When he expresses his admiration for the "continuous and constantly changing" beauty of the writer's oeuvre ([2003] 2004, 49), he concludes that it can only be approached and experienced via

> this *co-presence* in each novel, in each part or each chapter of each novel, of all the others at once, as the multiple perceptions of one self-same space that is constantly *unfolding*, of a totality not in progress but in continuous expansion, always the same and yet always new, always evident and always elusive.

The same is true for Leonard Cohen. Both in individual texts and in his oeuvre as a whole, the relationships between the recurring characters are unclear and sometimes interchangeable, past and present are concurrent, and themes develop in chaotic and sometimes conflicting ways. This was clear on his very first album in "The Stranger Song": "Please understand I never had a secret chart to get me to the heart of this or any other matter." In the sixty years between 1956 and 2016 he kept revisiting the themes I identified in the previous chapters. These themes had one thing in common: the aim was always to bring about some form of encounter or contact through words, sounds, and images. The attempted meetings could take on different forms and unfold from various positions. Be it from near or far, with or without power, the artist (in the guise of a character) or the character (in the guise of the artist) always wanted to come into contact with a woman, a reader or listener, a God, and ultimately with himself. On more than one occasion, the same passage could be read from various perspectives at once. This is the case in "The Eyes of Men," psalm 8 in *Book of Mercy*:

> In the eyes of men he falls, and in his own eyes too. He falls from his high place, he trips on his achievement. He falls to you, he falls to know you. It is sad, they say. See his disgrace, say the ones at his heel. But he falls radiantly toward the light to which he falls. They cannot see who lifts him as he falls, or how his falling changes, and he himself bewildered till his heart cries out to bless the one who holds him in his falling. And in his fall he hears his heart cry out, his heart explains why he is falling, why he had to fall, and he gives over to the fall. Blessed are you, clasp of falling. He falls into the sky, he falls into the light, none can hurt him as he falls. Blessed are you, shield of falling. Wrapped in his fall, concealed within his fall, he finds his place, he is gathered in. While his hair streams back and his clothes tear in the wind, he is held up, comforted, he enters into the place of his fall. Blessed are you, embrace of the falling, foundation of the light, master of the human accident.

Who is falling to whom? Is Cohen—as a believer—speaking in the third person about himself, as a man, as an artist? Does the fall culminate in contact with God (which the overall religious tenor of the piece seems to suggest), with the audience (in earlier work the "disgrace" often pertained to Cohen, who felt like he was slipping into a state of disgrace when he was on stage), or with himself? The identity of those involved remains unclear, but the longing for a form of contact is undeniable. The fact that many texts from *Book of Mercy* can be read from different angles is what makes this collection into what Marina Scarsella once called a "total" work of art: the encounter is divested of any specific meaning and all that remains is the event itself.

At the same time it is worth asking whether the characters in Cohen's universe ever succeed in making genuine contact with each other. The Hessian idea of fundamental loneliness may be a bit of a cliché, but it is another constant in his work, and when an encounter does take place, it is fragile and fleeting above all else. Accordingly, the actual moment is not often described, let alone explained, but captured in just a single word: "something like a second" (on "Light as the Breeze"), "a touch" (on "Suzanne"), "an embrace" (on "True Love Leaves No Traces"), "a fatal moment" (on "The Traitor"), and so on. "Closing Time" revolves around an amorous encounter, with Cohen assuring his listeners that he did everything he could to capture that one brief but essential moment in words: "I swear it happened just like this: / a sigh, a cry, a hungry kiss / the Gates of Love they budged an inch." He frequently uses metaphors that express this idea of transience particularly well: the falling leaf, smoke, mist, snow, particles of dust, dreams—or simply a song. In the documentary *The Song of Leonard Cohen*, Cohen illuminated his role as an artist:

> It's important to understand the difference between an artist and a theologian, or a politician. To me an artist does not have a platform, does not have a message, does not have a party. His only message, his only part[y] is the dissolution of differences. And we have to

leave it to these other kinds of experts to get us all inflamed about one particular view or another. But in the moment of a song or a poem or an embrace between a man and a woman, or a handshake, between two people, in that moment things are dissolved, and that's the artist's realm. (Cohen, in Rasky [2001] 2010, 123)

Naming, the key task of the artist who is credited with having once had a "famous golden touch" on "Dress Rehearsal Rag," could also be regarded as a kind of encounter, as a conflation of words and things. "I think that naming things is a great part of my craft," Cohen said back in 1969 (Harris 1969). Six year earlier, his alter ego, Lawrence Breavman, declared in *The Favourite Game*: "I want to touch people like a magician, to change them or hurt them, leave my brand, make them beautiful. I want to be the hypnotist who takes no chances of falling asleep himself. I want to kiss with one eye open" (Cohen [1963] 1994, 105). But such encounters are just as rare, which Breavman is only too aware of: "I hate all the things that can happen between the beginning of a sentence and the end" (177).

"Ballad of the Absent Mare" brings a few of these issues to a head. The song ends as follows:

> But my darling says, "Leonard, just let it go by
> that old silhouette on the great western sky"
> So I pick out a tune and they move right along
> and they're gone like the smoke
> and they're gone like this song.

In a lengthy analysis of this track, Ronald Green remarks that both the content and form of this final stanza draw twofold inspiration from Buddhism:

> First, there is the idea that we experience only provisional reality, that only Buddha Nature is ultimately real and unchanging. Many

Buddhist writings, including the *Lotus Sūtra*, describe our experience of provisional reality as being like clouds, smoke, bubbles, a mirage, or as Cohen put it earlier in his song, a dream. The second way the last verse fits with Zen is that it expresses non-attachment in the phrase "just let it go by," an idea that is actualized in the next phrase, "they're gone like the smoke and they're gone like this song." Again, while "they" seems to refer to the cowboy and the mare, it also implies all duality and the struggle to realize non-duality. (2017, 56)

The song "Hallelujah" similarly conveys this moment. In an interview, Cohen shed light on the track's real subject: "this world is full of conflicts and full of things that cannot be reconciled, but there are moments when we can transcend the dualistic system and reconcile and embrace the whole mess, and that's what I mean by 'Hallelujah'" (Light 2013, 30–31). In other words, the idea of an "encounter" goes beyond contact between two people to imply a sense of existential connection.

The ambition to realize an encounter is usually formulated in the work itself, but that has not stopped Cohen from repeatedly trying to achieve contact beyond it as well. His stint on the Israeli front in 1973, during the Yom Kippur War, is a good example of such an undertaking. He boarded the plane from "a sense of mission and a desire to take an active part in the war" (Bar-Yosef 2013) and embarked on an improvised tour to raise the spirits of the Israeli soldiers. He travelled from base to base and from hospital to hospital to meet as many military personnel as possible. Although Cohen has always expressed a close connection with the fate of the Jewish people, he has equally sought to transcend concrete political situations in his art and to hone in on human interactions. And indeed, "Lover, Lover, Lover," which he wrote in the Sinai Desert, does not include any direct references to the war. Moreover, when he introduced the track during one of his later gigs, he claimed to have written it for the soldiers on *both* sides of the frontline. Another example also dates back to the 1970s. During one of his tours, he reached out to a vulnerable but receptive audience. Between the official gigs, he performed at psychiatric institutions across Europe. "I really wanted to say that this is the audience that we've been looking for," he confessed during one such performance. Cohen was of the opinion that

> the experience of a lot of people in mental hospitals would especially qualify them to be a receptive audience for my work. In a sense, when someone consents to go into a mental hospital or is committed he has already acknowledged a tremendous defeat. To put it in another way, he has already made a choice. And it was my feeling that the elements of this choice, and the elements of this defeat, corresponded with certain elements that produced my songs, and that there would be an empathy between the people who had this experience and the experience as documented in my songs. (Simmons 2012, 224)

Finally, the intensity and the transience of the encounter often renders it ineffable. Again, "Ballad of the Absent Mare" serves as a good example. In one stanza Cohen touches on the crucial moment, describing it as a "binding" that takes place beyond space and time:

> So he binds himself
> to the galloping mare
> and she binds herself
> to the rider there
> and there is no space
> but there's left and right
> and there is no time
> but there's day and night.

In the original Buddhist parable, the encounter between the boy and the bull turns out to be merely a *representation* of the encounter with the self, an aid to visualize an abstract idea. The parable is illustrated with figurative woodcuts, but for this stage of the narrative the illustrator drew merely an empty circle. Several years later, the challenge remains just as pressing. In 2002, shortly after Cohen returned from Mount Baldy, he said he could not really talk about what had happened to him there, "because it's personal. I don't want to see it all in print"[3] (Gilmore 2008, 366). Although he devoted many years to Buddhist meditation and it is the foundation of many of his texts, he seldom spoke about the experience.

"THESE CRIES OF MINE"
THE OEUVRE AS PALIMPSEST

Ultimately, the encounter can also be viewed as a confrontation between the artist and the man he is. The opening track of *Old Ideas*, "Going Home," which features the artist addressing the man, revolves around just such a confrontation. The lyrics chime with those of "Different Sides," the album's final track, on which the man hits back at the artist. These two figures present themselves as two sides of one and the same body. Cohen expresses the wish that these two will one day find each other: "Though it all may be one in the higher eye / down here where we live it is two." Thirty years earlier, he described the meaning of "The Window" in similar terms. At a German gig in 1979 he spoke of a prayer, an attempt at "bringing together the two parts of the soul": a masculine and feminine element, yin and yang, a knot of spirit and matter.

As each text, each song, each artistic production can invariably be linked to the name "Leonard Cohen," the whole acquires an extraordinary continuity. In that sense, the use of the singular form in the title of the documentary *The Song of Leonard Cohen* was very apt. Its maker, Harry Rasky, wanted to highlight that Cohen's career is one sustained attempt at creating one (ultimate) song. On *Popular Problems* Cohen indicated that—in spite of everything—he has managed to perform that song, like a major, cathartic confession: "You got me singing / The only song I ever had." In the preceding pages, I have sought to illuminate a different side of this song in each chapter. Biographer Ira Nadel (1994, [1996] 2007) associates its genesis with the death of Cohen's father, which sparked off a lasting artistic impulse. Cohen's ex-partner Rebecca De Mornay, while also identifying a remarkable continuity in his oeuvre, attributes it to Cohen's extreme self-awareness. In her view, Cohen was

> searching all of his life to figure out, what is it, where is it, or maybe just, how do I get the hell out of here? Having all these relationships with women and not really committing; having this elongated history with Roshi and Zen meditation and yet always running away from it also, and having his long relationship to his career, and yet feeling like it's the last thing he wants to be doing. (Simmons 2012, 384–385)

Whatever the case may be, the themes that Cohen touched on in his very first work would stay with him forever. His family, his faith, his hometown, his teachers, his vocation, his obsessions—Cohen never fully moved on from them, but he also never simply accepted them. "What I loved in my old life [...] It lives in my spine," he writes in "Days of Kindness." Although he developed an extreme self-awareness in his artistic practice, he would never fundamentally change himself. So perhaps the course of his career can be better described as variations on or offshoots from those initial sources of inspiration (which is also why his work has been dismissed as monotonous), or in the words of François Ricard ([2003] 2004, 49) as an "unfolding" or "expansion" of one and the same space.

For the same reason Cohen's oeuvre can be seen as a palimpsest (Mus 2018b), a handwritten parchment from which the original words have been scraped off and replaced by new writing—a common procedure in historical Hebrew writing. The constant reworkings of his songs attest to this. The best-known example is probably "Chelsea Hotel," as the addition of "#2" explicitly alludes to the existence of an earlier, never officially released version. A further example is the reuse of texts that were first released as poems and later as songs. And even in the anthologies, (bigger and smaller) changes were still being made in the texts. Two tracks merit special mention in this respect. The process of superimposition is actually audible on "Joan of Arc": the track is a compilation of overlapping voices (all of them Cohen's) with the lyrics simultaneously recited and sung. "It was my idea," Cohen said, "and I had, as the model, manuscripts that you'd see with lines written over lines. I just thought it was appropriate at that moment. It's like the line of a Larry Rivers painting, you see the variations"[4] (Ruhlmann 1993, 17). "The Partisan" is another extraordinary example of a palimpsest. Both lyrics and music are based on a French resistance song from 1943, which was later translated into English. In his version Cohen combines the original with the existing adaptation, thus pushing the connection with the Second World War to the background. He starts off in English and switches to French before ending the first stanza in English again. The French piece here literally appears as a backdrop, like an echo or a trace of the original. The effect is heightened by a choir of female backing voices singing the French. During live performances Cohen occasionally plays with the hierarchy between the two texts. Sometimes he introduces additional lines from the original text: "I have changed my name so often / I have lost my wife and children / *Vous qui le savez / Effacez mon passage*" ("But those of you who know / You cover up my footprints," in Hy Zaret's translation). This artistic practice has not gone unnoticed by his musicians. Javier Mas (2013, 2) picked up on it in Cohen's rehearsals for his rehearsals for gigs: "Sometimes we play the same song for half an hour. It's like Arabian art, where one meaning is repeated 200,000 times. Every time he repeats the song he puts a little thing on the lyric, he adds a little change in the singing. That's the way he works: repetition." The relatively small number of albums and books that have been released is also indicative of this.

In short, Cohen does not take his quest *further* as much as he digs *deeper* in his obsessions. This labor has taken on different forms—a tough fight, a blind search, a strict order, a humble prayer, a real dialog—and has culminated in a body of daimons and positions, in and through which his identity kept taking on new forms, depending on the other the self kept addressing. Fundamentally dialogic, this identity is also plural and in flux. That is why it is impossible to formulate a clear-cut answer to the question with which I opened this book: Who is Leonard Cohen? Each of the six chapters offers a different answer. That is why I opted for the plural *demons* in the title, and thus to some extent appropriate the traditional interpretation of the Greek concept of the daimon. By now it should be obvious that the idea of "identity" is ubiquitous yet never fully defined in Cohen's oeuvre. On the contrary: from the 1980s onwards, the familiar game with pronouns—which are more indeterminate in that period than ever, "pure address, an emptying of the pronoun" in Scobie's words (1993)—is frequently replaced by the increasingly de-individualized "heart(s)." The emptying out that Cohen appears to aim for is partly achieved by the music. It is as if the words have to sing themselves free from their meaning and their maker.[5] It requires musicality to give language the scope it needs to let the polysemy of both man and world be seen and heard. This, together with the sounding board he always found in his listeners—and they in him—may explain why Cohen managed to sing and find an audience for half a century, "even though the world is gone."

NOTES

1 In *The Bob Dylan Encyclopedia*, Michael Gray (2006, 145) has noted that Cohen is "much more willing [...] than Dylan to discuss the processes of his work straightforwardly—to give good 'shop talk'—in public." Although Cohen had all but stopped giving interviews during the final years of his career, in the past he often elaborated on the hard work (song) writing was for him.
2 He did so in his autobiography *Voer voor psychologen* (Fodder for psychologists, 1960). The statement took on a life of its own and has since been (re)used in other contexts.
3 Sylvie Simmons claims that Cohen tried to explain the experience to her, but that in the end he chose not to have it published in her biography—either

because it was too personal or because the phrasing did not adequately reflect his actual experience. (Telephone interview with the author; for a summary, see Mus 2012b.)

4   Ruhlmann described the technique as "enormously effective," although it has been "relatively little used since. One thinks of Patti Smith's 1975 *Horses* album and John Trudell's 1992 record AKA *Grafitti Man*, but there are few other examples." (1993, 17)

5   I am paraphrasing the words of Dutch poet Martinus Nijhoff (1894–1953) in the poem "Tweeërlei dood" (literally "Two deaths," published in Dutch in the collection *Vormen*, 1924). Arguing that a good artist manages to disappear in his work, Nijhof shifted attention from the poet to the poem itself, which must lead a life of its own and be independent of its maker.

APPENDIX

À TOUT PRENDRE [TAKE IT ALL]

LEONARD COHEN, CLAUDE JUTRA AND THE ACADEMY OF MOTION PICTURE ARTS & SCIENCES

Montréal, le 29 janvier 1964.

Monsieur Gilles Marcotte,
La Presse,
7, rue St-Jacques ouest,
MONTREAL.

Mon cher Gilles,

L'anecdote que je relate ici est authentique. J'ai pensé qu'elle pourrait occuper de façon amusante un petit coin de la page deux.

Amicalement,

Claude Jutra

inc.

COLLECTION
CINÉMATHÈQUE
QUÉBÉCOISE

COPIE ARCHIVE

APPENDIX

M. Léonard Cohen, poète canadien-anglais éminent, partisan avoué et enthousiaste du fait français au Canada, téléphonait récemment à l'Academy of Motion Picture Arts and Sciences, à Hollywood. Ce dialogue se déroule en anglais, évidemment.

COHEN : Je voudrais présenter une candidature dans la section des films étrangers, pour le concours des Academy Awards. Le titre est A TOUT PRENDRE.

UNE DAME : A what ?

- C'est un titre français. Je l'épelle : A - T - T - O - U - T - ...
- Yeah ! I got that. A trout... A trout does what ?
- Non, pas une truite... Ecoutez, c'est en français.
- Mais nous avons déjà un film français.
- Je vous parle d'un film canadien.
- Les films canadiens passent dans la section des films américains.
- D'accord. Présentez-le dans la section américaine. Le titre est A TOUT PR...
- Mais c'est une langue étrangère !
- Pas au Canada, madame. C'est une langue officielle. Plus de cinq millions de canadiens parlent français du matin au soir. La plupart des longs métrages canadiens sont en français.
- Oh !
- Alors ? Quelle catégorie ?
- Je me le demande.
- Il faudra bien prendre une décision.
- Je le suppose... (UN TEMPS DE REFLEXION) De toute façon, pour cette année, c'est trop tard.
- (EN FRANCAIS) Au revoir, madame.

30

Mr. Leonard Cohen, well known Canadian writer is collaborating with Claude Jutra on the english version of his feature film (ATP) TAKE IT ALL. On his behalf, he was calling <u>The Academy of Motion Picture Arts & Sciences</u> in Hollywood.

Cohen — I would like to enter a film into Foreign Film category of the Academy Awards. The title is A TOUT PRENDRE.

A lady — A what ?

— It's a French title. I'll spell it : A - T - O - U - T -

— Yeah, I got that, A trout ... A trout what ?

— Not a trout. Listen, this is in French.

— We already have our French entry.

— This is a Canadian film.

— Canadian films are considered American films.

— All right, I'd like to enter it as an American film. The title is A TOUT PRENDRE.

— But that's a foreign language.

— Not in Canada. Is's an official language. Five million people speak it every day. And most of the features made in Canada are in French.

— Oh.

— So what category could we enter it under ?

— I really don't know.

— Could some decision be made ?

— I suppose so. Anyhow, you're too late this year.

30

CBC Information Services
Box 500, Terminal A, Toronto 1

CBC Television Network

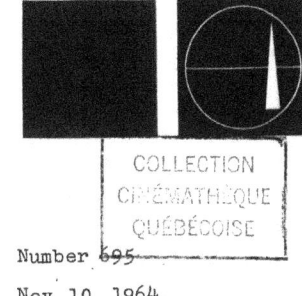

CBC ACQUIRES TV RIGHTS TO JUTRA FILM
ALSO TO HANDLE WORLD TV DISTRIBUTION

Number 695

Nov. 10, 1964.

    In an agreement with Orion Films Ltd. of Montreal, the Canadian Broadcasting Corporation has acquired TV rights to the English version of A Tout Prendre, a prize-winning French-Canadian feature film by Claude Jutra, for CBC-TV's Festival series. The full-length feature will be telecast on Festival in February, 1965.

    In addition, the CBC will act as international television sales agent for both English and French versions of A Tout Prendre, responsible for world distribution.

    Robert Hershorn, president of Orion Films and producer of the award-winning movie, states: "This is the first independently-produced Canadian feature film to be scheduled on nation-wide English-language TV in Canada. The international sales agreement marks another 'first' --and, I hope, the beginning of a new era of constructive co-operation between the corporation and the independent film producers in Canada."

    Representing the corporation, Bill Weston, manager of TV programs on film, referred to the agreement as "indicative of the growing recognition of Canada's outstanding film makers, about which the CBC is most happy."

- more -

CBC ACQUIRES   --2

A Tout Prendre won first prize at the Montreal Film Festival of 1963 as "the best Canadian feature film". The same year, it was winner of the National Film Award as "the best Canadian theatrical feature", the International Critics' Award at a Brussels film festival, and the Belgian radio and television prize. In production, it received a $6,000 subsidy from the ministry of culture of the Province of Quebec.

The English version to be seen on Festival next February was written by Leonard Cohen, Canadian poet and novelist, marking the first collaboration of the kind between artists from English and French-speaking Canada.

Two techniques are utilized in the English version to make the film understandable to English-speaking audiences. In scenes involving direct conversation, the dialogue is still in French but with English subtitles. In scenes with "thought dialogue" (stream of consciousness), the voice-over lines are spoken in English. The techniques are combined to eliminate the need for lip synchronization. Much of the film's dialogue is of the stream-of-consciousness variety.

Claude Jutra, director of A Tout Prendre, also stars in the film, with Victor Desy and Johanne, noted French-Canadian stage and television actors. Jutra is one of the new generation of young French-Canadian film makers now active in cinema-verite, an outgrowth of "new wave" films from France. A Tout Prendre is a frank and personal love story about a French-Canadian film producer who, at odds with his conventional background, falls in love with a beautiful Negro entertainer in a cabaret-coffeehouse milieu.

- 30 -

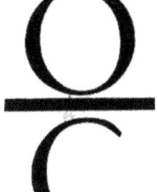

orion films/les films cassiopée/2152 mackay st. 937-2090

February 6, 1964.

Mr. Leonard Bernstein,
Columbia Pictures, Inc.,
72 Carlton Street,
Toronto 5, Ontario.

Dear Mr. Bernstein,

I'm enclosing the still of Johanne from which we're making the poster. No grey tones will be used; only blacks and whites.

On page 39 of Film Quarterly there is a superlative review of A TOUT PRENDRE. I thought you might want to look at it.

Everything seems to be moving in the right orbit.

All good things,

Leonard Cohen

COLLECTION
CINÉMATHÈQUE
QUÉDÉCOISE

COPIE ARCHIVE

PRIMARY SOURCES

BOOKS

1956	*Let Us Compare Mythologies*. McGill Poetry Series
1961	*The Spice-Box of Earth*. Toronto: McClelland and Stewart Ltd.
1963	*The Favourite Game*. London: Secker And Warburg Ltd. (1994, McClelland and Stewart Ltd).
1964	*Flowers for Hitler*. Toronto: McClelland and Stewart Ltd.
1966	*Beautiful Losers*. Toronto: McClelland and Stewart Ltd. (1991).
1966	*Parasites of Heaven*. Toronto: McClelland and Stewart Ltd.
1968	*Selected Poems: 1956-1958*. Toronto: McClelland and Stewart Ltd.
1972	*The Energy of Slaves*. Toronto: McClelland and Stewart Ltd.
1978	*Death of a Lady's Man*. Toronto: McClelland and Stewart Ltd.
1984	*Book of Mercy*. Toronto: McClelland and Stewart Ltd.
1993	*Stranger Music*. Toronto: McClelland and Stewart Ltd.
1994	*Musique d'ailleurs* (tr. Jean-Dominique Brierre and Jacques Vassal). Paris: Christian Bourgois.
2000	"A note to the reader" [foreword in the Chinese edition of *Beautiful Losers*] https://www.leonardcohenfiles.com/bl-chinese.html.
2000	*Étrange musique étrangère* (tr. Michel Garneau). Montréal: L'Hexagone.
2006	*Book of Longing*. Toronto: McClelland and Stewart Ltd. New York: HarperCollins.
2007	*Livre du constant désir* (tr. Michel Garneau). Montréal: L'Hexagone.

2008	*Le livre du Désir* (tr. Jean-Dominique Brierre and Jacques Vassal). Paris: Le Cherche Midi.
2012	*Fifteen Poems*. New York: Random House (eBook)
2018	*The Flame*. Toronto: McClelland and Stewart Ltd.

STUDIO ALBUMS

1967	*Songs Of Leonard Cohen*
1969	*Songs From A Room*
1971	*Songs Of Love And Hate*
1974	*New Skin For The Old Ceremony*
1977	*Death Of A Ladies' Man*
1979	*Recent Songs*
1984	*Various Positions*
1988	*I'm Your Man*
1992	*The Future*
2001	*Ten New Songs*
2004	*Dear Heather*
2012	*Old Ideas*
2014	*Popular Problems*
2016	*You Want It Darker*
2019	*Thanks for the Dance*

LIVE ALBUMS AND VIDEOS

1973	*Live Songs*
1994	*Cohen Live*
2001	*Field Commander Cohen: Tour of 1979*
2009	*Live in London*
2009	*Live at The Isle of Wight 1970*
2010	*Songs From the Road*
2012	*Live in Fredericton*
2014	*Live in Dublin*
2015	*Can't Forget: A Souvenir of The Grand Tour*

For a detailed overview of primary sources (bibliography and discography), see the excellent website www.leonardcohenfiles.com.

SECONDARY SOURCES

Adorno, Theodor. 2002. *Essays on Music*, edited by Richard Leppert. Berkeley, Los Angeles, London: University of California Press.
Adria, Marco. 1990. "Leonard Cohen: Icon of Popular Music." *Aurora Online*. http://aurora.icaap.org/index.php/aurora/article/view/36/47.
Albertazzi, Silvia. 2018. *Leonard Cohen: Manuale per vivere nella sconfitta*. Vedano al Lambro: Edizioni Paginauno.
Anon. 1968. "Pop Music Personalities: Leonard Cohen." March, 1968: 82.
Anon. 1971. "Le chanteur est aussi un romancier. " *La Quinzaine Littéraire*. September, 1971: 1.
Anon. 1971. "Ingeboekt." *Leeuwarder courant*. August 10, 1971: 5.
Anctil, Pierre. 2002. *La Main de Montréal*. Sillery, Montréal : Septentrion | Musée Pointe-à-Callière.
———. *Histoire des Juifs du Québec*. Montréal : Boréal.
Arend, Hannah. 1963. *Eichmann in Jerusalem: A Report on the Banality of Evil*. New York: Viking Press.
Arjatsalo, Jarkko. 2012. "Interview with Sylvie Simmons." https://www.leonardcohenfiles.com/sylvie-iv.html.
Atwood, Margaret. 1972. *Survival: A Thematic Guide to Canadian Literature*. Toronto: McClelland and Stewart Ltd.
Bar-Yosef, Neta. 2013. "A Poet Goes to War." *Israel Hayom Newsletter*. September 13, 2013.
Barthes, Roland. 1979. "The Wisdom of Art." In *Cy Twombly. Paintings and Drawings 1954–1977* (tr. Annette Lavers), 9–22. New York: Whitney Museum of American Art.

Batten, Jack, Michael Harris, and Don Owen. 1969. "The Poet as Hero." *Saturday Night* 84 (6): 23–32.
Beck, Roscoe. 2012. "I'm Still Trying to Find my Song." https://www.leonardcohenfiles.com/franciscus.pdf.
Benazon. Michael. 1986. "Leonard Cohen of Montreal." *Matrix* 23 (fall): 43–57.
Benson, Eugene, and William Toye. 1997. *The Oxford Companion to Canadian Literature*. 2nd ed. Toronto-Oxford-New York: Oxford University Press.
Berman, Antoine. 1991. *La Traduction et la Lettre ou l'auberge du lointain*. Paris: Seuil.
Bilefsky, Dan. 2018. "Is Leonard Cohen the New Secular Saint of Montreal?" *New York Times*. March 6, 2018, Section C, Page 1.
Biron, Michel, François Dumont, and Élisabeth Nardout-Lafarge. (2007) 2010. *Histoire de la littérature québécoise*. Montréal: Boréal.
Bloom, Myra. 2018. "The Darker Side of Leonard Cohen." *The Walrus*. April 12, 2018. https://thewalrus.ca/the-darker-side-of-leonard-cohen/.
Bougnoux, Daniel. 2013. "Leonard Cohen, scène zen." *Médium* 2 (23): 63–74.
Brisset, Annie. 2012. "The Search for a Native Language: Translation and Cultural Identity." In *The Translation Studies Reader*, edited by Lawrence Venuti, 281–311. London, New York: Routledge.
Brittain, Donald, and Owen, Don. (1965) 2000. *Ladies and Gentlemen... Mr. Leonard Cohen*. DVD. National Film Board of Canada.
Broackes, Vicky. 2018. "Sound and Vision: Curating Music Exhibitions for Museums." Conference paper delivered at Leonard Cohen. A Crack in Everything. Max and Iris Stern International Symposium. Montréal, April 7, 2018.
Broomfield, Nick. 2019. *Marianne and Leonard: Words of Love*. DVD.
Brusq, Armelle. (1996) 2009. *Leonard Cohen. Portrait intime*. DVD.
Bublitchi, Alexandru. 2013. "Flavours from the Past and Intriguing New Ideas: Javier Mas and Alexandru Bublitchi Talk About their Collaboration with Leonard Cohen." https://www.leonardcohenfiles.com/franciscus-2.pdf.
Burger, Jeff, ed. 2014. *Leonard Cohen on Leonard Cohen*. Chicago: Chicago Review Press.
Burnham, Clint. 1993. "How Postmodern is Cohen's Poetry?" *Canadian Poetry: Studies, Documents, Reviews* 33:65–73.
Byham, Ray D. 1971. "Letter to Henry D. Bicks, President." Dalhousie University Archives, 28.01.1971.
Casanova, Pascale. 2004. *The World Republic of Letters* (tr. M. B. De Bevoise). Cambridge, MA: Harvard University Press.
Chesterman, Andrew. 2016. *Memes of Translation: The Spread of Ideas in Translation Theory*. Rev ed. Amsterdam-Philadelphia: John Benjamins.
Cormier, Sylvain. 2008. "Leonard Cohen à traduire." *Le Devoir*. June 21, 2008. https://www.ledevoir.com/lire/194902/leonard-cohen-a-traduire.

SECONDARY SOURCES

Dalziell, Tanya, and Paul Genoni. 2018. "Mythmaking, Social Media and the Truth About Leonard Cohen's Last Letter to Marianne Ihlen." *The Conversation.* December 5, 2018. http://theconversation.com/mythmaking-social-media-and-the-truth-about-leonard-cohens-last-letter-to-marianne-ihlen-108082.

Damrosch, David. 2003. *What is World Literature?* Princeton and Oxford: Princeton University Press.

Daniell, Roy. 1957. "Poetry and the Novel." In *The Culture of Contemporary Canada*, edited by Julian Park, 1–81. New York: Cornell University Press.

Davey, Frank. 1974. *From There to Here: A Guide to English-Canadian Literature Since 1960 (Our nature, our voices).* Toronto: Press Porcépic.

———. 1994. *Canadian Literary Power: The Writer as Critic: IV*. Edmonton: NeWest Press.

———. 2000. "*Beautiful Losers*: Leonard Cohen's Postcolonial Novel." In *Intricate Preparations: Writing Leonard Cohen*, edited by S. Scobie, 12–23. Toronto: ECW Press.

De Botton, Alain. 2002. *The Art of Travel.* London: Penguin.

De Bruyn, André. 1976. "Interview Met Leonard Cohen." *'t Liedboek* 42:3–8.

———. 1980. "Poëzie in popformaat... Leonard Cohen." *Audio-Visueel* 6: 30–34.

———. 1985. "Interview Met Leonard Cohen." *Audio-Visueel* 1:44-48.

De Waard, Elly. 1985. "Leonard Cohen: 'we zijn een roofzuchtig ras.'" *Vrij Nederland.* January 5, 1985. https://www.vn.nl/leonard-cohen-we-zijn-een-roofzuchtig-ras.

Deshaye, Joel. 2009. "Celebrity and the Poetic Dialogue of Irving Layton and Leonard Cohen." *Studies in Canadian Literature* 34 (2): 77–105.

———. 2013. *The Metaphor of Celebrity: Canadian Poetry and the Public, 1955–1980.* Toronto: University of Toronto Press.

Djwa, Sandra. 1967. "Leonard Cohen Black Romantic." *Canadian Literature* 34:32–42.

Dragland, Stan. 1991. Afterword to *Beautiful Losers*, by Leonard Cohen, 261–269, Toronto: McClelland & Stewart Ltd.

Elicker, Martina. 2001. "Concept Albums: Song Cycles in Popular Music." In *Word and Music Studies: Essays on the Song Cycle and on Defining the Field*, edited by Walter Bernhart and Werner Wolf, 227–236. Amsterdam-Atlanta: Rodopi.

Enos, Elysha. 2017. "Montreal's Leonard Cohen Comes Home." CBC. November 29, 2017. https://www.cbc.ca/news2/interactives/leonard-cohen-montreal-legacy/.

Even-Zohar, Itamar. 1990. "Polysystem Theory." *Poetics Today* 11 (1): 9–26.

Fitzgerald, Judith. 2002. "Notes Towards A Definition Of A Masterpiece: *Ten New Songs.*" https://www.leonardcohenfiles.com/masterpiece.html.

Flynn, Kevin. 2000. "Balanced on Wooden Stilts and Dancing: What Irving Layton Taught Me about Leonard Cohen." In *Intricate Preparations: Writing Leonard Cohen*, edited by Stephen Scobie, 9–11. Toronto: ECW Press.

Footman, Tim. 2009. *Leonard Cohen—Hallelujah.* New Malden, UK: Chrome Dreams.

Foucault, Michel, Meaghan Morris, and Paul Patton. 1979. *Michel Foucault: Power, Truth, Strategy*. Sydney: Feral Publications.
Fournier, Michael, and Ken Norris. 1994. *Take this Waltz. A Celebration of Leonard Cohen*. Sainte-Anne-de-Bellevue, QC: The Muses' Company/La Compagnie des Muses.
Fremont-Smith, Eliot. 1966. "Books of the Times: Howl." *New York Times*. April 27, 1966: 45.
Garneau, Michel. 2011. "Les regards." *Revue de la Société historique de Montréal* 62:7.
Gasnault, François. 2015. "Hootenanny at the American Center: Inventing the Open Stage in France (1963-1975)." *L'Homme* 3 (215): 149–169.
Gilmore, Mikal. 2008. *Stories Done: Writings on the 1960s and its Discontents*. New York: Free Press.
Gray, Michael. 2006. *The Bob Dylan Encyclopedia*. London, New York: Continuum International Publishing Group Ltd.
Golsteijn, Jip. 1992. "Ladykiller Leonard Cohen (58) blijft 'meedogenloos' romantisch." *De Telegraaf* [Amsterdam]. December 24, 1992.
Green, Ronald. 2017. 'Teaching Zen's Ten Oxherding Pictures through Leonard Cohen's 'Ballad of the Absent Mare.'" *ASIANetwork Exchange* 24 (1): 29–58.
Grossman, David. 2015. "Breathing With Both Lungs" (tr. Jessica Cohen). Amsterdam: Nationaal Comité 4 et 5 mei. https://www.4en5mei.nl/media/documenten/5maylecture2015-grossmanen(1).pdf.
Guillot, Claire. 2016. "Leonard Cohen transforme le noir mat en noir brillant." *Le Monde*. November 11, 2016. https://www.lemonde.fr/musiques/article/2016/11/11/christophe-lebold-les-chansons-de-leonard-cohen-sont-consolantes-pas-deprimantes_5029823_1654986.html.
Halpern, Sheryl. 1984. "Cohen Calls Book 'An Address to God.'" Review of *Book of Mercy* (Leonard Cohen). *Catholic New Times*. July 8, 1984: 7.
Harris, Michael. 1969. "An Interview with Leonard Cohen." *Duel* 1 (winter).
Hofmann, Philipp. 2010. *Corporeal Cartographies. The Body in the Novels of Leonard Cohen*. Berlin: Lit.
Hutcheon, Linda. 1974. "Beautiful Losers: All the Polarities." *Canadian literature* 59:42–56.
———. 1980. *Leonard Cohen and His Works*. Toronto: ECW Press.
———. 1984. *Narcissistic Narrative: the Metafictional Paradox*. London: Methuen.
———. 1988. *The Canadian Postmodern: A Study of Contemporary English-Canadian Fiction*. Toronto; Oxford; New York: Oxford University Press.
Jones, Allan. 2017. *Can't Stand Up For Falling Down: Rock'n'Roll War Stories*. London: Bloomsbury.
Kapica, Jack. 1973. "The Trials of Leonard Cohen." *Montreal Gazette*. August 25, 1973: 37–38.
Keunen, Gert. 1998. "Het theatrale in de popmuziek." *Etcetera* 66:21–24.

———. 2002. *Pop! Een halve eeuw beweging*. Tielt: Lannoo.

Kirk, Kris. 1988. "As a New Generation Discovers Leonard Cohen's Dark Humour Kris Kirk Ruffles the Great Man's Back Pages." *Poetry Commotion*. June 18, 1988. http://www.webheights.net/speakingcohen/mus0788.htm.

Kloman, William. 1969. "Leonard Cohen." In *Songs of Leonard Cohen*, edited by Harvey Vinson, 4. New York-London: Collier Books/Collier-Macmillan Ltd.

Komrij, Gerrit. 1974. *Daar is het gat van de deur. Kritieken, Essays, Synopsis*. Amsterdam: De Arbeiderspers.

Kory, Robert. 2018. "Leonard's Conversations with Me about Creative Inspiration and Collaboration." Conference paper delivered at Leonard Cohen. A Crack in Everything. Max and Iris Stern International Symposium. Montréal, April 7, 2018.

Kristeva, Julia. (1974) 1985. *Revolution in Poetic Language* (tr. Margaret Waller). New York: Columbia University Press.

Kundera, Milan. (2005) 2007. *The Curtain*. London: Faber & Faber.

Lake, Steve. 1980. "Cohen plays a timeless game." *Melody Maker*. November 22, 1980: 12, 36.

Leach, Jim. 1999. *Claude Jutra Filmmaker*. Montréal and Kingston: McGill-Queen's University Press.

Leader, Darian. 2008. *The New Black: Mourning, Melancholia and Depression*. London: Hamish Hamilton.

Lebold, Christophe. 2013. *Leonard Cohen: L'homme qui voyait tomber les anges*. Rosières-en-Haye: Camion Blanc.

Lecker, Robert. 1994. "The New Canadian Library: A Classic Deal." *American Review of Canadian Studies* 24 (2): 197–216.

Leduc-Cummings, Maryse. 1992. "Lectures de la ville. Montréal dans la littérature." *Continuité* 55: 9–13.

Leonard Cohen Papers. University of Toronto, Manuscript Collection (Thomas Fisher Rare Book Library, Ms. Coll. 122)

Light, Alan. 2013. *The Holy or the Broken: Leonard Cohen, Jeff Buckley and the Unlikely Ascent of "Hallelujah."* New York: Atria Books.

Logan, William. 2019. "*The Flame*: Leonard Cohen's Posthumous Collection of Poems, Lyrics and Sketches." *New York Times*. January 2, 2019. https://www.nytimes.com/2019/01/02/books/review/leonard-cohen-flame.html.

Lunson, Lian. 2005. *Leonard Cohen: I'm Your Man*. DVD.

MacLeod, Meredith. 2016. "Music Experts Reflect on Legacy of Leonard Cohen, 'A National Treasure.'" *CTV News*. November 11, 2016. https://www.ctvnews.ca/entertainment/music-experts-reflect-on-legacy-of-leonard-cohen-a-national-treasure-1.3156352?cache=yes.

Maingueneau, Dominique. 2004. *Le discours littéraire. Paratopie et scène d'énonciation*. Paris : Armand Colin.

Mandel, Eli. 1978. "Leonard Cohen's 'Con Game'" *Saturday Night.* November: 51-53.

Marshall, Tom. 1980. *Harsh and Lovely Land: The Major Canadian Poets and the Making of a Canadian Tradition.* Vancouver: UBC Press.

Mas, Javier. 2013. "Flavours from the Past and Intriguing New Ideas: Javier Mas and Alexandru Bublitchi Talk about their Collaboration with Leonard Cohen." https://www.leonardcohenfiles.com/francismus-2.pdf.

McClelland, Jack. 1977. "Note to Anna Porter." McMaster University Archives (McClelland files), 25.11.1977.

McLeese, Don. 2019. "The New York Times Sends an Assassin to Kill Leonard Cohen." *Book & Film Globe.* January 8, 2019. https://bookandfilmglobe.com/creators/new-york-times-sends-an-assassin-to-kill-leonard-cohen/.

Meizoz, Jérôme. 2007. *Postures littéraires. Mises en scène modernes de l'auteur.* Genève: Slatkine.

Meuleman, Bart. 2009. *De donkere kant van de zon. Over popmuziek.* Amsterdam: Querido.

Montpetit, Caroline. 2007. "Leonard Cohen ou la constante quête de beauté." *Le Devoir.* May, 5, 2007. https://www.ledevoir.com/lire/142205/leonard-cohen-ou-la-constante-quete-de-beaute.

Mus, Francis. 2012a. "Thoughts on Sylvie Simmons' *I'm Your Man.*" *Consequence of Sound.* November 27, 2012. https://consequenceofsound.net/2012/11/thoughts-on-sylvie-simmons-im-your-man-the-life-of-leonard-cohen/.

——. 2012b. "De onbekende in de bekende blauwe regenjas. Francis Mus in gesprek met Cohen-biografe Sylvie Simmons." *De Leeswolf* 9 (December): 612–614.

——. 2017. "Passive (Re)translations and Identity Struggles in the Poetry of Leonard Cohen. A Comparison of Three Translations of *Book of Longing* (2006)." *Cadernos de Tradução* 39 (1): 145–167.

——. 2018a. "Leonard Cohen in French Culture: A Song of Love and Hate. A Comparison Between Musical and Literary Translation." *JoSTrans. The Journal of Specialised Translation* 29. https://www.jostrans.org/issue29/art_mus.php.

——. 2018b. "L'écriture comme palimpseste. Une exploration archéologique de l'œuvre de Leonard Cohen." Conference paper delivered at Leonard Cohen. A Crack in Everything. Max and Iris Stern International Symposium. Montréal, April 7, 2018.

Nadel, Ira B. 1993. "Ten or More Questions I Should Have Asked Leonard Cohen." *Canadian Poetry* 33:108–121.

——. 1994. *Leonard Cohen: A Life in Art.* Toronto: ECW Press.

——. (1996) 2007. *Various Positions: A Life Of Leonard Cohen.* Toronto: Random House of Canada.

——. 2018. "Cohen à la Mode, or Back on Boogie Street." Conference paper delivered at Leonard Cohen. A Crack in Everything. Max and Iris Stern International Symposium. Montréal, April 7, 2018.

New, William Herbert, ed. 2002. *Encyclopedia of Literature in Canada*. Toronto: Toronto University Press.
Nijhoff, Martinus. 1924. *Vormen*. Bussum: C.A.J. van Dishoeck.
Nolens, Leonard. 2011. *Zeg aan de kinderen dat wij niet deugen*. Amsterdam: Querido.
Norris, Ken. 1987. "Healing Itself the Moment It Is Condemned: Cohen's Death of a Lady's Man." *Canadian Poetry* 20. http://www.canadianpoetry.ca/cpjrn/vol20/norris.htm.
———. 1994. "'From this Broken Hill': Leonard Cohen's Stranger Music." *The American Review of Canadian Studies* 24 (3): 363-375. http://www.canadianpoetry.ca/cpjrn/vol20/norris.htm.
O'Neil, Mary Anne. 2105. "Leonard Cohen, Singer of the Bible." *Cross Currents* 65 (1): 91-99.
O'Riordan, Brian, and Bruce Meyer. 1982. "Working for the World to Come: an Interview with Leonard Cohen." *Descant* 37:113-129.
Ondaatje, Michael. 1970. *Leonard Cohen*. Toronto: McClelland and Stewart Ltd.
Oz, Amos, and Fania Oz-Salzberger. 2014. *Jews and Words*. New Haven, CT: Yale University Press.
Palmer, Tony. (1974) 2010. *Leonard Cohen: Bird on a Wire*. DVD.
Pezzarello, Christopher Joseph. 1997."'You Have Sweetened Your Word': Sincerity and Prayer in Leonard Cohen's Book of Mercy." Master's thesis, McGill University.
Pleshoyano, Alexandra. 2016. "L'américanité des 'Perdants magnifiques de Leonard Cohen' : cinquante ans plus tard. Une quête identitaire entre la jouissance et le désespoir.' In *Les révolutions de Leonard Cohen*, edited by Chantal Ringuet and Gérard Rabinovitch, 213-227. Québec: Presses de l'Université du Québec.
———. 2019. "Steering Our Way into Leonard Cohen's Archive." November 14. Conference paper delivered at the University of Antwerp, Belgium.
Rae, Ian. 2008. *From Cohen to Carson: The Poet's Novel in Canada*. Montréal and Kingston: McGill-Queen's University Press.
Rasky, Harry. (2001) 2010. *The Song of Leonard Cohen*. Oakville, ON: Mosaic Press.
Ratcliff, Maurice. 2012. *Leonard Cohen: The Music and the Mystique*. London: Omnibus Press.
Ravvin, Norman. 1993. "Writing Around the Holocaust: Uncovering the Ethical Centre of *Beautiful Losers*." *Canadian Poetry* 33. http://canadianpoetry.org/volumes/vol33/ravvin.html.
Reid, Malcolm. 2010. *Deep café – Une jeunesse avec la poésie de Leonard Cohen*. Laval, QC: Presses de l'Université de Laval.
Remnick, David. 2016. "Leonard Cohen Makes it Darker." *The New Yorker*. October 17, 2016. http://www.newyorker.com/magazine/2016/10/17/leonard-cohen-makes-it-darker.
Ricard, François. (2003) 2004. *Agnes' Final Afternoon: An Essay on the Work of Milan Kundera*. New York: Harper Perennial.

Ringuet, Chantal. Gérard Rabinovitch. 2016. *Les révolutions de Leonard Cohen*. Québec: Presses de l'Université du Québec.

Rolling Stone. 1969. "Is Your Name Leonard Cohen?" *Rolling Stone*. May 17, 1966.

Ruhlmann, William. 1993. "The Stranger Music of Leonard Cohen." *Goldmine*. Vol. 19 No. 4, Issue 328: 10–20, 56.

Said, Edward. 2017. *On Late Style. Music and Literature Against the Grain*. London-New York: Bloomsbury.

Schnabel, Tom. 1988. *Stolen Moments: Conversations with Contemporary Musicians*. Los Angeles: Acrobat Books.

Scobie, Stephen. 1978. *Leonard Cohen*. Vancouver: Douglas & McIntyre.

———. 1991. "Leonard Cohen, Phyllis Webb, and the End(s) of Modernism." In *Canadian Canons. Essays in Literary Value*, edited by Robert Lecker, 57–70. Toronto: University of Toronto Press.

———. 1993. "The Counterfeiter Begs Forgiveness: Leonard Cohen and Leonard Cohen." *Canadian Poetry* 33:7–22.

———. 1997. "Racing the Midnight Train. Leonard Cohen in Performance." *Canadian Literature* 152/153:52–68.

———. 2002. "Ten Reasons To Toast Him On His Birthday." https://www.leonardcohenfiles.com/scobie02.html.

Shepard, Richard F. 1968. "Disks Wear Art on Their Sleeves to Woo Buyers." *New York Times*. March 12, 1968.

Siemerling, Winfried. 1994. *Discoveries of the Other: Alterity in the Work of Leonard Cohen, Hubert Aquin, Michael Ondaatje and Nicole Brossard*. Toronto: University of Toronto Press.

Simmons, Sylvie. (2012) 2017. *I'm Your Man: The Life of Leonard Cohen*. London: Jonathan Cape.

Simon, Sherry. 2006. *Translating Montreal: Episodes in the Life of a Divided City*. Montréal and Kingston: McGill-Queen's University Press.

———. 2012. *Cities in Translation: Intersections of Language and Memory*. London, New York: Routledge.

Simonart, Serge. n.d. "De liefdes van Leonard Cohen." *Midi Libre* (broadcast on Belgium's Radio 1 station).

Skelton Grant, Judith. 1977. "Leonard Cohen's poems-songs." *Studies in Canadian Literature/Études en littérature canadienne* 2 (1): 102–107.

Slabbinck, Sammy. 2017. Personal conversation. Bruges.

Smith, Rowland J. 1970. Introduction to *The Favourite Game*, by Leonard Cohen. Toronto: McClelland and Stewart Ltd.

Söderlind, Sylvia. 1991. *Margin/Alias: Language and Colonization in Canadian and Québécois Fiction*. Toronto: University of Toronto Press.

Stacey, Robert David. 2014. "Mad Translation in Leonard Cohen's *Beautiful Losers* and Douglas Glover's *Elle*." *English Studies in Canada* 40 (2–3): 173–197.

Susam-Sarajeva, Şebnem. 2008. "Translation and music: Changing perspectives, frameworks and significance." *The Translator* 14 (2): 187–200.
Tanasescu, Raluca, and Louis Alberti. 2016. "Leonard Cohen: Un auteur majeur et ses traducteurs en 'mode mineur.'" In *Les révolutions de Leonard Cohen*, edited by Chantal Ringuet and Gérard Rabinovitch, 229–252. Québec: Presses de l'Université du Québec.
Taubin, Amy. 2019. "Not my man." *Artforum*. July 11, 2019. https://www.artforum.com/film/amy-taubin-on-nick-broomfield-s-marianne-and-leonard-2019-80270.
Toews, Jennifer. 2011. Personal conversation. Toronto.
Tordjman, Gilles. 2006. *Leonard Cohen*. Pantin: Le Castor Astral.
Toye, William, ed. 1983. *The Oxford Companion to Canadian Literature*. Toronto, Oxford, New York: Oxford University Press.
Trehearne, Brian. 2013. "Layton as Ethical Subject: The Later Poetry and the Problem of Evil." *Canadian Poetry: Studies, Documents, Reviews* 73:8–31.
———. 2013–2019. Personal conversations. Montréal.
Van der Hout, Bram. 2003. "Abraham, Isaak en het postreligieuze tijdperk. Woody Allen en Leonard Cohen over 'De binding van Isaak.'" *Vooys* 21: 16–21.
Van Dijck, Ira, Maarten De Pourcq, and Carl De Strycker. 2013. *Draden in het donker: intertekstualiteit in theorie en praktijk*. Nijmegen: Vantilt.
Van Doorne, J. 1971. "De glorierijke verliezers van Leonard Cohen." *Trouw*. July 3, 1971: 19.
Van Stiphout, H. 1971. "Leonard Cohens 'vulsel-boek.'" *Het Parool*. Septembre 18, 1971: 9.
Vassal, Jacques. 1969. "Dylan contre Cohen." *Rock et Folk* 29:33–61.
———. 1977. *Folksong: racines et branches de la musique folk aux États-Unis*. Paris: Albin Michel.
Visker, Rudi. 2007. *Lof der zichtbaarheid. Een uitleiding in de hedendaagse wijsbegeerte*. Amsterdam: SUN.
Walsh, John, 1994. "Leonard Cohen." *Mojo*. Septembre: 58.
Webster, Derek. 2018. "Montreal Poetry after Leonard Cohen." *Canadian Notes & Queries* 101 (Winter Issue). http://notesandqueries.ca/essays/montreal-poetry-after-leonard-cohen-by-derek-webster/.
Wieseltier, Leon. 2005. "Letters for Leonard." *Arts and Opinion* 4 (2). https://www.artsandopinion.com/2005_v4_n2/cohen.htm.
Wilkins, Peter. 2000. "'Nightmares of Identity': Nationalism and Loss in *Beautiful Losers*." In *Intricate Preparations, Writing Leonard Cohen*, edited by Stephen Scobie, 24–50. Toronto: ECW Press.
Zollo, Paul. 1997. Songwriters on Songwriting. Boston: Da Capo Press. https://www.leonardcohenfiles.com/zollo.html.

CANADIAN STUDIES

Series editor: Pierre Anctil

The Canadian Studies collection touches upon all aspects of Canadian society in all disciplines with a special focus on Canadian women, cultural and religious minorities, and First Nations. The collection is also devoted to regional studies, local communities, and the unique characteristics of Canadian society. Among the topics privileged in this collection are all contemporary issues, especially in the domain of the environment, with regards to large urban centres and new forms of art and communications.

PREVIOUS TITLES IN THE CANADIAN STUDIES SERIES

Pierre Anctil, *A Reluctant Welcome for Jewish People: Voices in Le Devoir's Editorials, 1910–1947*, 2019.

Le Mawiomi Mi'gmawei de Gesp'gewa'gi, *Nta'tugwaqanminen – Notre histoire : l'évolution des Mi'gmaqs de Gespe'gewa'gi*, 2018.

Pierre Anctil, *Jacob Isaac Segal: A Montreal Yiddish Poet and His Milieu*, 2017.

Hughes Théorêt, *The Blue Shirts: Adrien Arcand and Fascist Anti-Semitism in Canada*, 2017.

For a complete list of the University of Ottawa Press, visit:
www.press.uOttawa.ca

www.ingramcontent.com/pod-product-compliance
Lightning Source LLC
Chambersburg PA
CBHW041733300426
44116CB00019B/2971